Social Work with Substance Users

Social Work with Substance Users

Anna Nelson

Los Angeles | London | New Delhi
Singapore | Washington DC

SAGE Publications Ltd
1 Oliver's Yard
55 City Road
London EC1Y 1SP

SAGE Publications Inc.
2455 Teller Road
Thousand Oaks, California 91320

SAGE Publications India Pvt Ltd
B 1/I 1 Mohan Cooperative Industrial Area
Mathura Road
New Delhi 110 044

SAGE Publications Asia-Pacific Pte Ltd
33 Pekin Street #02-01
Far East Square
Singapore 048763

Library of Congress Control Number: 2010941766

British Library Cataloguing in Publication data

A catalogue record for this book is available from the British Library

ISBN 978-1-84860-221-2
ISBN 978-1-84860-222-9 (pbk)

Typeset by C&M Digitals (P) Ltd, Chennai, India
Printed by MPG Books Group, Bodmin, Cornwall
Printed on paper from sustainable resources

Mixed Sources
Product group from well-managed
forests and other controlled sources
www.fsc.org Cert no. SA-COC-1565
© 1996 Forest Stewardship Council
FSC

For Ben and Trilby

Contents

Acknowledgements

Writing this book has been a huge undertaking for me, but one that, for all the sacrifices, has been remarkably fulfilling. First and foremost, my special thanks to all my social work service users who have faced problematic substance use. Seeing your beauty in the face of adversity inspired me to write this book. Thanks to all my friends and family whose unfaltering encouragement helped me along the way. Due special thanks is Trish Hafford-Letchfield, an amazing woman, who had faith in my ability and role-modelled mind-blowing academic ability, coupled with incredible energy, integrity, support and friendship throughout the project. Thanks to Sage and my original editor Susannah Trefgarne for believing in me from the start, as well as to Zoë Elliott-Fawcett and Emma Milman who helped me get the job done with practical support and encouragement right to the end. Last but by no means least, my special thanks, love and hugs to my husband Ben and our daughter Trilby, who will now have their wife and mummy back.

Praise for the book

'Writing in clear, accessible language, this excellent book will be useful for students and practitioners.'
Rachel Fyson, Centre for Social Work, University of Nottingham

'Social workers are often seen to fail substance users despite extensive evidence on the scale and impact of these issues on most of those they work with. Nelson's comprehensive and detailed text is a timely and welcome contribution to an area of practice where there is surprisingly little research and literature. Written by someone with substantial policy knowledge and practice expertise in the field, her approach will help to inspire social workers confidence by drawing on common discourses about substance users and working to embed a partnership approach. Highly recommended for both pre- and post qualified practitioners!'
Trish Hafford-Letchfield, Teaching fellow, Interprofessional Learning, Middlesex University

Introduction

The fact that so many social workers feel so poorly prepared for working with substance use issues, that so many of their clients experience difficulties related to drug or alcohol use and that social work courses tend to provide so little training on the issue is inexcusable. (Galvani and Forrester, 2008: 5)

Whilst this book is necessarily concerned with our response to and support of people who use substances problematically, it must not be assumed that all substance use is, or will become problematic. Where substance use is problematic, however, it is recognised as a problem across a range of social work settings and service user groups. Problematic substance use can and does exacerbate problems in all areas of social work practice, such as increasing the likelihood of child neglect and destabilising mental health problems. There have been ongoing calls from the Advisory Council on the Misuse of Drugs (ACMD) (2003), academics (Ahmed, 2007; Galvani, 2007; Galvani and Forrester, 2008), drug and alcohol charities (Addaction, 2007) and stakeholders (Bootle, 2007), for social work education to improve information given to students about problematic substance use. Not all social workers are necessarily required to be substance misuse specialists; however, they are expected to be able to work effectively with services users who may be using substances problematically, regardless of the social work setting that they are currently practising in.

Working with problematic substance use has to become a core theme underpinning academic social work programmes because it so often plays a role in the lives of individuals and families who access social work services. To this end, Galvani and Forrester (2009) have developed a Social Policy and Social Work Subject Centre (SWAP) learning and teaching guide *Social Work and Substance Use: Teaching the Basics* aimed at supporting social work lecturers and tutors teaching about problematic substance use to their social work students. It is vital that any social work academic seeking to teach about problematic substance use uses this guide coupled with a text such as this.

How to use this book

The book is set out in four separate parts, with introductions to each part, summaries at the end of each chapter, questions for the reader to reflect on and relevant case studies. The reflective questions at the end of each chapter challenge the reader to think about and consider each chapter in relation to their thoughts, feelings and attitudes as well as their own direct social work practice.

The case study examples provide valuable insight into how social workers might acknowledge and work with problematic substance use in each of their practice settings.

In recognition of the need for students to be more aware of problematic substance use in their social work practice, this book is aimed first and foremost at social work students; however, it is also very useful for qualified social workers in a variety of settings. In contrast to the bureaucratic and managerialist functions of social work, where social workers are often 'therapeutically deskilled' while they concern themselves with budgets and risk, this book offers a number of meaningful models for therapeutic social work practice with service users who have problematic substance use.

This book aims to:

- Provide social workers with an understanding of historical and current policy relating to prohibition, drug use and problematic substance use, in an anti-discriminatory context.
- Provide information to social workers to raise awareness about a range of substances and their potential effects on service users.
- Provide social workers with the knowledge to be able to screen adequately for problematic substance use and where referral to a specialist service is not required, use key skills to offer brief intervention, motivational approaches, harm reduction and relapse prevention.
- Provide social workers with an awareness of the particular issues and special needs of specific service user groups who may be experiencing problematic substance use.
- Provide social workers with an understanding of the issues relating to problematic substance use in a variety of practice settings.

Service users with problematic substance use deserve a fair, equitable, anti-discriminatory and relevant service no matter which social work service they attend for help. This book sets out to begin to make this possible.

Part 1

Historical and Contemporary Context

Part 1 of this book sets the scene for anti-discriminatory social work practice with people who may use substances problematically. The first chapter, 'A social history of problematic substance use', provides a brief history of substance use prior to prohibition and regulation, describing how substances and users of them were first medicalised and then criminalised. In this historical light the chapter then describes more recent policy and legislation related to alcohol and drug use, outlines some of the language used to describe problematic substance use, and covers some of the main theories and models that may help us to understand problematic substance use. Chapter 2, 'Anti-discriminatory/anti-oppressive practice and partnership working', focuses on the main components of working in an anti-discriminatory and anti-oppressive way with service users who may have problematic substance use. The importance of social workers working in partnership and collaboration with substance misuse specialists, including service users and peer support services is also covered in this chapter. Chapter 3, 'Substances and their effects', concludes Part 1 by covering some of the main types of substances that are used problematically, their effects and dependence potential.

1

A Social History of Problematic Substance Use

Social workers require knowledge and understanding of the socio-political and historical context of the issues with which they work. In order to understand why we meet with individuals, families, groups and/or communities we must understand not only their personal stories but the context and nature of the issues that they bring. In this way then it is important for social workers to understand some of the history of substances, their use and the political and socio-cultural factors that led to their prohibition or strict regulation. It is important to understand this history as it helps to explain why users of substances are often portrayed negatively, and why people who may have problematic substance use are marginalised and criminalised. To truly understand the nature of the problem or perceived problem provides an anti-oppressive footing, which should be at the heart of all social work practice.

The normalisation of substance use

'Attempts to govern morals pervade the history of human societies' (Rimke and Hunt, 2002: 60). Around the world society's attempt to govern the use of substances has been profound, but it has not always been this way. Substance use for many centuries was seen as a religious experience, as providing creative inspiration, self-medication and/or recreation, with little or no moral condemnation or social control (Bennett and Holloway, 2005). Medicinal use of cannabis in China and the chewing of coca leaves for energy and strength in South America have been documented as dating back several thousand years (Bennett and Holloway, 2005). Throughout history, the use of alcohol, cocaine and opium was unexceptional among people of all classes and backgrounds, including great poets, writers, artists and medical professionals and until the 1960s most known 'addicts' in Britain were 'professionals' (doctors, dentists and pharmacists) who had direct access to morphine and other substances (Bennett and Holloway, 2005; Davenport-Hines, 2004). In the eighteenth and first half of the nineteenth century, Britain had a well-established lay and commercial opium trade primarily with Turkey and imported stocks of opium and associated paraphernalia, that was distributed throughout pharmacies and grocers around the country (Strang and Gossop, 2005). Alcohol has played and continues to play an important role in many civilisations around the world (Lloyd, 2010). Britain in particular has a long proud history of making ales and beer and over the course of history alcohol use and indeed drunkenness among all classes has not been uncommon.

The use of substances throughout history was normal, and there was very little if any moral judgement of it. It was only later that health and social concerns leading to medicalisation and then a criminalisation of substance use transpired.

Health and social concerns

In London in the early to late 1700s, the concern regarding drinking, and specifically drinking gin, became known as the 'gin epidemic'. Gin was known as 'mother's ruin' and the 'demon drink' and was blamed for social unrest and absenteeism among the working classes. It is argued by some, however, that in reality gin was merely a concomitant factor in these issues alongside overcrowding and poverty (Abel, 2001). Health concerns regarding alcohol use were officially published by American Benjamin Rush in 1790, when he released *An Inquiry into the Effects of Spirituous Liquors on the Human Body and the Mind*, more commonly known as the 'Moral Thermometer'. The thermometer provided a visual depiction of the 'horrors' of drunkenness and was later used to support the temperance movement.

Concerns about other substances were also raised when health and social problems relating to their use also started to surface. Alongside public drunkenness and absenteeism, accidental overdosing was quite common. Had it not been for the fact that these health and social problems began to impact on economic productivity, the 'ruling classes' may not have cared about the impact substance use was having on the working classes. Abel (2001) argues that the ruling classes strongly endorsed 'poverty theory' at this time, the premise of this theory being that the working classes needed to be paid little and kept in poverty so that exports remained competitive. This also kept commodities out of their reach, which in turn meant that they had to work hard to survive, which further supported the continuation of the class system.

In line with poverty theory and over concern about decreased productivity, the 'ruling classes' argued that substances and those who used them needed controlling; that individual conduct should be governed in the interests of the nation (Rimke and Hunt, 2002). So began the inextricable link between the use of substances and wider social and cultural concerns and a campaign that would eventually see many substances prohibited or highly regulated (Mold, 2007):

> The respectable classes experienced deep apprehensions about the declining hegemony of the traditional authority of the social, political and religious establishments. They responded with a disparate array of projects of moral regulation. (Rimke and Hunt, 2002: 66)

The medicalisation of substance use

Following Benjamin Rush's earlier work on the 'moral thermometer' and during the last quarter of the nineteenth century, the medical profession was beginning to theorise about substance use, associated health problems and 'addiction'. The term 'addiction' first emerged in the nineteenth century as an explanation for the overwhelming desire to use alcohol (Mold, 2007). While addiction was initially seen as a disease caused by the consumption of alcohol, the concept soon began to be located in the 'alcoholic' rather than the alcohol itself (Mold, 2007). An alliance in the form of the 'social and moral hygiene' movement soon formed from the moral codes rooted in religious views and that of the 'new' medical institution (Rimke and Hunt, 2002: 61). Medical professionals began to refer to 'addiction' as a moral pathology, which saw those who were 'addicted' as having an 'impaired moral faculty' (Mold, 2007: 2). 'History can provide numerous examples of how the application of scientific knowledge to a "problem" such as drug use is not value free: but socially and culturally shaped' (Mold, 2007: 6).

So, while the use of substances began to be prohibited and restricted due to the real and perceived health and social problems they created, the users of the substances themselves also began to be vilified. The association between the use of substances, immorality and disease had begun.

Towards the end of the nineteenth century, doctors favoured a combination of medical treatment and 'moral enlightenment' in order to treat the 'disease' of 'addiction', and the medical profession had control over this treatment (Bennett and Holloway, 2005). The 1920 Dangerous Drugs Act permitted doctors to prescribe 'dangerous' drugs even to known 'addicts' if it was deemed medically necessary. This medical approach is often called the 'British System' and was unique to Britain at a time when America was demanding complete prohibition around the world. The 'British System' evolved with the publication of the *Rolleston Committee Report* in 1926. This report supported the continuation of this prescribing strategy, reaffirming the 'disease' model of 'addiction' and placing the responsibility for the treatment of 'addiction' with medical professionals (Bennett and Holloway, 2005; Strang and Gossop, 2005). It was argued that this decision to 'medicalise' the problem rather than 'criminalise' it at this stage, which was different to other countries (including America), was due to the fact that Britain had at this time in reality only a small problem with the use of drugs (Bennett and Holloway, 2005).

The criminalisation of drug use

While the medical profession was still the dominant force in the treatment of 'addiction', in the early 1900s the British government began to take more of an interest in 'drug addiction'. It was at this time that thinking about the criminalisation of substance users began. For the same reasons that drug use was medicalised, drug users slowly began to be criminalised.

Opium use amongst the working class was thought to be damaging to morality and detrimental to production, echoing elements of the temperance movement's attack on alcohol. (Mold, 2007: 3)

The Opium Convention, signed by 12 nations at The Hague in 1912, proposed among other things the closing down of opium dens and that the possession and sale of opiates (morphine, opium and heroin) to unauthorised persons should be punishable by law (Bennett and Holloway, 2005). Following the signing of the Opium Convention, the British Home Office began to take responsibility for matters relating to dangerous drugs (in June 1916). This included a focus on international distribution and consumption.

The Dangerous Drugs Act of 1920, while placing the prescribing of drugs in the hands of the doctors, prohibited the importation of raw opium, morphine and cocaine, and allowed the Home Office to regulate the manufacturing, sale and distribution of dangerous drugs (Bennett and Holloway, 2005). This appeared to mark the beginning of the criminalisation of drug use in Britain, and ratified the principles of an even earlier Defence of Realm regulation that came into force in 1915, that was concerned with the use of drugs by the British armed forces in the First World War. Britain made cannabis illegal in 1928 as it had been previously omitted from the Dangerous Drugs Act.

Following the introduction of these policies, substance use and the number of known 'addicts' remained relatively low and constant in Britain until the 1960s. The 1960s, however, saw a marked increase in the use of drugs by a wide range of people from all social backgrounds. This increase in the use of what were now 'illegal' substances appears to have come about due to younger people having more personal income, more movement of people and substances around the world and the sixties culture encompassing 'freedom' and the importance of spiritual experiences. The use of heroin registered the biggest rise at this time, but cannabis and cocaine were also regularly used, especially in London's 'music scene'. At this time, some of the powers that medical professionals had enjoyed under the 'British System' began to be limited by the Home Office. It was thought at the time that the marked increase in drug use that was being seen was as a result of over-prescribing by a small number of doctors. Following this 'explosion' in the use of substances, there was a perceived need to regulate further and criminalise the use of drugs.

Drug policy and legislation

The 1960s

The Interdepartmental Committee on Drug Addiction, chaired by Sir Russell Brain (the *First Brain Report*), reinforced the findings of the earlier 1926 *Rolleston Report* and favoured the continued use of drug prescription for 'addicts' where necessary, and emphasised the relatively minor scale of drug use in the UK. While this report was widely criticised at the time for not recognising the changing drug-using culture in the UK, the media had begun to pick up on these changes. It was at this time that sensationalist reporting of the dangers of the 'drug epidemic' began.

The 1961 UN drugs convention, the Single Convention on Narcotic Drugs, marked a key turning point in global prohibition, safeguarding prohibition in domestic law around the world, and closing down any possibility of regulated models of the production and supply of illicit drugs (paradoxically, alcohol and tobacco were excluded) being introduced by individual countries. The Brain Committee was reconvened in 1964 following pressure from the media and the public. While this report (the *Second Brain Report*) was more realistic, it is said to have focused too narrowly on the London scene and neglected other parts of the UK, where drug use culture was also changing (Yates, 2002).

The UN Drugs Convention and the *Second Brain Report* informed the implementation of the Dangerous Drugs Act 1967, which effectively saw the beginning of the end of the 'British System' of opiate prescribing. The Dangerous Drugs Act introduced the notification of 'addicts', wide-ranging restrictions on the prescribing rights of doctors, and the establishment of special treatment centres or clinics for the provision of drug treatment (Drug Dependency Units or DDUs). The right to prescribe heroin and cocaine to 'addicts' was now limited to specialist psychiatrists working in these clinics and equipped with a licence from the Home Office (Lart, 2006). The quantity of these drugs that was prescribed was also dramatically reduced, with the heroin substitute methadone often being supplied in their place (Transform Drug Policy Foundation, 2009). The limitations placed on the prescribing of opiates and cocaine by the Dangerous Drugs Act 1967 came at a time when the black market for drugs was becoming established, especially in London. Whether or not this new legislation caused the black market, or was in response to the beginnings of it, is arguable, but what was clear was that the number of drug users continued to increase through the 1960s and well into the 1970s (Yates, 2002).

The Misuse of Drugs Act 1971

The 1971 Misuse of Drugs Act 1971 established the Advisory Council on the Misuse of Drugs (ACMD). ACMD was set up to advise the government about drug misuse prevention, and how to deal with social problems related to drug misuse (Yates, 2002). The Misuse of Drugs Act also implemented the 'schedule' system in accordance with the judgement of the UN Commission on Narcotic Drugs as to the potential for abuse and the therapeutic value of each drug. These schedules govern possession and supply of drugs controlled under the Misuse of Drugs Act as well as prescribing, safe custody, importation, exportation, production and record keeping. These criteria still underpin UK drug policy today. Under the Misuse of Drugs Act it is an offence to possess a controlled substance unlawfully; possess a controlled substance with intent to supply it; supply or offer to supply a controlled drug (even if it is given away for free); or allow a house, flat or office to be used by people taking drugs.

Table 1.1 Drug classification under the Misuse of Drugs Act 1971

	Drugs (including but not limited to)	Penalty for possession	Penalty for dealing/ supply
Class A	Ecstasy, LSD, heroin, cocaine, crack cocaine, magic mushrooms, amphetamine (if prepared for injection)	Up to 7 years in prison or an unlimited fine or both	Up to life in prison or an unlimited fine or both
Class B	Amphetamine, cannabis, methylphenidate (Ritalin), pholcodine, mephedrone	Up to 5 years in prison or an unlimited fine or both	Up to 14 years in prison or an unlimited fine or both
Class C	Tranquilisers, some painkillers, gamma hydroxybutyrate (GHB), ketamine	Up to 2 years in prison or an unlimited fine or both	Up to 14 years in prison or an unlimited fine or both

Source: Home Office, 2009a

Drugs are scheduled as either class A, B or C according to how damaging they are thought to be to individuals and communities. The different classes carry different penalties for possession and supply. A simple table (Table 1.1) is presented that helps to make sense of these classes.

All of the drugs identified in this schedule under the Misuse of Drugs Act are considered to be controlled substances and are illegal to use, except where they have been prescribed. Class A drugs are those that are thought to be the most dangerous to individuals, families and communities, while Class C drugs are thought to be the least harmful.

This scheduling system has been severely criticised over the years. According to Nutt et al. (2007) 'the process by which harms are determined is often undisclosed, and when made public can be ill-defined, opaque and seemingly arbitrary' (p. 1047). This appears to be due to the fact that drug-related harms are complex, multi-dimensional and evolve over time in unpredictable ways. Some drugs, like cannabis, have been moved between classes. For example, in 2004, cannabis was downgraded to a class C drug, only to be upgraded again in 2009 to class B because of concerns about the strength of hybrid types of cannabis known as 'skunk', and its detrimental effects to users' mental health.

It also appears, however, that history, politics and the subsequent discourse regarding what are 'good' substances and what are 'bad' substances (legal and illegal) has also influenced not only society's perception of these substances and those who use them, but also the official UK classification system and its associated penalties. This is especially true if we look at the research. According to Nutt et al.'s (2007) research based on experts' understandings of the scientific evidence of substance-related harm, if we kept the same structure for classification that is currently used in the UK and based it on 'harm', alcohol would almost certainly be classified as a class A drug, while ecstasy would probably be class C. That is, experts in the field believe that there is much more evidence to suggest that alcohol is overall far more harmful than ecstasy.

Based on these types of evidence, the Royal Society of Arts' (RSA) *Commission on Illegal Drugs, Communities and Public Policy* (2007) stated that the Misuse of Drugs Act should be repealed entirely and replaced with a Misuse of Substances Act which should incorporate alcohol, tobacco, solvents and over-the-counter and prescription drugs.

The 1980s

In 1979, there was another huge rise in the availability and use of heroin throughout most cities in the UK. This heroin was mostly from the Middle East and was smoked. By the early 1980s, there was huge public concern about this 'blight' on society, and the drug problem, especially the inner city heroin problem, became a serious political issue. In 1982, following a report from the ACMD, the Conservative government announced a central funding initiative to begin to establish a network of drug treatment services. This new funding, coupled with the HIV epidemic, saw a rapid change in UK drug policy (via recommendations from the ACMD) and the availability of services. The concern that HIV would be spread via injecting drug users meant that harm minimisation, methadone maintenance and needle exchange became a priority for drug services. Alongside these changes to drug services, the 1980s also saw a huge resurgence in the use of psychedelic drugs, namely ecstasy. This necessitated a further expansion in the repertoire of drug services which were used to working with injecting and other 'hard' drug users, and now had to begin thinking about ways of reaching out to drug users in the 'rave scene'.

The 1990s and beyond

Since the 1990s, consecutive governments have published a number of pertinent documents as well as developed comprehensive drug strategies in an attempt to reduce drug-related harm to individuals, families and communities. These drug strategies have included: *Tackling Drugs to Build a Better Britain* (Home Office, 1998); *Drugs: Protecting Families and Communities* (Home Office, 2008) and *The Road to Recovery: A New Approach to Tackling Scotland's Drug Problem* (Scottish Government, 2008a). Under each of these strategies, a number of key initiatives were introduced, including:

- The establishment of Drug Action Teams (DATs) set up around the country to implement drug strategy at a local level.
- In 1997, the appointment of the UK's first 'drug czar' (the UK anti-drugs co-ordinator).
- In 2001, the establishment of the National Treatment Agency (NTA) to improve availability, capability and effectiveness of drug services.
- A substantial increase in the availability of drug treatment, including treatment accessed through the criminal justice system (Drug Intervention Programme).
- Drug supply and enforcement approaches.
- A focus on drug services working with drug-using parents.

- A focus on getting people into training, education and employment following their attendance at treatment services.
- A move from harm reduction strategies back to 'recovery' and abstinence focused strategies (for example, the Scottish Government's (2008a) *The Road to Recovery: A New Approach to Tackling Scotland's Drug Problem*).

It is clear, however, that despite these best efforts the demand for drugs remains. The makers and supplies of illicit substances are becoming more productive, and enforcement agencies cannot begin to compete with the criminal element that rules the illicit drug trade. According to a report by the RSA:

> Drugs Policy in its present form has largely been a failure. We know it has sub-stantially failed because in the nearly four decades since the Misuse of Drugs Act came into force the number of addicts and others dependent on drugs has soared and the social problems associated with substance abuse have wors-ened dramatically. (2007: 21)

Critics of prohibition still believe that we will never be able to reduce drug related harm until drugs are decriminalised and/or legalised, because the prohibitive nature of the regulation in itself can create harms for individuals and communities (Haden, 2006). Since the establishment of the Coalition government in 2010 the outlook for the health and social care sector appears uncertain. This is especially true given the release of the Coalition government's new *Drug Strategy 2010 Reducing Demand, Restricting Supply, Building Recovery: Supporting People to Live a Drug Free Life* (Home Office, 2010). This Drug Strategy replaces the strategy *Drugs: Protecting Families and Communities* (Home Office, 2008) which had been established under the previous Labour government. The new strategy is structured around three themes: reducing demand, restricting supply and building recovery in communities. It has two overarching aims: to reduce illicit and other harmful drug use, and to increase the numbers recovering from substance dependence. It has a number of ambitious objectives and it remains to be seen whether these goals will be met in the future.

The UK Drugs Policy Commission (UKDPC) has historically been concerned that so little is known about 'what works' in regards to drug policy. They advocate for more resources to be put into further study and research into the components of the strategies so that regular and independent evaluation can be made regarding what is proving to be effective (UKDPC, 2007). They express concern that 'tough' measures and zero tolerance are ineffective. Continued focus on the implementation and evaluation of projects, programmes and initiatives that support the aims of any new Drug Strategy is paramount if its objectives are to be met.

According to Reuter and Stevens (2007):

> The arena where government drug policy needs to focus further effort and where it can make an impact is in reducing the levels of drug related harms (crime, death and disease and other associated problems) through the expansion of and innovation in treatment and harm reduction services. (p. 11)

Alcohol policy and legislation

Issues related to problematic alcohol use have historically been superseded politically by the issues relating to problematic drug use; however, there have been a variety of responses to problematic alcohol use throughout the twentieth century and around the UK. Public health measures in the 1970s included a focus on alcohol awareness campaigns, education and prevention, while the adoption of drinking 'units' or 'standard drinks' in the 1980s helped to quantify and identify unsafe or problem drinking (Lloyd, 2010). Since this time, however, the issue of problematic alcohol use has become a major policy issue, with concerns about binge drinking, young people's underage drinking and anti-social and disorderly behaviour leading to a number of government strategies focused on these areas. As a result of key alcohol harm reduction strategies (Prime Minister's Strategy Unit, Cabinet Office, 2004; Department of Health (DoH), Home Office, Department for Education and Skills (DfES), Department of Culture, Media and Sport, 2007) these measures have included increasing the price of alcohol, controlling alcohol advertising, increasing the minimum age for buying alcohol, and restricting opportunities to buy alcohol. Other measures have included the advertising of health information on bottles of alcohol, in 2005 the implementation of the Licensing Act 2003 (which brought in '24-hour drinking'), sharpened criminal justice interventions for drunken behaviour, more help available for people who may want to drink less (telephone hotlines, websites and support groups), and where Scotland is concerned a focus on the importance of culture change aimed at 'de-normalising' alcohol consumption (Lloyd, 2010).

The Coalition government elected in 2010 criticised the previous Labour government's alcohol strategy for having too much of a public order focus. The Coalition government suggests its alcohol strategy will be based on reducing demand through more public education and will include:

- A ban on the sale of alcohol below cost price.
- A review of alcohol taxation to tackle binge drinking.
- An overhaul of the Licensing Act to give local authorities and police more powers.
- A doubling of the fine for underage alcohol sales. (UK Alcohol Alert, 2010)

The actual changes to alcohol policy and legislation under the Coalition government, and their subsequent effects remain to be seen.

Historical legacy

There is no denying that substance use can be harmful (see Chapter 3), but there are also harms associated with prohibition. 'Drug prohibition itself creates violence, crime, corruption, disease, and creates a robust black market, which engages youth and makes drugs widely available' (Haden, 2006: 126). Alongside this, the harm that comes from having a criminal record can lead to unemployment, stigmatisation and benefit dependence, all of which probably does very little to reduce the likelihood of continued drug use. When social workers think about and work with service users who may have problematic substance use, it is important for them to recognise the potential harms from the criminalisation of drug use as well as the harms from the substance use itself.

It is also important to think about the reasons why some substances are illegal and others merely regulated, and why this may be the case. There are a number of theories on why this might be. For example, as we have seen earlier in this chapter, some of the first policies that sought to control the use of alcohol and other substances in the UK were aimed at the working class and were in effect 'classist'.

The 'war on drugs', especially in the United States, has also often been labelled as 'racist', and the influence of these policies internationally cannot be overlooked. Some examples of this include:

- Opium use linked predominantly to Chinese immigrants in the US at a time when anti-Chinese sentiment was being fuelled by concern about cheap Chinese labour. (This led to opium importation being prohibited and the US Chinese Exclusion Act of 1882.)
- Cocaine use being linked to black communities in the 1900s when stories proliferated about 'cocaine crazed negroes'.
- The use of cannabis by both black and white people who enjoyed the jazz music scene being used in the racist anti-marijuana propaganda which used this disintegration of racial barriers as an example of the degradation caused by marijuana.

Moral crusaders exploited endemic racism to spread the prohibition message by linking substance use with ethnic minority populations. Exaggerated claims and racial stereotyping featured prominently in the propaganda that was used to support prohibitionist legislation, which was further supported by the commercial sector and industry, which were worried about maintaining a productive, industrious and sober workforce (Woodiwiss, 1998). In the shadow of this history, policies including racial profiling and extensive sentencing for drug trafficking, dealing and drug use are still disproportionately carried out against minorities in both the UK and the US (Drug Policy Alliance, 2001; Ministry of Justice, 2009). The consequences of these disparities are evident in the poor economic and political health of the communities that those imprisoned leave behind. While policies and laws relating to substances, especially drugs, may no longer be as racist by design, they appear to remain racist (Provine, 2007).

Other hypotheses as to why some substances have been criminalised and others have not, include the argument that some policies have at their basis the protection of corporate profit. For example, it is argued that a legal opiate trade would be a huge competitor to the pharmaceutical industry. Conversely, alcohol which while regulated is still legal despite the harms it causes, means the liquor industry remains a powerful economic player. Whatever the reasons, on the face of it the fact that some substances are illegal and some are not is difficult to understand. According to the House of Commons Science and Technology Committee (2006), the way that the Advisory Council on the Misuse of Drugs (ACMD) makes recommendations to the government about the classification of drugs is ad hoc, arbitrary and not based on evidence.

This short history of the use of substances helps us to appreciate better some of the context in which the current understandings of problematic substance use have developed. It appears that which substances have been made illegal and which remain merely regulated has not necessarily been based on scientific evidence of their harms and has been heavily influenced by social and political factors, including classism, racism and capitalism. This knowledge should help social workers understand that people who use substances, whether they are illegal or regulated, are not necessarily bad or immoral (as this is socially constructed) and therefore deserve a fair, equitable and non-discriminatory service.

Understanding the language

Language and definitions of problematic substance use, substance misuse, substance abuse, addiction and dependence still vary internationally and across professional disciplines. The disciplines of medicine and psychiatry still prefer 'addiction' and 'dependence' to encompass either physiological and/or psychological dependence on a substance or substances. The terms 'substance abuse' and 'dependence' continue to have diagnostic criteria for diagnosis included in the American Psychiatric Association's (2000) *Diagnostic and Statistical Manual of Mental Disorders*, and the World Health Organization's (1992) *ICD 10: International Classification of Mental and Behavioural Disorders*. Those working in the field of social work and social care, however, tend to use the term 'substance misuse' to include misuse and dependence on alcohol and/or drugs (Hafford-Letchfield and Nelson, 2008). The terms 'addiction', 'substance abuse' and 'substance misuse' while still commonly used have culturally constructed negative connotations attached to them, which as social workers we must try to move away from. The term 'problematic substance use' is used throughout this text to include the entire continuum of problematic substance use from severe end dependence through to problem use. This language also identifies the problem as being with the use of the substance (including alcohol), rather than a problem with the person who uses the substances. Such contested use of language is indicative of the struggle between practitioners, service users, patients, government, medicine and psychology for authority in theorising about problematic substance use and providing treatment solutions.

Theory and models

Objective knowledge about problematic substance use has been developed over time from a variety of hypotheses and studies of substances and the people who use them. Models and theories about problematic substance use include the 'moral model' – where substance users are seen as 'sinful' and 'weak willed' – the 'disease' model (Jellinek, 1960; Levine, 1978), as well as psychological (Reinout and Stacy, 2005), genetic (Blum et al., 1990), social learning (George, 1989) and socio-cultural models of understanding (Furnham and Thompson, 1996).

Disease models have probably been the most historically significant, as this concept underpins the powerful and popular 12-step fellowship programmes, including Alcoholics Anonymous (www.alcoholics-anonymous.org.uk) and Narcotics Anonymous (www.ukna.org) that have been influential in providing substantial support for people with problematic substance use worldwide. The 'disease' model perceives 'substance misuse' as the behavioural consequence of pre-existing and permanent physical vulnerability that 'addicts' have to substances (Barber, 2002). Behavioural learning theories emphasise the influence of learning to use substances through personal experience and the influence of others such as parents, peers, the media or other sources. This theory also encompasses socio-cultural perspectives, where the use of substances can be seen as helping to alleviate personal and social difficulty by 'self medicating against life's negative experiences' (Taggart et al., 2007: 360), thus reinforcing substance-using behaviour. What is clear is that environmental influences cannot easily be separated from genetic ones (Hafford-Letchfield and Nelson, 2008). None of these theories, however, really provides us with all the answers to problematic substance use, as there are a remarkable number of variables that may contribute to some people developing problematic substance use where others do not. These variables are often referred to as 'risk' and 'protective' factors.

Risk and protective factors

What causes individuals to develop problems with their use of substances will be different for different people. However, there have been a number of 'risk' and 'protective' factors that have been identified. These are variables that are thought to put people at risk of developing problematic substance use or conversely may provide some protection from problems. Social workers may find these factors helpful as a guideline when seeking to understand service users with problematic substance use. According to the American National Institute on Drug Abuse (NIDA) (2008) the risk and protective factors to look out for come in five domains. These five domains are individual, family, peer, school and community. Risk and protective factors are often associated with experiences that people have had in their childhood. 'Children's earliest interactions within the family are crucial to their healthy development and risk for drug abuse' (NIDA, 2008: 1). Risk factors are associated with negative behaviours or experiences in each of these domains, while protective factors are seen as useful or positive behaviours, experiences and support in each of these domains.

We know that a lot more people use substances than develop problematic substance use. Thinking about risk and protective factors helps us to identify why some people may be more likely to develop problematic substance use than others. For instance, it is not unusual for higher education students to experiment

Table 1.2   Risk and protective factors for problematic substance abuse

Risk factors	Domain	Protective factors
Early aggressive behaviour	Individual	Self-control
Poor social skills	Individual	Positive relationships
Lack of parental supervision	Family	Parental supervision
Substance use	Peer	Academic achievement
Substances easily available	School	Substances difficult to get
Poverty	Community	Strong sense of positive community

Source: Adapted from the American National Institute on Drug Abuse (NIDA), 2008

with the use of substances, but not all of them will develop problematic substance use. This might be because they have a number of protective factors working for them, and very few risk factors. For example, it is likely that many students entering into higher education have good family support, positive relationships and academic competence, compared to young people from deprived communities who may have left school early and be unemployed (risk factors). Adverse life events in childhood (like abuse and neglect) and beyond, lead to limited opportunities and put people at risk of being more likely to develop problematic substance use. Some examples of risk and protective factors that you should be aware of are noted in Table 1.2.

With the confusion and lack of consensus around what causes and sustains problematic substance use, it may be more helpful that social workers are aware of these factors rather than know all the details of the vast number of theories that there are about problematic substance use. It is important to note, however, that even if someone presents with all of these risk factors, it does not necessarily mean that a problem will develop, and conversely someone with a number of these protective factors may still develop a problem. Use them purely as a guide to your work with service users.

Summary

History provides us with some understanding of how and why we view substances and the people who use them the way we do. Substances have not always been illegal or highly regulated, or seen as immoral, and have been used for centuries in many communities around the world. Real concern regarding health and social problems, alongside socio-cultural and political agendas, have influenced the medicalisation, criminalisation and subsequent prohibition and regulation of substances. This in turn has led to marginalisation for people in our societies who use substances. The historical context has also influenced the language we use and the theories and models that try to explain problematic substance use. There are no clear and precise understandings of problematic substance use; however, there are some real risk and protective factors that are useful for us to be aware of when working with service users who have problematic substance use.

Since the 1960s, there have been a number of policies and strategies throughout the UK aimed at reducing the harm of alcohol and other drugs, to individuals, families and communities. Governments have implemented a variety of measures, including ongoing education and communication to reduce substance-related harm, supply-side enforcement, enforcement to reduce anti-social behaviour and crime associated with alcohol and drug use, and faster access to better drug treatment services. Critics of policy argue that we do not know enough about what is working in regards to drug policy and that too often zero tolerance and so-called 'tough' measures that are unsupported by the evidence are counterproductive (UKDPC, 2007). While previous governments have readily accepted that a focus on harm reduction measures is integral, the Coalition government's drug strategy (Home Office, 2010) focuses on the importance of 'recovery' for individuals and communities with problematic substance use. What is clear is that any new alcohol or drug strategy needs to be more aligned to evidence-based interventions, and that more rigorous and independent research is needed to evaluate its effectiveness.

Reflections

Think about your own personal views of people who may use substances. If you are honest about this, what do you think of them?

Does understanding some of the history of substance use and how it has influenced contemporary thinking change your views at all? If so, in what ways?

Have you been aware of some of the strategies outlined in this chapter? For example, were you aware that raising the level of tax on alcohol and limiting alcohol advertising sought to reduce alcohol-related harm. Do you believe that any of these strategies have been effective?

Further readings

Davenport-Hines, R. (2004) *The Pursuit of Oblivion: A Social History of Drugs.* London: Phoenix.

Lloyd, C. (2010) 'How we got to where we are now', in J. Barlow (ed.), *Substance Misuse: The Implications of Research, Policy and Practice.* London: Jessica Kingsley Publishers, pp. 19–38.

2

Anti-Discriminatory/ Anti-Oppressive Practice and Partnership Working

Understanding the history of the use and problematic use of substances, previous and present legislation, as well as theories of why people use or 'mis-use' substances can help social workers understand why people who use substances have become an oppressed and often criminalised group of people in our society. It may also help you to feel more comfortable about providing anti-discriminatory interventions for this much marginalised section of the community. Much has been written about anti-discriminatory and anti-oppressive practice in the social work literature (Dominelli, 1998, 2002; Smith, 2008; Thompson, 2001, 2006). Much has been written about how this relates to minority groups, for example black and other ethnic minorities, women, gay, lesbian, bisexual and transgendered people, people with disabilities and people with mental health problems. Very little, however, has been written about how anti-discriminatory practice may relate to working with service users who may use substances problematically, and people who use substances may still face discrimination when encountering social work services. It appears that the use of substances is often misunderstood and sometimes seen as morally objection-able, especially where it is illegal. The previous chapter, however, has attempted to put some of these possible perceptions into context.

Societies all around the world have used a variety of substances for a variety of reasons for centuries. People of all classes, genders, ages and ethnicities have used substances and some have developed problems with this use. The way substances have been either normalised or vilified has changed over the course of history and for a variety of reasons (health and social issues, classism, racism, capitalism and politics), but is entirely socially constructed. There is no arguing that problematic substance use can have very serious negative health and social consequences. However, the condemnation of people who use substances is a construct in our society that is arguably unnecessary. If social workers are able to recognise this historical legacy, coupled with an understanding of some of the theories as to why people may develop problematic substance use, then anti-discriminatory practice becomes easier.

It is sometimes difficult to understand problematic substance use, even with this knowledge especially if service users present intoxicated, drunk, put their children at risk, are abusive and/or are engaged in criminal behaviour. If practitioners[1] can stop to think and consider this behaviour and see it in its socio-political and historical context, it is easier to understand that the use of substances could well be a defence mechanism, a survival strategy and/or a way of coping that is no longer working. The role of the social worker in these scenarios is to see through the presenting behaviours that are sometimes difficult to deal with and offer, where possible, some alternative coping strategies that are more appropriate and cause less damage to the service user, their families and the community. Social workers ought to be the type of people drawn to working with 'the multiply excluded and widely despised' (Ashton, 2007: 13). To see the human side of these service users is to begin to be anti-discriminatory.

Not everyone with problematic substance use will require an intervention and many may enter into a 'natural recovery' or 'spontaneous remission' in their own way without help. Alternatively, we must also remember that for many people, substance use is pleasant and enjoyable and does not become problematic. For many others, however, problems develop that require a lot of ongoing support. Problematic substance users are an oppressed group of people who may need advocacy, advise or support through a multitude of difficult times, regardless of whether they continue to use substances or not. In your role as a social worker or social work student you are charged with making sure people who use substances are not discriminated against.

Anti-discriminatory and anti-oppressive practice

Historically, social work has been criticised for not having its own theory from which to base its interventions on, and for borrowing from other professions such as counselling and psychology. What has always made social work unique, however, is it's fervour for social justice and social change. Social workers should not only be interested in individual or family change, but should also be interested in societal change. As a profession, social workers are, or should be, interested in political and structural change of that which supports the oppression and discrimination of minority groups in our communities. We should see our service users in their socio-political and historical contexts and understand that the issues that they bring to us are as a result of not only their own choices and individual experiences, but of a variety of structural and historical legacies that have often made them powerless. Understanding how social structures and

---

[1]The term 'practitioner' is used throughout the text not only to include the social work practitioner, but also to recognise other health and social care practitioners that the text may relate to.

social divisions based on such things as class, race, age and gender create power differentials, is to begin to understand why some groups in our society have more status and power than others. By its very nature, social work is concerned with working among the people who are the least powerful and most vulnerable in society. It is essential that social workers understand the history of oppression that has occurred for these groups in society at the hands of the more powerful groups, if they are to begin to do justice to the role of social work. While this way of thinking and working has come to be described as 'radical social work', it could be argued that this is at the heart of all social work and is what makes social work unique. Out of this uniqueness have come the approaches known as 'anti-oppressive' and 'anti-discriminatory' practice. The belief is that it is not enough just to 'not be' oppressive or discriminatory, but that social workers must be anti-oppressive and anti-discriminatory.

The terms 'anti-oppressive' and 'anti-discriminatory' practice are often used interchangeably. They may be understood as very similar, especially if you take the broadest definition of anti-discriminatory practice which encompasses socio-political and economic concerns. At the same time, however, it is helpful to clarify the difference. According to Dalrymple and Burke (2006), anti-oppressive practice is about acknowledging differing power relations in society, which in practice requires social workers to be empowering, liberating and reflective of their own, their agency's and their society's value base. Anti-discriminatory practice may be defined as working with a range of governmental legislation, laws, policies and practices to challenge discrimination. Dalrymple and Burke (2006) believe that anti-discriminatory practice may be limiting in its ability to challenge oppression if it merely works within these narrow legal requirements. To be truly anti-oppressive has much broader implications and responsibilities. It is going beyond that which is merely legally required, or can be legally challenged, to confront power differentials and oppression wherever and whenever they are unearthed; which by the very nature of the social worker/service user relationship is everywhere.

In order to understand this further it may help to think about what Thompson (2001) terms 'PCS analysis'. The PCS (personal, cultural, structural) model provides us with a framework from which to theorise about oppression. This model of analysis allows us to move beyond merely focusing on the 'personal' issues that services users may bring to us, but also to recognise the place of the 'cultural' and 'structural' factors within the difficulties that may present. The personal sphere is shaped by the cultural sphere that we all inhabit, that in turn is shaped by the structural sphere we find ourselves in. The personal sphere includes all of our individual thoughts, feelings and actions, and these will be shaped by our personal experiences to some degree (Thompson, 2006). The cultural level, however, which includes shared ways of seeing, thinking and behaving (that are common and taken for granted within cultures), will also influence how we personally think, feel and behave. Culture is therefore very influential in us, determining what we consider 'normal', and therefore what we might also consider 'abnormal' (Thompson, 2006). The structural level refers to the network of social divisions such as those identified earlier (class, race, gender, age) and the power relations between them. At this level of analysis, we can recognise oppression and discrimination and how it is 'institutionalized and thus "sewn in" to the fabric of society' (Thompson, 2006: 28). Thompson (2001) states that ideology or a 'set of ideas believed to be true and right' is the glue that holds the three spheres together. This ideology, for example, may include the idea that 'drug users are criminals and bad people'. This thinking then justifies the personal discrimination and societal oppression that drug users experience that in turn legitimises the current power structures. On a personal level, some social workers may also believe that 'drug users are criminals and bad people', too, because their personal choices, thoughts and feelings are strongly influenced by the cultural and structural spheres of their lives, in turn heavily influenced by dominant ideology. Social workers must acknowledge their own prejudice, thoughts and feelings towards people who may have problematic substance use, whilst also acknowledging that as social workers they are bound by anti-discriminatory and anti-oppressive practice.

An understanding of the historical and socio-political context, coupled with a commitment to self-reflection and the notions of justice, equality and participation will support the social work practitioner in being anti-oppressive and anti-discriminatory in the work they do. It will also allow them to recognise that in order to tackle discrimination and oppression they need to do more than just work with individuals, families and communities in their social work practice. Social workers need to be able to challenge dominant discriminatory structures and ideology wherever and whenever they are found.

Partnership and collaboration

In seeking to understand discrimination and oppression it is essential that social workers begin to challenge ideas that suggest that there may be 'one truth' or hierarchies of knowledge about what is right and what is wrong. That is, they must challenge the assumption that some people (usually those in power) are more knowledgeable, or that their knowledge is more worthy. This sort of thinking, which tends to support the dominant ideologies in society that are likely to oppress 'other' or 'different' ways of thinking, should be replaced with more social constructivist understandings of reality that recognise multiple 'truths' and appreciate alternative views (Wilson et al., 2008). One such dominant ideology in social work might be that 'professionals are experts on their service users'. If social workers are to be anti-discriminatory and anti-oppressive in the way they work, then this is one of the very first assumptions that they must seek to discredit. Social workers may be well educated, trained and in positions of power, but they are not experts on their service users. Problems experienced by individuals, families and communities may have a number of explanations (at personal, cultural and structural levels) as well as a number of potential solutions to be explored. Partnership working with other services, professionals and, most importantly, service users themselves is an important task in helping to identify these explanations and solutions, and is an essential element (among many) of anti-discriminatory and anti-oppressive practice.

The language around 'partnership' and 'collaboration' is difficult as the two terms are often (wrongly) used interchangeably (Lymbery, 2006). The term 'partnership' relates to when two or more agencies or services have established arrangements that enable them to work together, while the term 'collaboration' refers to the activities undertaken in establishing the partnership and the continued activities undertaken within the partnership (Lymbery, 2006). The development of partnership working and collaboration in social work appeared to happen alongside consumerism and the rise of service user movements in the 1980s. Consumer-led groups questioned the authenticity of social work values like empowerment and self-determination, given the reality that users of services rarely had much of a say in their own care plans let alone service development. Coupled with this was also a recognition that social work and other health and social care services did not work well together or communicate effectively. Since this time, UK governments have focused on encouraging service user involvement, and partnership and inter-agency working as an appropriate way of approaching difficult and complex social issues with a variety of service user groups. Because of these influences there has been a huge cultural shift in the way that social work is undertaken, with a concentrated emphasis on partnership working and collaboration both with service users and other professionals.

Collaboration with service users

Anti-oppressive/anti-discriminatory practice, partnership working and collaboration cannot be discussed without clearly identifying the importance of service user involvement in their own social work services. Social workers would continue to be oppressive if they were merely to 'do' social work 'to' service users with problematic substance use. Service users should be involved in the development of the services social workers provide as well as their own individual or family care plans.

While there is generally a lack of research regarding the views and needs of services users who have problematic substance use, we do know that, 'In the UK user involvement has been identified as an important element in the development of effective drug treatment services' (Schulte et al., 2007: 278). As well as service users being involved in the development of 'professional' organisations, there are a number of peer-led services for people with problematic substance use in the UK. Peer-led services are run by fellow problematic substance use service users and have been set up primarily as 'aftercare' services for people who have left treatment and need further support in the community (Home Office, 2005).

Current research tends to be focused on users of specialist 'substance misuse' services (Fischer et al., 2007; Schulte et al., 2007) and while this view is obviously important, people with problematic substance use may also access a number of other social work and/or health services. What we do know about users of 'substance misuse' services is that they want changes to services, including a reduction in waiting time, more staffing and resources and more access to counselling and psychological services (Schulte et al., 2007). Increasing non-specialist social worker knowledge about problematic substance use increases the capacity for all services to meet the needs of these service users better. While we know very little from the research about problematic substance users who access generic social work services, it is clear that the social workers' ability to work in an anti-oppressive and anti-discriminatory way with people with problematic substance use, wherever they may meet them, will be incredibly beneficial to service users. People with problematic substance use must not be pathologised, because if anything substance use is 'normal' across space and time, and certainly within the range of ordinary human behaviour (RSA, 2007).

There has been much debate and criticism that service user involvement can easily become tokenistic and that social work has failed to live up to the promises it has made about being anti-oppressive. Over time, service users appear to have lost some of their trust in social workers and the role of the social work profession. One of the biggest reasons for service users' cynicism about social workers is due to the practical realities of the role that sometimes appears in stark contrast to social work values. In reality, social workers have different roles to play and different expectations to meet. They are often caught in the 'social care versus social control' bind, which can often put the wants and needs of service users second to other considerations.

Inter-agency and inter-professional working

'Inter-agency working' encompasses work across different agencies, while 'inter-professional working' covers work with practitioners from different professional disciplines. Inter-professional working may need to happen within the same agency, for example if there is a multi-disciplinary team. The lack of appropriate and good inter-agency, inter-professional working and communication have been named as some of the main failings of social work and other health and social care services in a number of the social enquiry reports that have been published over the years in the UK (Laming, 2003; London Borough of Greenwich, 1987; Scotland et al., 1998). The 'new' Labour 'modernising government' agenda attached great importance to partnership working, or the 'joined up' approach and wrote the need for this into many social policies at the time, including the Social Services White Paper *Modernising Social Services* (Department of Health (DoH), 1998) and the Green Paper *Every Child Matters* (Department for Education and Schools (DfES), 2003) which both specifically call for partnership working and more thorough communication systems. The importance of effective communication and working in partnership, including with service users, is obviously best practice. It improves effectiveness, sees service users as a source of knowledge, ensures the rights of service users are central, and enhances empowerment (Hatton, 2008). Partnership working fits well with social work values that guarantee a voice for all and acknowledge the service user as the expert on themselves.

When working with people who may have problematic substance use it may be necessary to refer on, or co-work with more specialised 'substance misuse' services, including peer support services. In these circumstances, inter-agency and inter-professional working will be vital. It is likely that a service user with problematic substance use may have a variety of professionals working along-side them. These professionals may include psychiatrists, psychologists, Drug Intervention Programme (DIP) workers, nurses, specialist social workers, counsellor/therapists and probation officers, among others. In these instances, social workers need to be very clear about the official policies and informal proc-esses that are already established that should guide their partnership working. In some areas of social work, for example children's services, there will be very clear guidelines and protocols governing working in partnership with other agencies and services. In other areas, these protocols will be more informal and based on relationship building.

There have always been moral, political and social responses to issues of substance use that different agencies and professions have different ways of understanding and responding to, so inter-agency and inter-professional working is not always easy. If social workers are to be effective in their inter-professional work, then competent communication and relationship building is paramount. Social workers should be respectful of the other professionals' opin-ions but also be prepared to advocate strongly for their perspective if they believe it is in the best interests of the service user, or if the service user has asked for this advocacy. Wherever and whenever you do partnership working, it is likely that it will present challenges, especially where problematic substance use is concerned. Some of the issues that you may encounter are historical, while others have come about due to political changes in the way social workers are expected to work.

> The new managerialism and the emphasis on external scrutiny, accountability, performativity, and cost effectiveness has reconstructed notions of professional expertise ... Emphasis on external regulation and scrutiny does not necessarily sit easily with notions of professionalism, inter-professional collaboration and 'good practice'. (Harris, 2003: 312)

Practice realties

In practice, social workers find it increasingly difficult to be anti-oppressive, anti-discriminatory and work in honest, equal partnership with their service users. They can also find it practically quite difficult to work in collaboration with different agencies and professionals. Social workers have to balance com-peting and complex perspectives, experiences, knowledge, alliances, wants, needs, resources, policies and laws. What this means in reality is that the social work role can be difficult, divisive and fraught with confusion over these competing domains. This can be especially tricky if working with service users who are engaged in illegal activity, like drug-taking. On the one hand, social workers may recognise the importance of harm reduction initiatives that might include continued drug use, while on the other hand they might be obligated (in some circumstances) to inform criminal justice authorities, whom they are working in partnership with, about this use.

Social workers have to be accountable, they have large amounts of paperwork and time constraints regarding how long they can work with service users and how often they can see them, they have limited resources, statutory obligations and often highly prescribed roles within organisational structures that allow for very little therapeutic work or flexibility. These are some of the practice realties for social workers and social work students. The social worker must walk the fine line between being anti-oppressive and fulfilling their statutory obligations. They must run the gauntlet between offering services users real choice and the reality of a limited budget from which to buy these services. While this position is unenviable, it does not make good social work impossible. Social workers must create effective, therapeutic relationships with service users and good working relationships across agencies and professions, all within these organisational and structural constraints (Wilson et al., 2008). In order to overcome some of these structural obstacles and constraints, it is recommended that social workers go back to basics. We cannot escape the power dynamics in our interactions with service users, but by being genuine, honest, equitable and authentic in our dealings with service users we may be as anti-oppressive as possible in a potentially oppressive situation. Social workers and social work students most likely came into the profession to make a difference to individuals, families and communities, not to do paperwork, or hold budgets, but in reality they can and will do all of these things.

Summary

Understanding the social history of substance use and its impact on current policy and legislation helps us to put the problematic substance use of our service users into perspective. Understanding that public perceptions of problematic substance users are socially constructed by this history enables social workers to be better at working anti-oppressively and in an anti-discriminatory way. Anti-oppressive and anti-discriminatory practice also requires ongoing self-reflection, partnership working (especially with service users) and skills in being able to work effectively across agencies and professional disciplines. This will ensure that service users with problematic substance use are offered the best possible service, regardless of where they present. While practice realties, including resource constraints, accountability and the 'social care versus social control' bind, can make working in an anti-oppressive and anti-discriminatory way difficult, this is a skill that social workers and social work students must master, whatever their practice setting.

Reflections

What do you think are some of the attitudes and stereotypes that society has about people with problematic substance use? How would you seek to challenge this in your anti-discriminatory practice?

How can you make sure that the level of service user involvement you have in your social work practice is not merely 'tokenistic'?

Partnership working and collaboration can present many challenges. Do you think that the cultures of manageralism and accountability in social work can make partnership working particularly difficult? If so in what way?

Further readings

Beresford, P., Branfield, F., Lalani, M., Maslen, B., Sartori, A., Jenny, Maggie and Manny (2007) 'Partnership working: Service users and social workers learning and working together', in M. Lymbery and K. Postle (eds), *Social Work: A Companion for Learning*. London: Sage, pp. 215–39.

Thompson, N. (2006) *Anti-discriminatory Practice*. 4th edn. Basingstoke: Palgrave Macmillan.

Websites

For free resources on partnership working, inter-professional and inter-agency collaboration from the Social Care Institute for Excellence, see: http://www.scie.org.uk/publications/elearning/ipiac/index.asp.

3

Substances and their Effects

It is vital that social workers, regardless of where they work, or with whom, have at least a basic knowledge of the variety of substances that their service users could have difficulty with. This chapter aims to provide some of this knowledge by covering the most commonly used substances and their effects and may be used as an ongoing reference when necessary. It is not possible to cover every potential substance that people can develop a problematic relationship with, because this would necessitate covering every conceivable substance. If the substance you are interested in finding out more about does not appear in this chapter, please see the recommended reading and website list at the end of the chapter.

While there are a number of complex classifications for drugs due to their chemical compositions, to keep it simple it is most useful to think about and classify substances in groups according to their physiological effects. For the purposes of this chapter, the most commonly used substances that will be discussed will be divided into three categories: stimulants, depressants and hallucinogens. Where a substance fits into more than one of these categories it is noted. These categories may include illegal, legal and prescribed substances. Some key terms that you will need to understand will also be discussed in relation to each substance.

Dependence and tolerance

Some substances are more or less likely to cause physical dependence and/or psychological symptoms that make them very difficult to stop using. These psychological symptoms are sometimes known as 'psychological dependence' or 'psychological habituation'. This dependence or habituation is demonstrated through a compulsion to take the substance either periodically or continuously (Petersen and McBride, 2002). Some believe that the distinction between physiological and psychological dependence is a false dichotomy. However, it can be helpful to think about the different ways in which substance use affects the user. Physical dependence means that the user's body has become dependent on having the drug in its system, and usually means that if a user stops using the substance, they will experience physical withdrawal symptoms. These withdrawal symptoms will be different depending on the substance or substances being used. Psychological symptoms can develop when people feel the need to use these substances to have a good time or escape from the realities of life. In this case, they may not have physical withdrawal symptoms, but may experience psychological or emotional difficulties if they give up these substances. Whether substances have the ability to induce physical and/or psychological dependence will be discussed for each of the substances examined.

Tolerance to some substances will develop relatively quickly, while tolerance to others may not occur at all. This will depend on the substance or substances being used. If tolerance develops, users will usually find that they require more and more of the substance in order to induce the required effects from the drug. When tolerance to a substance develops it is likely that the user has become physically dependent. Whether substances have the ability to create tolerance in the user will be discussed for each of the substances covered in this chapter.

Throughout this chapter and for all the substances discussed, please keep in mind that most substances may have both positive or pleasant effects and/or negative or unpleasant effects depending on a number of variables, including: amount taken, route of administration (whether it is ingested, smoked or injected), previous experience of using the substance, whether it is used alongside other substances, the environment in which it is taken and the individual taking it. Also remember,

> The evidence suggests that a majority of people who use drugs are able to use them without harming themselves or others. They are able, in that sense, to manage their drug use ... The harmless use of illegal drugs use is possible, indeed common. (RSA, 2007: 11)

Stimulants

These substances increase activity in the nervous system. They speed users up, keep users awake, make users feel more energised and alert and give users a sense of well-being. They may also cause anxiety, restlessness and insomnia.

Tobacco (also commonly referred to as cigarettes, ciggies, rollies, roll-ups, cigars, chewing tobacco)

Various types of the nicotiana species of plant are more commonly referred to as tobacco plants, and are grown in many countries around the world. These plants are commonly grown for their leaf, which is used to make tobacco products such as cigarettes, cigars and chewing tobacco. Tobacco contains the chemical nicotine (among others), which has a stimulant effect on the user. Tobacco is usually smoked but can also be chewed. Tobacco is a legal substance in the UK and can be bought from a number of outlets, including supermarkets and newsagents.

Effects of use

The use of tobacco products containing nicotine increases the heart rate and can also improve mood and increase the user's ability to concentrate. How long this stimulant effect lasts will depend on the user's level of tolerance, that is, how used to the nicotine their bodies and minds have become. It is likely that for most regular users of nicotine, this stimulant effect will be short-lived and that they will soon require more of the substance (for example another cigarette) to relieve their withdrawal symptoms. In between use of nicotine, the user may become irritable and anxious as the hormone levels that have been stimulated with the use of nicotine begin to drop (NHS, 2010). It is likely that if the user does not maintain their levels of nicotine that they will begin to experience more difficult withdrawal symptoms within 24 hours.

Tobacco use also has very serious long-term health effects that are caused by the variety of different chemicals (including nicotine) that are found in tobacco products like cigarettes. Smoking tobacco causes the majority of cases of lung cancer, and is also linked to other cancers. It is also a major factor in the cause of heart attacks, heart disease, stroke, and respiratory diseases such as emphysema and chronic bronchitis. It is thought that smoking tobacco products may also cause blindness, impotence and infertility (NHS, 2010).

Potential for dependence

Physical dependence is likely to develop for regular users of tobacco products because they contain nicotine. Nicotine induces tolerance in the user, so that they will need to use more of the substance to get the desired effect. It also means that regular users of nicotine will develop uncomfortable and difficult withdrawal symptoms within 24 hours of not using the substance, including: a depressed mood, difficulty sleeping, frustration or anger, difficulty concentrating, restlessness, a decreased heart rate, dizziness and an increased appetite. It is also likely that psychological habituation may develop. Stopping the use of tobacco products containing nicotine is likely to be very difficult for regular users, and they may require help and support in the form of counselling and/or nicotine replacement therapy (NRT). NRT comes in the form of patches, gum, lozenges, nasal sprays and inhalers, most of which are available on prescription from general practitioners. NRT helps people to stop using tobacco products such as cigarettes by replacing the nicotine in the tobacco (that they have become dependent on) with another form of nicotine. Reducing the smoking of tobacco products containing nicotine reduces much of the harm caused from all the other damaging chemicals found in the tobacco products.

Cocaine (also commonly referred to as coke, charlie, toot, Bolivian marching powder)

Cocaine comes from the leaves of the coca bush, which is primarily grown in South American countries, including Bolivia and Columbia. Cocaine is usually found in the form of a white or slightly off-white powder, and is sold by the gram(s) to personal users. By the time it is sold to personal users, it is often reduced in purity by as much as 70 per cent by being cut with various forms of glucose and lactose (Emmett and Nice, 2006). While this substance is usually snorted, it may also be prepared for injection by some users.

Effects of use

As with all stimulants, users of cocaine will feel energised, alert and have a sense of well-being and often euphoria. Users often feel confident, and appear excitable and talkative. Whatever the route of administration, users will usually get these effects quite swiftly; however, these feelings tend to be short-lived. How long these feelings last will depend on the user's tolerance, that is, how used to the drug their bodies and minds have become, and the purity of the drug. A regular user may only experience the positive effects of cocaine for a very brief period, as little as a couple of minutes, whereas an irregular user may experience the effects for longer.

After this period of increased stimulation induced by the use of cocaine, the user may experience a 'come down', where they may feel lethargic, tired and possibly depressed. The 'come down' experienced by the user will probably depend on a number of variables, including the person's tolerance, how often they use the drug and the purity of the drug. A regular heavy user may experience more of a 'come down' and potentially feelings of depression and anxiety as well as weight loss, insomnia, damage to the nose (if snorting) or infections of the veins or skin (if injecting). In some cases, very heavy users of cocaine may experience paranoia and sometimes psychosis. Always remember, however, that while generalisations can be made about the effects of heavier drug use, every individual user of a substance may experience the use of that substance quite differently:

> The way in which a drug affects the person who has taken it depends as much upon the psychological characteristics of the individual (their personality, how they believe the drug will affect them, their emotional state, and so on) as upon the chemical properties of the drug itself. (Gossop, 2000: 16)

Overdose can occur with cocaine and this is usually due to the often 'unknown' purity of the drug, but will also depend on the variables mentioned above. The amount that induces an overdose for one person may not cause an overdose for another. This can make using cocaine unpredictable and dangerous. If an overdose occurs, the heart rate and body temperature of the user will increase, potentially resulting in convulsions, cardiac and/or respiratory failure, coma and possibly death (Emmett and Nice, 2006).

Potential for dependence

There has always been debate about whether it is possible to be physically or physiologically dependent on cocaine. According to Emmett and Nice (2006), it is possible but rare, while other authors believe that cocaine is not physically addictive as are alcohol or heroin (Gossop, 2000). More likely is the potential for psychological dependence or habituation. A heavy user may continue to take the drug because they do not want to experience the inevitable 'come down' which can be very unpleasant. While the 'come down' can lead to depression, anxiety and insomnia, which are distressing, there are usually no life-threatening physical withdrawals from cocaine. Of more concern is the potential for suicide or self-harm, which may result from feelings of anxiety and depression. For this reason, a heavy cocaine user should always seek some help and support before they attempt to discontinue cocaine use on their own.

Crack and freebase cocaine (also commonly known as rocks, white)

Crack and freebase cocaine are chemically identical, but produced in slightly different ways. They are both produced by 'freeing' the cocaine from its chemical base, in relatively crude chemical processes. The resulting substance is a more pure form of cocaine that can easily be smoked and that gives the body a more intensive 'high'. Freebase is a white powder that can be up to 95 per cent pure, and is not usually cut with anything. Crack comes in the form of white or off-white (slightly yellow or pinkish) crystals that vary in size from small granules to larger rocks (up to 1 cm across). Crack can be up to 100 per cent pure (Emmett and Nice, 2006). While these substances are usually smoked in pipes, they too can be prepared for injection by some users.

Effects of use

The effects of crack and freebase use are very similar to the effects of cocaine but occur almost immediately after use, and are much more intense. These feelings include intense euphoria, boundless energy and an almost 'superhuman' feeling. The intensity of these feelings is very short-lived and can last as little as 15 minutes (Emmett and Nice, 2006). How long these feelings last will, however, depend on the user's tolerance, that is, how used to the drug their bodies and minds have become.

As with cocaine, after this intense high, a 'come down' often occurs. The 'come down' effects are the opposite of the intense high and therefore can include fatigue, depression and anxiety. The short-lived 'high' followed by the 'come down' can encourage users to continue to use to avoid the inevitable. The 'come down' experienced by the user will probably depend on a number of variables, including the person's tolerance and how often and for how long they have been using the drug. A regular heavy user may experience more of a 'come down' and potentially feelings of depression and anxiety as well as weight loss, damage to the lungs and insomnia. In some cases, users of crack and freebase may experience paranoia and sometimes psychosis. The potential for this is higher than for cocaine use, and in severe cases, this paranoia may require a period of treatment by mental health services. Always remember, however, that while generalisations can be made about the effects of drug use, every individual user of a substance may experience the use of that substance quite differently.

Overdose can occur with crack and freebase but will depend on the variables mentioned above. An overdose for one person may not be an overdose for another. An overdose can result in convulsions, cardiac and/or respiratory failure, coma and possible death (Emmett and Nice, 2006).

Potential for dependence

As with cocaine, there is an ongoing debate about the potential for users of crack and freebase to be physically or physiologically dependent. The potential of psychological dependence or habituation is, however, amplified, due to the more intense 'high' and potentially more powerful 'come down'. That is, users want more of the substance because they enjoy the high and loathe the low. More concerning than any physical withdrawal symptom, therefore, is the potential for suicide or self-harm which may accompany the 'come down' feelings of anxiety and depression. For this reason, a regular crack or freebase user should always seek some help and support before they attempt to discontinue crack or freebase use on their own.

Amphetamine and amphetamine-like stimulants (ATS) (commonly known as speed, whizz, base and uppers)

These substances are synthetically produced, manufactured and prescribed. They have historically been given to troops in combat to enable them to battle without fatigue for longer periods of time and given to the general public to help with weight loss and sleep disorders. ATS are also prescribed to children for hyperactivity disorders. The most common among these is methylphenidate (Ritalin), given to children diagnosed with Attention Deficit Hyperactivity Disorder (ADHD). When given to people with ADHD, these substances have a paradoxical effect and usually 'calm' the user. The illicit manufacturing of these substances is a relatively crude process and is common throughout Europe, Asia and Australasia. Amphetamine that is produced legally comes in tablet form in a range of colours. Illegally manufactured amphetamine usually comes in a white, off-white or cream powder. This powder is usually coarser than powder cocaine and is not usually particularly pure (only 8 to 12 per cent), often being cut with glucose, milk powder, paracetamol or caffeine (Emmett and Nice, 2006). Amphetamine can also come in a grey, off-white paste form which tends to be more pure. Legally manufactured tablets are taken orally, and while powder forms of this substance can be taken orally (dissolved in a drink or rubbed on the gums), it is more commonly snorted or smoked straight off tin foil. In its paste form, the substance is usually rapped in cigarette paper and swallowed. These substances can also be prepared for injection.

Effects of use

The usual effect of amphetamine use is increased energy, confidence and feelings of euphoria and elation. The user may also experience a reduction in the need for sleep and a reduction in appetite. How long these feelings last will depend on the user's tolerance, that is, how used to the drug their bodies and minds have become, as well as how much they have taken and the 'route of administration'.

Injection of the drug is likely to quicken the onset of these effects but will usually mean that they are short-lived, while ingesting the substance orally may mean the effects take longer to be felt and feel less intense. The effects of these substances can, however, last for several hours. As with other stimulants, the adverse effects of the use of amphetamines are often the converse of the 'high'. Users can experience tiredness, anxiety and depression as well as, in severe cases, paranoia and psychosis. The 'come down' experienced by the user will probably depend on a number of variables, including the person's tolerance, how often they use the drug and the purity of the drug. A regular heavy user may experience more of a 'come down' and potentially feelings of depression and anxiety as well as weight loss, disturbed sleep patterns, damage to the nose (if snorting) or infections of the veins or skin (if injecting). Always remember, however, that while generalisations can be made about the effects of heavier drug use, every individual user of a substance may experience the use of that substance quite differently.

Overdose is possible with the use of amphetamines, although relatively high doses of the drug are usually needed. The body temperature can increase to dangerous levels, leading to convulsions and in some cases death. Potential harm can also be caused by ingesting high levels of 'cutting agents', for example paracetamol.

Potential for dependence

There is little evidence of physical dependence developing with the use of amphetamine. It is likely, however, that psychological symptoms or habituation can develop. That is, users want more of the substance because they enjoy the high and dislike the 'come down'. Because of this, users of the substance are more likely to feel psychologically as if they 'need' the substance. For this reason, a regular amphetamine user may need some help and support before they attempt to discontinue amphetamine use on their own; however, to discontinue to use will not in itself be physically dangerous.

Methamphetamine (commonly known as ice, pure (P), crystal, crystal meth)

This substance is synthetically produced and is closely related to amphetamine. It is commercially produced for the pharmaceutical industry but more often illegally produced in clandestine 'labs'. While it can come in powder and sometimes tablet form, it is most commonly found in crystal or 'rock' form. This crystal form can range in colour from ice clear to light brown, and range in size from small granules of up to 1 cm across (Emmett and Nice, 2006). Methamphetamine is taken in the same way as amphetamine. The powder form can be taken orally in drinks or rubbed on the gums or, less commonly, snorted. The powder form can also be prepared for injection. Methamphetamine in crystal from is usually smoked in a glass or metal pipe or inhaled off metal foil. Methamphetamine is usually more potent than amphetamine and users find they require much less of this in order to get the same effects.

Effects of use

The usual effect of methamphetamine use is increased energy, supreme confidence and feelings of absolute euphoria and elation. The user may also experience a reduction in the need for sleep, a reduction in appetite and potentially an increased sexual appetite. How long these feelings last will depend on the user's tolerance, that is, how used to the drug their bodies and minds have become, as well as how much they have taken and the 'route of administration'. Injection of the drug is likely to quicken the onset of these effects compared to smoking or ingesting it. All methods of use, however, tend to produce relatively long-lasting effects, usually between 2 and 16 hours. The adverse effects are similar to those of amphetamine, but tend to be more intense. Users can experience tiredness, anxiety and depression as well as, in severe cases, paranoia, delusions and psychosis. The 'come down' experienced by the user will probably depend on a number of variables, including the person's tolerance, how often they use the drug and the purity of the drug. A regular heavy user may experience more of a 'come down' and potentially feelings of depression, anxiety and paranoia as well as weight loss, disturbed sleep patterns, damage to the nose (if snorting) or infections of the veins or skin (if injecting). This drug has also been linked to aggression and lack of control in users (Emmett and Nice, 2006). However, always remember that while generalisations can be made about the effects of drug use, every individual user of a substance may experience the use of that substance quite differently.

Overdose of the drug is possible but will depend on a variety of variables, including the person's tolerance, how often they use the drug and the purity of the drug. Overdose can result in severe convulsions, coma and death.

Potential for dependence

Unlike amphetamine, there is evidence to suggest that users of methamphetamine can become both physically dependent and suffer from negative psychological symptoms as a result of using the substance. That is, the body can have physical withdrawals as well as the user feeling that they need and crave the drug. The withdrawal symptoms can be both physically and psychologically very uncomfortable and because of this it is recommended that anyone wanting to cut down or come off the drug seeks support from a drug professional.

Khat (also commonly known as qat, quat, gat, chat, graba, Miraa)

Khat (Catha edulis) is a leaf that is chewed over a number of hours, used widely in Somalia, Yemen, Eritrea and Ethiopia as a stimulant. It is also widely used in the UK, particularly by people from these countries. It is legal in the UK, but illegal in many other countries around the world, including the US. Khat is imported into the UK and can be bought at greengrocers, especially in areas such as East London where there is a large Somali population. It sells at about £4 a bunch and is strongest when the fresh leaves are chewed. It can, however, also be made into a tea or chewable paste (DrugScope, 2010)

Effects of use

Khat can induce mild euphoria and excitement and make the user talkative and alert with increased energy levels. Regular use of khat can lead to insomnia, low mood, anxiety, irritability, frustration and even anger in some people either while they are using it or as an unpleasant after-effect. Long-term khat use can exacerbate mental health problems, pre-existing heart conditions, bronchitis, cirrhosis, dizziness and impaired concentration (Cox and Rampes, 2003). Although rare, it is possible to overdose on khat, which results in agitation, paranoia, rapid heartbeat and breathing, high body temperature and convulsions (Isse, 2004).

While some generalisations can be made about the effects of khat use, every individual user may experience use of the substance quite differently.

Potential for dependence

Cathinone is the dependence-producing active ingredient in khat leaves, although it is more likely that a user will become psychologically dependent rather than physically dependent on khat. That is, regular users of khat may feel as though they need khat in order to get through their day, and feel low in mood if they do not have it, but are unlikely to suffer from any physical withdrawal symptoms. According to Cox and Rampes (2003), however, some withdrawal symptoms have been documented, including 'lassitude, anergia, nightmares and slight trembling, which appear several days after ceasing to chew' (p. 459). If a regular user of khat wants to cut down or give up their use, it is likely that they would benefit from some further support in order to do this.

Depressants

Depressants are drugs that slow down the central nervous system, and because of this they are sometimes called 'downers'. They have the opposite effects of stimulants in that they make people feel sleepy, relaxed and calm.

Alcohol

Alcohol is made by fermenting yeast with grains, fruits or vegetables. This fermentation process produces ethyl alcohol, or ethanol. Beer, lager and cider are usually about 1 part ethanol to 20 parts water, although some brands may be stronger. Wine is about twice to four times as strong and distilled spirits such as whisky, rum and gin are about half water and half ethanol. The more ethanol in the drink, the more 'alcoholic' it is to drink. Therefore distilled spirits are stronger and have more alcohol in them than beer or wine. Alcohol comes in liquid form and is usually drunk. An alcoholic unit is 8 grams, or about 10 ml, of pure alcohol – regardless of how diluted it is. For example, one pint of strong lager (alcohol 5 per cent volume) = 3 units; one pint of standard strength lager (alcohol 3–3.5 per cent volume) = 2 units; one 275 ml bottle of an alcopop (alcohol 5.5 per cent volume) = 1.5 units; one standard (175 ml) glass of wine (alcohol 12 per cent volume) = 2 units and one measure (25 ml) of a spirit strength drink = 1 unit. Current UK guidelines recommend that men limit their intake to no more than 3 or 4 units of alcohol a day (up to 21 units a week), and that women drink no more than 2 or 3 units a day (up to 14 units a week). These 'safer drinking' guidelines suggest at least one day a week should be alcohol free. Units should not be consumed all at once as this is considered 'binge drinking' and can cause long-term health effects.

Effects of use

Alcohol tends to relax people, reduce their inhibitions and stimulates sociability. It can also cause impaired motor co-ordination and cause slowed reaction times. How long these feelings last will depend on the user's tolerance, that is, how used to the alcohol their bodies and minds have become, as well as how much they have taken, whether they have eaten recently and how hydrated their bodies are. Long-term regular heavy use can lead to severe health problems, including cirrhosis of the liver, high blood pressure, damage to the brain and severe vitamin deficiencies. Alcohol use is also strongly related to accidental death, violent crime and absenteeism. Overdosing on alcohol can lead to vomiting, 'blackouts' (amnesia), acute poisoning, unconsciousness, coma and death. Always remember that while generalisations can be made about the effects of alcohol use, every individual user of alcohol may experience the effects of use quite differently. 'The precise expression of alcohol intoxication will vary widely because it is largely determined by the individual's personality and by social and cultural expectations about the effects of drink' (Gossop, 2000: 72).

Potential for dependence

Physical dependence and tolerance can develop so that people need to drink more and more in order to get the same effects and can suffer withdrawal symptoms such as trembling, sweating, anxiety and delirium if they try to stop without support. It is essential that alcohol dependent people seek medical advice when thinking about stopping. Stopping drinking without medical advice once dependence has developed can be very dangerous and can lead to seizures.

Cannabis (commonly known as marijuana, hash, pot, weed, grass, dope, bud). (Please note that cannabis is also sometimes classified as a hallucinogen)

Most types of cannabis come from the plant cannabis sativa, which can be grown in most countries around the world. It is most commonly available in either herbal, resin (hash) or oil form. The herbal form is dried plant material, similar to tobacco that is green or brown in colour. The resin is dried, compressed sap from the plant usually found in blocks that range in colour, size and consistency (from oily to dry and crumbly), but when sold for personal use are no more than 1 inch square. Cannabis oil is obtained by extraction from the resin in a relatively basic chemical process. The oil is usually brown or dark green and can be sold in a 'cap' or capsule-like pill. While cannabis can be baked into food or eaten it is most commonly smoked, but in a variety of ways. It can be rolled into a cigarette or 'joint' either on its own in herbal form or the leaf can be mixed with tobacco. The resin may be burnt off the block and be flaked into a cigarette usually with tobacco, and the oil may be soaked into the cigarette paper before a tobacco cigarette is made. It can also be smoked in a pipe or 'bong' (a smoking device usually made from glass or plastic filled with water to 'filter' the smoke). Cannabis resin and oil can also be used in any way whereby it is heated to release the drug and then inhaled. For example, a common method for using cannabis oil is to put a 'spot' of oil between two heated knives and inhale the drug that is released. This is sometimes known as spotting or 'hot knives'.

Effects of use

Using cannabis can result in a carefree mood, euphoria, muscular relaxation, bodily warmth and intensified visual and auditory perceptions. Many users suggest it gives them creative insights and is a mind-opening experience. How long these feelings last will depend on the user's tolerance, that is, how used to the drug their bodies and minds have become. A first-time user may only require a few draws or 'tokes' on a joint before feeling 'stoned', and this feeling may last for several hours. A regular user will require more of the drug to reach the required effect and it may be that the effects wear off sooner than for a first-time user. At low levels of use, people can have lung damage, increased appetite, short-term memory loss, impaired judgement, bloodshot eyes, dry mouth and lethargy. For regular heavy users, adverse effects may include anxiety, paranoia, psychosis and depression. As with all substances, while generalisations can be made about the effects of cannabis use, every individual user of cannabis may experience the effects of use quite differently. It is not thought to be possible to overdose from cannabis.

Potential for dependence

Physical dependence is thought to be very rare, if not impossible; however, psychological dependence or habituation is very real. That is, users want more of the substance because they enjoy the feeling it induces and dislike how they feel without it. While irregular users may not experience any 'after-effects' of using cannabis, regular heavier users may experience symptoms, including disturbed sleep patterns, anxiety and irritability. Because of this, users of the substance are more likely to feel psychologically as if they 'need' the substance. If a cannabis user wants to cut down or give up their use, as long as there are no other physical or mental health contraindications, it is relatively safe to do so on their own without any form of medical intervention. However, support can be beneficial to help them through the process, because it can be difficult.

Benzodiazepines (including diazepam, 'Valium', temazepam, nitrazepam, 'Mogadon' and others; commonly known as benzos)

Benzodiazepines are synthetically produced prescribed medications for anxiety, insomnia and depression. They are sometimes referred to as anxyiolytics, hypnotics, tranquillisers and sleeping pills. Benzodiazepine users may develop problematic use of these substances either from buying them illicitly, or if they have been prescribed them and are not carefully monitored. Benzodiazepines usually come in pill form and will be in a variety of shapes, sizes, doses and colours, depending on the type. They are usually taken orally, but can also be crushed, dissolved, filtered and injected.

Effects of use

Benzodiazepines reduce anxiety and induce sleep. When used in higher doses, users may experience euphoria, dreaminess and disinhibition. Adverse effects may include over-sedation, mood swings, aggression, lethargy, tiredness and disorientation. As with all substances, while generalisations can be made about the effects of benzodiazepine use, every individual user of these drugs may experience the effects of use quite differently. Overdose is relatively easy, especially if benzodiazepines are mixed with other depressants, like alcohol. Overdose can result in convulsions, respiratory depression, coma and death.

Potential for dependence

Regular use of these substances (even as prescribed) can lead quickly to physical dependence. Tolerance also develops very quickly, and the user will need to use more and more of the drug to get the required effect. The physical and psychological withdrawal symptoms that can occur on cessation of benzodiazepines are thought to be some of the most difficult and unpleasant to experience. Sudden withdrawal from benzodiazepines without medical assistance is not advised as this can lead to convulsions and even death. Do not encourage regular users to give up without support. Withdrawal from benzodiazepines can take place over the course of several weeks or even months and will usually require specialised medical intervention.

Opiates and opioids (heroin, codeine, pethadine, methadone; commonly known as brown, junk, smack, H, done)

Opiates are derived from the milky sticky liquid that is taken from the Asian opium poppy and include drugs like morphine, codeine and after-chemical processing diamorphine (heroin). These drugs are pharmaceutically produced primarily for pain relief and can be found in tablet form as well as in injectable ampoules. These are sometimes available on the street illegally if doctors' surgeries, hospitals or pharmacies have been broken into, or if those prescribed the medication are selling it on, or are vulnerable to friends or family members exploiting their supply. The more likely form of opiate to be found on the street is heroin in the form of a coarse brown powder. Street samples of the drug are usually about 20 per cent pure (Emmett and Nice, 2006). Opiates including heroin are most often smoked or injected. When smoked, it is often inhaled off metal foil through a tube. This is sometimes called 'chasing the dragon'. Heroin can also be mixed with cannabis or tobacco and smoked in cigarette form. Heroin in the form of the coarse brown powder is not readily injectable as it is not water soluble, so it needs to be heated with citric acid or lemon juice to help it dissolve and be prepared for injection.

Opioids have been the name traditionally given to synthetic drugs that have been developed to have the same action and effects as natural opiates, derived from the poppy (raw opium). These drugs are commonly prescribed for pain relief and for 'substitution therapy', and include pethadine and methadone. While use of these drugs can also be problematic and these drugs can be obtained illegally on the street, they are very carefully monitored and held under tight security at hospitals and pharmacies. Opioids are now the name that tends to be used to describe both opiates and the synthetic alternative. The next part of this section refers primarily to heroin, which remains the most widely available and used illicit opioid in the UK.

Effects of use

For illicit users of opioids and in particular heroin, the effects of use can be euphoria, blissful apathy and dreamy, drowsy warmth. Feelings of anxiety, worry, fear or pain disappear and users feel at peace. How long these feelings last will depend on the user's tolerance, that is, how used to the drug their bodies and minds have become. A first-time user may actually feel quite nauseous at first, but the euphoric feelings could last from two to six hours. A regular user will require more of the drug to reach the required effect and it may be that the effects wear off sooner than for a first-time user. The effects of heroin as with other substances will depend on its purity. Heroin bought on the street can be particularly dangerous because of its unknown purity. A higher than expected dose of heroin can depress the heart rate and respiratory system, causing the user to lose consciousness and die. As with all substances, effects depend on a number of variables, including: amount taken, route of administration (whether it is ingested, smoked or injected), previous experience of using the substance, whether it is used alongside other substances, the environment in which it is taken and the individual taking it.

Potential for dependence

When prescribed for pain relief or substitution therapy, opioids are used to stop pain or reduce withdrawal effects. It is likely that people who are prescribed opioids will become dependent on them. This is not the same thing as developing problematic substance use. These drugs induce physical dependence whether used as prescribed or used problematically. Both physical and psychological heroin dependence can also develop relatively quickly. A tolerance will develop in regular users, which means that they will need to use more and more of the drug in order to acquire the same effects. Eventually, unpleasant withdrawal symptoms develop, and the user has to continue to use the drug in order to relieve these. Using more of the drug more often will be necessary if they are to obtain the desired pleasant effects. Withdrawal effects from regular use of the drug can include flu-like symptoms, muscular aches and pains, hot and cold sweats, diarrhoea, vomiting, muscle spasms as well as psychological cravings for the drug. Withdrawing from opioids unassisted is often called 'going cold turkey', and can be very difficult without support.

Volatile substances (glue, solvents, petrol, lighter gas and others)

Most volatile substances are complex hydrocarbons which pass rapidly to the brain. Volatile substances are many and varied and are found in a range of domestic and commercial products. The range of substances with the potential for abuse is huge and includes glue, aerosol propellant gases, petrol, lighter fluid, paint thinners, nail polish remover, paint and paint remover. These substances are usually sprayed directly into the mouth and inhaled deeply, and/or put into a plastic bag, on to a rag, cloth or sleeve and inhaled deeply from here.

Effects of use

Low doses of volatile substances tend to have a similar effect to alcohol, but with larger doses users can experience powerful intoxication, excitability and hallucinations. Intoxication can occur within seconds and may take several hours to wear off, depending on the amount taken. Adverse effects can include short-term memory loss and problems with speech and balance. The use of volatile substances is linked to sudden death by asphyxiation, caused by swelling of the throat and inhalation of vomit. Overdose is also possible, leading to coma and death. As with all substances, while generalisations can be made about the effects of volatile substance use, every individual user of these substances may experience the effects of use quite differently.

Potential for dependence

It is not thought possible that use of volatile substances can create a physical dependence, but it is likely that psychological symptoms may develop, in that people feel the need to use these substances to have a good time or to escape from the realities of life. It is therefore unlikely that users will have any difficult or dangerous physical withdrawal symptoms if they stop using them but they may require some support to come off and stay off these substances if they are very used to relying on them. Tolerance to these substances can build up relatively quickly, with the user finding that they need more and more of the substance to induce the required effects.

Hallucinogens

Hallucinogens are taken so as to produce a sensory experience of something that does not exist outside the mind (a hallucination). They are naturally occurring in certain fungi, cacti and plants, but are also often manufactured in laboratories.

Ecstasy (MDMA) (commonly known as E, tabs, beans, pills)

Ecstasy is a difficult drug to classify as it has stimulant-like properties and leads to changes in the user's state of consciousness. However, it does not cause hallucinations as such in most users. It is, however, often categorised as a hallucinogen and will be for the purposes of this text. Ecstasy is a completely synthetic substance originally produced in Germany as an appetite suppressant. Ecstasy in its pure form is a white powder, but more often comes in a tablet or capsule form that can vary in shape, size and colour. The tablets often have an image imprinted on them to identify the type or make. It is not uncommon for the 'tabs' to be less than pure and they are often 'cut' with a number of different agents, including amphetamines and ketamine. Pure ecstasy powder and ecstasy in tablet form are usually taken orally.

Effects of use

Ecstasy can generate feelings of warmth and happiness, take away fear and lead to overwhelming feelings of peace, sociability and empathy towards others (feeling 'loved up'). Common side effects can include tension in the jaw and grinding of the teeth, anxiety and heart palpitations. Ecstasy has also been implicated in death by users overheating. However, the risk of this is thought to be relatively low. There is also some evidence of the drug being associated with mental health problems such as depression, although there are no clear conclusions about this. According to some authors, 'Excessive doses of ecstasy can lead to collapse, coma, permanent brain damage and death' (Emmett and Nice, 2006: 122). As with all substances, while generalisations can be made about the effects of ecstasy use, every individual user of ecstasy may experience the effects of use quite differently.

Potential for dependence

There is little evidence that users can become physically dependent on ecstasy; however, a psychological habituation may develop if users feel that they need to use the substances to feel sociable and have a good time. Tolerance can develop for regular users, who may need more and more of the drug in order to produce the same effects. Most ecstasy users will not experience any physical complications as a result of stopping their use; however, they may be inclined to feel depressed and anxious and may require some support to help them stop using it.

Ketamine (special k, vitamin k)

Ketamine was originally developed as an anaesthetic for use by the US forces in the Vietnam War. Today, it is still manufactured legally for surgical procedures in some humans and animals. While ketamine is illicitly manufactured, most of it found on the street is diverted from legal supplies. It is usually found illicitly in the form of a white powder, but is sometimes found in capsule form. For medical purposes, it is produced in vials or bottles for injection. Ketamine is most commonly snorted, or if in tablet form taken orally. It is sometimes mixed with cannabis and/or tobacco and can be smoked. While it could also easily be injected, it is thought that this happens less regularly because the effects of the drug occur almost instantly when used in this way, making it difficult for the user to have the time to finish injecting.

Effects of use

According to Emmett and Nice (2006), ketamine is a 'dissociative anaesthetic'. Users can experience a euphoric rush similar to that caused by cocaine and/or mild dream-like feelings, as well as powerful hallucinations. Users sometimes report that use of the drug can cause 'out of body' or 'near death' experiences. This experience is sometimes referred to as being in a 'K-hole'. Sometimes muscle rigidity can occur so that users of the drug remain in the same position until the drug has worn off, on average up to about three to four hours. Adverse effects of ketamine can include interference with speech, vision and attention, as well as paranoia, agitation and aggression. Convulsions and vomiting have also been noted. There is overdose potential when using ketamine because users can be unsure of the doses they are taking and the purity of the drug. Overdose can lead to death through cardiac and respiratory failure. As with all substances, while generalisations can be made about the effects of ketamine use, every individual user of ketamine may experience the effects of use quite differently.

Potential for dependence

It is thought that over time, regular heavy users will develop a tolerance to the drug and will therefore require more and more of it in order to produce the required effects. It is thought that strong psychological habituation may also develop in regular users, but there are no known withdrawal symptoms associated with stopping regular ketamine use. Most ketamine users will not experience any physical complications as a result of stopping their use; however, they may be inclined to feel depressed and anxious and may require some support to stop them using it.

Magic mushrooms

Magic mushrooms come in the form of naturally occurring fungi. Although there are a number of varieties of hallucinogenic mushrooms, the two most widely used are called the 'liberty cap' and the 'fly agaric', which can be found growing in woodland and domestic gardens. They come in a variety of shapes and sizes and can be picked by the user themself, or when out of season can be found dried and bagged or in powder and capsule form. Magic mushrooms are usually taken orally, eaten raw or cooked, baked into a variety of dishes or made into a tea. In capsule form, they are usually swallowed. Dried mushrooms can also be taken with cannabis and/or tobacco and smoked.

Effects of use

The effects of magic mushrooms can vary greatly because the dose is difficult to regulate. Taking magic mushrooms is, however, likely to cause euphoria, animation and happiness. Users may also experience hallucinations and mild visual disturbances. It is thought that the 'mind-set' of the user and the environment in which they are taken may have an influence on whether the user experiences these hallucinations as pleasant or not. When users experience unpleasant hallucinations this is often referred to as a 'bad trip'. Because some users find it difficult to be sure that they are taking the right type of fungi (and not a poisonous variety) as well as the correct dose, adverse effects may include dizziness and nausea and in some rare cases depression and delusions. The overdose potential with 'real' magic mushrooms is negligible, but the danger comes from overdosing accidentally on the wrong, more poisonous variety of mushroom. As with all substances, while generalisations can be made about the effects of magic mushroom use, every individual user of magic mushrooms may experience the effects of use quite differently.

Potential for dependence

A tolerance to magic mushrooms can develop quite quickly, and that means that users may need to take more and more mushrooms to induce the required effect. Sometimes, the required effects become illusive and the user will need to take some time off to reduce their tolerance. Because of this, it is very unlikely that a user would become psychologically dependent on the drug, as its effects over time just cease. This means that it is highly unlikely that there will be any withdrawal effects and users are usually able to stop taking mushrooms with little or no support.

Lysergic acid diethylamide – LSD (trips, tabs, acid)

Lysergic acid diethylamide (LSD) is produced by the chemical processing of a substance contained in a naturally occurring fungus called 'ergot'. It was first produced in 1938 by a Swiss chemist called Albert Hoffman who was experimenting with ergot for medical purposes. Pure LSD occurs in the form of colourless crystals, but this is usually impregnated on small pieces of blotting paper when sold for personal use. These pieces of blotting paper, often referred to as 'trips' or 'tabs', are usually small, square pieces of paper with a picture on them. According to Emmett and Nice (2006), the amount of the actual drug found in 'tabs' on the street has significantly decreased from approximately 120–150 micrograms to 40–60 micrograms since the 1960s. LSD can also be found in the form of 'microdots', which are pinhead-sized pills of various colours, made from impregnating a small square of gelatine with LSD. These 'tabs' or microdots are usually taken orally, but microdots are also taken by placing them under the eyelids, where the blood vessels in the eye absorb the drug quickly.

Effects of use

After approximately 40 minutes, the user of LSD will start to feel that their perception of the world around them is changing. They are likely to experience visual, auditory and tactile hallucinations. Often, the user can feel as though they have entered into an entirely different world or dimension. These effects can be pleasant or very disturbing for the individual user, depending on a number of things, including dose, environment and mood of the user. The effects can vary and can last between 6 and 24 hours. There are very few physical effects of using LSD. The main potential problem may come from the types of hallucinations that the user may experience, which could cause them harm. For example, if they are hallucinating that they have special powers and can fly, or have special strengths to fight would-be attackers. As the LSD wears off, users may feel tired and disorientated at first, but will be left with no physical side effects. They may, however, be left with memories of the hallucinations, and when these are re-experienced they are called 'flashbacks'. There is some evidence to suggest that these flashbacks can be related to future mental health problems.

Potential for dependence

Tolerance to LSD can develop over time, meaning that a regular user may need to use more and more of the drug to get the same effects from it. This tolerance is rapidly lost after a week or so off the drug. People who stop using the drug will not experience any physical discomfort or withdrawal symptoms. It is, however, possible to develop a psychological habituation to the drug.

Summary

All substances can induce both pleasant and unpleasant effects. While it is impossible to deny that substances can cause very real damage to people's health and lives in a variety of ways, it is also important to remember that not all drug users will experience these problems. While generalisations can be made about substances, and many of these have been discussed here, the effects of any substance will always depend on a number of variables, including amount taken, route of administration (whether it is ingested, smoked or injected), previous experience of using the substance, whether it is used alongside other substances, the environment in which it is taken and the individual taking it. Use this chapter as a guide only for your work with people who may use substances problematically. Always seek specialised advice if you are unsure as to whether it is safe to support a service user to cut down or stop using their substance(s) of choice. Remember that in some cases, for example alcohol, it is actually more dangerous to encourage a user to stop their use suddenly. Always seek urgent medical attention if you suspect an overdose of any kind.

Reflections

Imagine you meet a service user who explains to you that they are using cocaine on a regular basis at the weekends. Would you feel comfortable working with this service user in a non-judgemental way?

What if they were a regular crack user? A daily drinker? Do you think that it matters what substances they might use? Why?

How do you feel about injecting drug users?

Further reading

Emmett, D. and Nice, G. (2006) *Understanding Street Drugs: A Handbook of Substance Misuse for Parents, Teachers and Other Professionals*. 2nd edn. London: Jessica Kingsley Publishers.

Websites

Helping to Document the Complex Relationship between Humans and Psychoactives, at: http://www.erowid.org.

Informing Policy and Seeking to Reduce Risk, at: http://www.drugscope.org.uk.

For the A to Z of drugs, see FRANK, at: http://www.talktofrank.com/.

Part 2

Diverse Populations

Part 2 covers problematic substance use among a number of diverse populations. This part assumes some general knowledge about these specialist populations and acknowledges that readers may currently work with or intend to work with these service user populations. Chapter 4 centres on 'Problematic substance use across the lifespan', with a special focus on working with younger and older people. Chapter 5 covers working with 'Gender and problematic substance use', covering pregnancy, sex work and interpersonal violence, while Chapter 6 covers 'Working with criminal justice service users who have problematic substance use'. Chapter 7 covers 'Problematic substance use in black and minority ethnic (BME) communities', including asylum seekers and refugees. The final chapter covers 'Problematic substance use in lesbian, gay, bisexual and transgendered (LGBT) communities'. For each of these diverse populations, a number of key vulnerabilities are explained and best practice guidance is discussed.

4

Problematic Substance Use Across the Lifespan

Lifespan or life course is the progression and path an individual takes from conception to death (Crawford and Walker, 2003). When working with service users, it is necessary to pay special attention to where people are at in their development along the lifespan if we are to make the most of the interactions we have with them. This chapter will explore problematic substance use across the lifespan and look specifically at these issues as they relate to younger and older service users. There is not enough scope in this chapter to cover this topic in any great depth. However, it will introduce you to the importance of considering your service users' developmental life stage while engaging them in behaviour change. There are a range of approaches to understanding human development (sociological, physiological and psychological). Approaches that take into consideration a range of variables to theorise about human development provide us with a comprehensive understanding of issues relevant to maturity through the life course. The different ways in which social workers work with people across the lifespan stem from these ways of understanding human development. Being able to take into consideration these special needs and work creatively using the basic approaches outlined in Part 2 of this text will make your work with people in these age groups more effective.

Working with young people

There has been increasing concern regarding the problematic substance use of our young people. While often seen as a rite of passage into adulthood, substance use by younger people is often experimental. That is not to say, however, that younger people cannot or do not develop serious problematic substance use and/or dependence. Recent statistics (National Treatment Agency for Substance Misuse (NTA), 2010) indicate that younger people are tending to stay away from 'harder' drugs like heroin and crack cocaine and the number of teenagers entering treatment for heroin and crack has fallen by a third in four years (NTA, 2010).

Alcohol, cannabis and 'dance drugs' like ecstasy, and amphetamines continue to be the mostly widely used substances by adolescents in the UK.

Adolescence is defined as the transition from childhood to adulthood and usually includes the age ranges from puberty to late teens or early twenties. The terms 'young person' or 'youth' are generally more widely defined and could include people outside of these age ranges if they appear to be 'young people' developmentally. 'Tasks' that are associated with this transition from childhood to adulthood include the physical changes of puberty and increased sexual feelings, a move from concrete to abstract thinking, risk taking, role experimentation and independence from family. Some of these 'tasks' of adolescence may include the use of substances (e.g. where risk taking and role experimentation is concerned) (Jarvis et al., 2005). These 'tasks' are based on generalisations about adolescent development and are typically based on Western cultures. Not all young people will perform all of these tasks on their journey to adulthood and it will also be important to bear in mind other cultural and religious developmentally appropriate tasks for the young people you work with.

According to NTA (2009c), young people should have their needs identified and met where possible in 'universal' or 'targeted services'. Universal services are those that are accessible to all young people, for example schools and doctors. 'Targeted services' are accessible by young people who are vulnerable or who have been identified as requiring some low intensity intervention and monitoring. As a social worker you may work in either of these types of services, and should be aware of the possibility of problematic substance use. Wherever necessary, you will also need to know how to refer young service users on to specialist services.

Effective social work with young people

When working with young people who have problematic substance use, there are some important yet simple things to bear in mind. It will be important to think about where and when you see them. It may not be helpful to see the young person in your office. Those of you who are familiar with working with young people will be aware of the importance that setting and environment can have when engaging young people in such a way as to facilitate behaviour change. Take time to complete any screening you may do and really listen to what the young person has to say. You have the opportunity to make a huge difference to the life of your young service user if you do the basics right. Take time to build rapport and trust and listen to their stories.

If social workers see young people with problematic substance use, it is likely that they will be seeing them initially for reasons other than their substance use, or because they have been coerced into seeing a social worker by family, their school or social services. With this in mind, it is vital that you also bear in mind being non-judgemental and anti-discriminatory in your work with them. You need to engage them in a valuable relationship, not judge their behaviours or try and 'force' them to change. According to Luckock et al. (2006), social workers should consider the 'rights and rescue stance' when working with young people. This means recognising that the young people we are working with can be both vulnerable and capable and intentional. We need to consider this vulnerability, but not at the expense of stifling their independence, and we need to encourage their capabilities but not at the risk of putting them in jeopardy.

Whether they come to us because they have been coerced or by their own volition, it is important to recognise that when working with younger people there are often daunting legal considerations. Confidentiality may be very important to the young person, but depending on their age and ability to give consent legally (be Gillick competent), this issue can be difficult to negotiate. Being Gillick competent, which is a term used in medical law, means a person under the age of 16 has been deemed competent and fit to consent to their own medical treatment without the permission of their parents or guardian. Young people may not want their parents/guardians to be aware of their problematic substance use; however, if they require treatment of some sort, the consent of their parent/guardian(s) may be a requirement. It is recommended that, if possible, caregivers and family are involved in the early stages of any ongoing work you may do regarding problematic substance use. This may be something you work towards with the young person in the early stages of your work together. If the young person will not engage unless there is strict confidentiality, always seek supervision on this issue as the legal implications are complex and untested in the 'substance misuse' field. You should still be able to work with the young person, but it may mean that some of their choices for onward referral and treatment options may be limited. Having family involved can support the young person's long-term behaviour change and is a protective factor against continued problematic substance use. Increasing protective factors in the young person's life while reducing risk factors will be important steps to take in improving the likelihood of long-term behaviour change. For more information about other risk and protective factors that relate to young people please see Chapter 1.

Risk management regarding their current substance use is also a complex issue. This is the case for all service users with problematic substance use, but particularly young people because their experience with using substances and their tolerance levels are more likely to be unknown. There are a number of specialised youth problematic substance use screening tools, including the Drug Use Screening Tool (DUST) (Department for Children, Schools and Family, n.d.), and the Substances and Choices Scale (SACS) (Christie et al., 2007) that can help you elicit some of this important information. Harm reduction education (Chapter 10) is also vital as you seek to reduce the risks associated with their substance use. You may find using a motivational approach (Chapter 11) as well as relapse prevention (Chapter 12), especially the coping skills training (for example, assertiveness training and communication skills) which is part of this model useful for working with young people.

In summation then, when working with young people who have problematic substance use:

- Use developmentally appropriate interventions. Young people are not adults.
- Think about confidentiality and the limits to it. Seek supervision when working in complex legal situations.
- Strengthen support from family and significant others, and involve them as much as possible.
- Reduce the harm associated with substance use as much as possible by teaching harm reduction education.
- Reduce risk factors and enhance protective factors.
- See young people somewhere other than in your office if possible.
- Use a motivational approach and teach coping skills.

These are a few of many considerations to take into account when you embark on working with young people who may have problematic substance use.

Working with older people

Problematic substance use by older people is often missed, ignored or assumptions are made that older people do not use substances. The myth that 'there are no old drug users', which assumes that all drug users die before reaching old age, perpetuates these assumptions. While substance use may decrease with age, it is still a relevant and often overlooked problem in older people. While findings from the *2008/9 British Crime Survey: England and Wales* show that the use of drugs is less prevalent amongst older people, our aging population means that the problem is likely to increase over time (Home Office, 2009b). Estimates indicate that by 2025, more than 25 per cent of the UK's population will be over 60 years of age. This is a generation that has grown up during a time when drug and alcohol use became more prevalent and therefore are more likely than previous generations to have problematic substance use.

When working with older people who may have problematic substance use, it is important to bear in mind a number of things that are specifically related to this age group. As people age, there are a number of physiological changes that occur that make older people generally less tolerant of substances. Some of these physiological changes include:

- A fall in ratio of body water to fat.
- Decreased hepatic blood flow.
- Inefficiency of liver enzymes.
- Altered responsiveness of the brain. (Institute of Alcohol Studies (IAS), 2009: 3)

All of these physiological changes mean that older people are more likely to have an increased concentration of substances in their system and therefore an enhanced probability of toxicity (Williamson, 2002). Substances are more likely to affect older people at lower doses.

While problematic substance use among older people is most likely to be linked to alcohol use, benzodiazepines and other prescribed or over the counter medications, older people may also use a range of other substances.

Alcohol

The number of older people who drink may be increasing, and there is evidence that today's population of older people may be heavier drinkers than previous generations (Institute of Alcohol Studies, 2009). This is possibly as a result of being from a generation in which there was a high availability and social acceptance of alcohol use. There are thought to be two types of drinkers in older adulthood. These types are known as 'early onset' and 'late onset' drinkers. Early onset drinkers are drinkers who started drinking early on in life and may have had problematic alcohol use throughout their lives. Late onset drinkers start drinking later in life, perhaps as a result of aging and the issues associated with it such as illness, pain and loss, or because they have more free time. Both types of drinkers are vulnerable to problems related to their drinking because of the aforementioned physiological changes that occur as people age.

Prescribed and over the counter medication

Older people are more likely to be on prescribed medication and use over the counter medications than the general population (Williamson, 2002). These medications have the potential to become problematic when taken more often or in higher doses than prescribed or recommended. There are also potential problems when prescribed and over the counter medications are taken together when service users have little knowledge of their combined effects. These medications also have the potential to cause more problems in older people due to the aforementioned physiological changes that occur as people age. Medications such as benzodiazepines, a group of minor tranquilisers including diazepam (Valium), are often prescribed to older people. These medications are usually prescribed to help people to relax, stay calm and sleep. When these types of medications first became available in the 1960s, they were thought to be very harmless and were seen as a safer alternative to barbiturates that were previously prescribed for similar problems. In time, however, it became apparent that these medications were highly 'addictive', that is, that people became heavily dependent on the use of them, and that the withdrawal from them was very difficult. Often prescribed long term, especially to women, for anxiety and depression in the 1960s, drugs like Valium became known as 'mother's little helper'. Unfortunately, the long-term impact of this was that many women remained dependent on this type of medication well into their older adult life. While these people are usually taking this medication as prescribed, the use quickly becomes problematic because they are highly dependent on the medication and coming off it is particularly difficult. These days, benzodiazepines are usually only prescribed in a very short course, which has lessened the dependence potential and problematic use of them. Awareness of the potential for people to be using prescribed and over the counter medications in a problematic way is important when working with older service users. Using medications in higher doses and for longer periods of time than prescribed or recommended can be problematic, as can the unknown combined effects of using a range of both prescribed and over the counter medications. Some of the issues that present as a result of this problematic use of alcohol and prescribed or over the counter medications can mimic other physical and/or mental health problems that also become more prevalent as people age. This in turn can confuse diagnosis of problematic substance use in the older person.

Identification of problematic substance use

It is thought that problematic substance use among older people is under-reported. Because many of the symptoms of problematic substance use, as well as the effects of it, can mimic other physical and mental health problems, it is thought that it often goes unrecognised. Problematic substance use may be implicit in many of the health problems or accidents older people have, for example dementia, falls, memory loss, incontinence and malnutrition. Without thorough investigation, these could be assumed problems of older age, when they are in fact a result of problematic substance use. If you work with older people in any setting it is important to consider potential problematic substance use, including 'misuse' of prescribed or over the counter medications when identifying health problems.

The models of practice outlined in Part 3 of this book may be useful for you to consider when working with older people with problematic substance use. Taking a motivational approach and believing that behaviour change is possible for older people is paramount. In summation, the key points to consider when working with older people who may have problematic substance use are:

- Older people can and do use a range of substances.
- We are likely to see an increase in problematic substance use among older people as our population ages.
- Most problematic use is associated with alcohol, prescribed and over the counter medications.
- Physiological changes that occur as people age can make older people's substance use potentially more problematic.
- Problematic substance use in older people is often misdiagnosed or ignored.
- Older people deserve to be offered effective treatment for their problematic substance use.

Summary

Working with service users across the lifespan who may have problematic substance use requires an awareness of some of the things that make these age groups unique. You will need to work differently with service users, depending on where they are in their life course. This chapter has provided a brief overview of what some of these considerations and differences may be. Use these ideas to think and reflect further on how you might use some of the models covered in Part 3 of this book in a more age appropriate manner.

Reflections

Are you aware of specialised youth substance misuse services that you could refer to if necessary?

How do you think you would feel offering harm reduction education to a young person? What if they were only 14?

How would you feel asking an older person if they take more medication than they are supposed to?

Further readings

Baer, J. and Petersen, P. (2002) 'Motivational interviewing with adolescents and young adults', in W. Miller and S. Rollnick (eds), *Motivational Interviewing: Preparing People for Change*. 2nd edn. New York: Guilford Press, pp. 320–32.

Davis, P. (2007) *Substance Misuse in Young People: A Brief (One Session) Intervention (BI) Framework for Reducing Hazardous or Harmful Use*, at: http://www.nta.nhs.uk/uploads/brief_adolescent.pdf.

Websites

For information about alcohol and older people see: http://www.rcpsych.ac.uk/mentalhealthinfoforall/problems/alcoholanddrugs/alcoholandolderpeople.aspx.

Also, see FRANK at: http://www.talktofrank.com/.

5

Gender and Problematic Substance Use

There is evidence that women and men differ in the causes and the progression of their problematic substance use. Men still use alcohol and most drugs more heavily and more problematically than women (Hoare, 2009; Health and Social Care Information Centre, 2010). However, women are more likely to have problematic use of prescribed medications like benzodiazepines (Women's Health Council, 2009), and are more susceptible to substance misuse-related interpersonal problems, trauma, mental health and medical problems (Greenfield et al., 2003 cited in NTA, 2005). Drug treatment services regularly report a 3:1 ratio of men to women attending their services. For example, in 2008/9, 151,064 men compared to 56,516 women aged 18 or over accessed treatment services in England (Hoare, 2009). While there is some evidence to suggest that women experience more barriers when accessing specialist services (Greenfield et al., 2007), other studies show that they are likely to seek services earlier in their substance-using careers (Office for Substance Abuse Services, 2004) and have overall better treatment outcomes (Greenfield et al., 2007).

While historically men have been more likely than women to drink heavily and use drugs, a younger generation of women is emerging that appears to be matching their male counterparts. According to an NTA media release (2009a), while less women entered treatment for crack and heroin treatment in 2008/9 compared to 2005/6, there was a huge increase in the number of women under 35 entering treatment for cocaine use in the same time frame (up 60 per cent). Recent Irish research found that girls are drinking almost as often as boys, and more girls (29 per cent) than boys (25 per cent) reported being drunk during the previous month. In the same research, slightly more girls than boys reported binge drinking (Women's Health Council, 2009). According to the European Monitoring Centre for Drugs and Drug Addiction (EMCDDA) (2006) and Fagan et al. (2008) (cited in Women's Health Council, 2009: 4), an equal proportion of boys and girls aged 15 to 16 have ever used cannabis, slightly more girls in this age group have used ecstasy regularly and both sexes are equally at risk of problematic opiate use.

In your social work role, it will be important to be aware of some of the differences in the way that men's and women's problematic substance use progresses, manifests and presents, as well as how this is predicted to change over time.

Vulnerabilities to problematic substance use

Physical health

Women appear to be more vulnerable to developing physical health problems as a result of their substance use. They seem to develop physical health problems sooner in their drinking and drug using careers (Cormier et al., 2003; Cox and Lawless, 2000). Women metabolise alcohol and other substances a lot slower than men do, which means that the harmful metabolites last for longer in their system and therefore cause more health problems. For example, they are more likely to develop and die from cirrhosis of the liver after a shorter length of time drinking compared to men (Women's Health Council, 2009). According to Cormier et al. (2003), women are also more likely to have brain shrinkage and impairment, breast cancer, gastric ulcers and alcohol hepatitis after drinking lower levels of alcohol over shorter periods of time.

While it is important to be aware of these physical vulnerabilities for women, the fact remains that men are much more likely to use substances, and use them more heavily than women (Hoare, 2009). This means that it is also important to be aware of the potential physical health problems that men may develop as a result of their problematic substance use (please see Chapter 3 for more information). For example, more men than women die from alcohol-related causes in England (Office for National Statistics, 2008).

Trauma and mental health

It is estimated that two-thirds of women with problematic substance use may also have a mental health problem such as depression, post-traumatic stress disorder (PTSD), panic disorder and/or eating disorder (Cormier et al., 2003). According to NTA (2005), women in drug treatment are two to three times more likely to report symptoms consistent with post-traumatic stress disorder, and have greater psychological needs. There is also evidence that there is a positive and significant relationship between the experience of child abuse, neglect and problematic substance use in men (Brems et al., 2004; Rostami et al., 2010). For example, according to Neaigus et al. (2001, cited in NTA, 2005), up to 45 per cent of drug-injecting women and 17 per cent of drug-injecting men in treatment have been sexually abused. Both of these figures are significantly high compared to the general population.

It is thought that people who have experienced some type of abuse or trauma may use substances to cope with the emotional and psychological pain that such events might create. There is also a strong link between childhood or historical sexual abuse and other mental health problems, including depression and post-traumatic stress disorder. Co-existing problems are therefore fairly common in the general problematic substance using population. It appears, however, that some mental health problems such as suicidality, deliberate self-harm and depression are much more likely to affect female problematic substance users. Please see Chapter 15 for further information about these co-existing problems, often referred to as 'dual diagnosis'. An awareness of the problematic substance users' vulnerability to mental health issues is vital when working with both men and women who may have problematic substance use.

Pregnancy and childcare

Substance use during pregnancy can have a direct impact on the foetus. Use of alcohol and drugs, coupled with poor nutrition, poor general health of the mother, experience of mental health problems and trauma as well as a lack of antenatal care makes pregnant women vulnerable to miscarriage and puts the unborn child at serious risk of birth defects (Cormier et al., 2003). When a woman drinks during pregnancy, the alcohol passes from her blood stream through the placenta and into the baby's blood stream. High intakes of alcohol can lead to Foetal Alcohol Spectrum Disorders in the child (for example, Foetal Alcohol Syndrome). These are a range of problems (physical, behavioural, cognitive) that may result after drinking in pregnancy. While the Department of Health recommends that women give up all drinking prior to becoming pregnant, experts remain unsure whether drinking at lower levels is dangerous or not. Several scientific reviews of the research have found no consistent evidence of adverse effects of drinking at low (under 2 units per day) to moderate levels (2 to 5 units a day). However, the best advice you can give your service user is not to drink at all (Royal College of Obstetricians and Gynaecologists (RCOG), 2006). Educating women about the potential harm is vital, and women with problematic substance use who are unable to stop using substances themselves will require specialist treatment. Your ability to engage these women and encourage and support them in a non-judgemental way throughout this time is imperative. Make sure that you are aware of any specialist maternal/pregnancy 'substance misuse' services in your area that you can refer your female service user on to. They should be offered highly specialised integrated care by these teams to help reduce serious problems such as Foetal Alcohol Syndrome, low birth weight and perinatal mortality.

Supporting women following the birth of their children to continue to reduce or stop their substance use is also crucial. Harm reduction education around safer substance using practices when caring for children is critical. Please see Chapter 16 on parental substance use and working with families for a more in-depth discussion of this complex area of social work practice.

Sex work and criminal offending

There is a correlation between women who sex work and dependent substance use. Women may use sex work as a way to fund their substance use. Sex work is a high-risk behaviour because there is more risk of sexually transmitted infections and unwanted pregnancy, and sex work is associated with high incidences of violence (Becker and Duffy, 2002). That is not to say, however, that all women with problematic substance use are sex workers, or that all sex workers have problematic substance use – this is not the case. The correlation does exist, however, and it will be necessary for you to be aware of potential problematic substance use if you regularly work with sex workers. While there has been much less research conducted with male sex workers, it is clear that male sex workers, especially those who work on the street, also engage in substance use and other high-risk behaviours (unsafe sex, injecting drug use) (Timpson et al., 2007). According to Hser et al. (2003) and the Office of Substance Abuse Services (2004), however, where women may turn to sex work, men are more likely to turn to more serious criminal behaviour to support their substance use. Criminal offending is strongly linked to both male and female problematic substance use, but men have much higher rates of offending, especially in relation to acquisitive crimes (Home Office, 2009b). Please see Chapter 6 for more information about working with service users involved in the criminal justice system.

If service users are supported to reduce or stop substance use this can in turn reduce sexually risky behaviour, the criminal activity associated with sex work and other offending behaviours. If you work with men or women who sex work, and/or who are involved with other criminal activity, it will be important to bear in mind the high correlation between these two things and problematic substance use. Your ongoing support in reducing the harm associated with problematic substance use, sex work and criminal activity will be essential.

Interpersonal relationships and violence

There is a strong correlation between problematic substance use and domestic violence. Histories of domestic violence are more prevalent among women who seek substance misuse services, and similarly women seeking services for domestic violence have a higher prevalence of substance misuse than women in the general population (Bennett and O'Brien, 2007). Women who access specialist 'substance misuse' services are more likely to be in relationships with substance using partners and identify relationship problems as being a cause of problematic substance use (Office of Substance Abuse Services, 2004). While women in heterosexual relationships are not the only people to experience domestic violence, they continue to be by far the main victims of abuse. A UK study which undertook a one-week snapshot of women's services in three 'substance misuse' agencies found rates of domestic violence of between 40 and 62 per cent (Greater London Authority (GLA), 2005). According to the same research, 50 per cent of women presenting at domestic violence agencies report problematic substance use themselves and/or in their partner. For women who accessed domestic violence outreach/tenancy support this was even higher, with 92 per cent reporting problematic substance use as an issue. Almost two-thirds of the women in this study accessing domestic violence services reported that they began problematic substance use after experiencing domestic violence, and most reported that they thought that this was to dull both physical and emotional pain associated with these experiences. Social workers working with vulnerable women and those who have experienced domestic violence should be aware of this correlation and the implications it has for the lives of their service uses.

Approximately 63 per cent of men attending perpetrator programmes report dual problems of substance use and domestic violence, and 93 per cent report that they had problematic substance use prior to becoming domestically violent (GLA, 2005). Clearly, any social work intervention with this service user group needs to take the high correlation between problematic substance use and 'being violent' into consideration. There is not a simple causal link between problematic substance use and domestic violence, however, as there are many variables that compound the complexity of the issues. Substance use should never be accepted as an excuse for violent or abusive behaviour, and neither should survivors' substance use be used to justify the use of violence against them (The Stella Project, 2007).

Effective social work with problematic substance-using men and women

Women are faced with an array of barriers if they wish to seek help and support for their problematic substance use. These barriers are also relevant for women accessing other health and social care services. Reducing these barriers in your own practice will limit the extent to which these barriers stop women accessing the help they need. Because women are usually the primary caregivers for children, it will be important that you are able to offer childcare, or see the women in a space conducive to working together while their children are playing around them. If services expect women to have their own childcare and do not allow women to bring their children to a service then they are creating a barrier for these women, who in turn will be much less likely to try and access the support that they require. While not all women are parents, or the main caregivers for their children, childcare is an important practical barrier to overcome for any social worker who works with parents. Issues of safeguarding children are also a potential barrier for parents accessing services. If they have problematic substance use for which they are seeking help, they are likely to feel like 'bad' parents and be concerned that accessing services means that they will be judged and potentially that their children will be removed from their care.

Women are traditionally seen as carers and nurturers and when faced with the reality of their problematic substance use they can feel very shamed, and are very often ostracised by society. It is thought that the stigma attached to men's problematic substance use is not as extreme as that experienced by women, primarily due to these traditional stereotypes that are attributed to women, and their roles. Being non-judgemental and empathic towards parents and in particular women who present with problematic substance use is essential, coupled with good risk management regarding any children in their care.

It may be useful to think about how your service operates in terms of what it offers. Think about whether your service is a safe place for both men and women to attend. Depending on where you work and the type of work you do, it may be possible to offer women only spaces where women might feel more comfortable, or women-only opening hours when your service just makes appointments for women and their children (offering childcare during these times would also be important). While most of the women we work with will be strong, purposeful people, they may also be vulnerable and it is important to reflect on the potential need for a women's only space (space and/or time) in your service. Further thought should also be given to ethnic minority women for whom accessing services is even more difficult (Becker and Duffy, 2002). Stigma attached to their problematic substance use is often even further intensified because of cultural or religious expectations. Offering services and spaces where black and minority ethnic women feel safe to attend would bridge a huge gap in service provision, regardless of where you work as a social worker.

The models outlined in Part 3 of this book have been proven to be effective for working with both men and women who have problematic substance use. However, it will be important to bear in mind and reflect on how they might best be used to meet the unique requirements of both genders. Working holistically and in an integrated way with the complex needs that your service users may have, regardless of their gender, is paramount. Services that are able to offer an array of support, including specialist problematic substance use treatment, alongside childcare, gynaecological care, parenting courses, counselling, job training and housing support, would provide a welcome integrated approach. However, while these types of services are thin on the ground, it will be up to you to work in partnership with specialist 'substance misuse', peer-led or other services as required.

Summary

Men and women with problematic substance use do have unique and different needs. Women are more likely to develop physical health problems after a shorter period of problematic substance use and are also more likely to have had previous trauma or current mental health problems than their male counterparts. However, men are more likely to use substances and use them more heavily than women, and those that do experience problematic substance use are much more likely to have experienced abuse and neglect than those without substance use issues. Both men and women who are sex workers are vulnerable to developing problematic substance use, but women who have problematic substance use are more likely than their male counterparts to turn to sex work to support their substance use. Men are more likely to turn to serious criminal activity. Women are much more likely to have been the current victims or survivors of domestic violence, whereas men are usually the perpetrators. Victims, survivors and perpetrators all have high rates of problematic substance use.

Women's specific reproductive role means that they put their children at risk of perinatal mortality, being born with low birth weight and having problems such as Foetal Alcohol Syndrome if they use substances while they are pregnant. Engaging with and supporting this service user group through their pregnancy and beyond is vital. While stigma about having problematic substance use affects everyone, women with problematic substance use are thought to be more severely stigmatised because usually they have been attributed stereotypical characteristics such as being caring and nurturing – especially if they are mothers. This means that they are judged by others much more harshly, and are more likely to feel guilt and shame, which act as barriers to accessing treatment. Women are more likely to be the caregivers for children, when in a partnership or while lone parenting, which means that childcare and concerns about safeguarding children are barriers to accessing treatment that tend to affect women to a higher degree.

While historically men have been more likely than women to drink heavily and use drugs, a younger generation of women is emerging that appear to be matching their male counterparts. While the prevalence of women accessing specialised substance misuse treatment is usually about 3:1 in favour of men, recent research shows that younger women's use of certain drugs (cocaine) is increasing, and that some girls are now drinking and using drugs to the same extent as boys. This means that in the future, women may be more likely to present to all types of social work services with problematic substance use. This reality means that we need to think about reducing the barriers to accessing our services by doing things like providing childcare, offering women's only spaces or times, being aware of support agencies (counselling and support groups) in our communities that they could be referred to if necessary, and providing an holistic, integrated response in partnership with these services to meet their complex needs.

All of the models from Part 3 of this book can and should be used with problematic substance-using men and women. Use them alongside this chapter so as to reflect on the distinctive needs of service users in terms of gender and problematic substance use. It may be that earlier interventions using brief interventions, harm reduction, relapse prevention and the motivational approach can help to cease the progression of their problematic substance use, alongside social work interventions for other areas of concern in their lives.

Reflections

How well does your service or practice learning placement work with women?

Can you recognise any barriers to women accessing the support you offer? Are there any barriers for men? If so, what are they, and what could be done differently to reduce these barriers?

In what way does your own gender affect your ability to work with men and women?

Further readings

Greater London Authority (GLA) (2005) *Alcohol and Drugs in London: Improving the Options for Women*. London: GLA.

Stella Project, The (2007) *Domestic Violence, Drugs and Alcohol: Good Practice Guidelines*. London: The Stella Project.

6

Working with Criminal Justice Service Users Who have Problematic Substance Use

Service users with links to the criminal justice system are worked with and supported by social workers in a variety of settings. A common term to describe these types of service users is 'offenders'. While such a description may be true in one sense, it does nothing to reduce the stigma attached to people involved with the criminal justice system, and of course does not clearly articulate the other aspects of their character. To describe someone as an offender is not usually a useful term. It is especially unhelpful where problematic substance use is concerned because, unless they are using legal substances as prescribed (alcohol, prescription medication), they are by virtue of the problem (illegal drug use) 'offenders'. This chapter will, however, refer to these types of service users as 'offenders' but it does so with caution.

There is a well-documented association between substance use and crime, with offending rates rising and falling in association with levels of substance use (Klag et al., 2005). While there is a definite correlation between these two variables, no exact understanding of any causal link has yet been established. The substance use crime issue is a complex one, with some studies suggesting substance use starts prior to offending behaviour (VanderWaal et al., 2001), and others suggesting the opposite (Moss and Kirisic, 1995). Generally, their interactions can be explained by four hypothesis: criminal involvement causes drug use; drug dependence causes crime; complex interaction or shared common cause (something else causes both, for example 'poverty') (Greaves et al., 2009).

Recent research suggests that 65 per cent of all prison 'inmates' in the US meet the Diagnostic and Statistical Manual of Mental Disorders (*DSM IV*) criteria for 'substance abuse', and that drugs and alcohol are implicated in 78 per cent of violent crimes and 83 per cent of property crimes (National Centre on Addiction and Substance Abuse (CASA), 2010). UK data suggests that 50 per cent of all shoplifting, burglary, vehicle crime and theft is committed by class A drug users and that this is because up to 75 per cent of these class A drug users commit crimes to support their drug habits (Bennett and Holloway, 2004). The socio-economic costs of drug 'misuse' are estimated to be up to £18 billion per year (Holloway et al., 2005). Crime associated with the use of legal substances is also significant, with links between alcohol and offending being well established (Matthew and Richardson, 2005).

Because of these links between substance use and crime, several initiatives have been launched to help offenders access treatment for their problematic substance use through the criminal justice system. Offenders with problematic drug use are identified through arrest, in court or on arrival at prison and are offered treatment. This treatment can be voluntary or court ordered. It is estimated that at least a quarter of the 188,000 service users that accessed community drug services in England and Wales in 2008 were identified via the criminal justice system (NTA, 2009b). Depending on where they are in the UK, drug-using offenders may also be dealt with in special 'dedicated drug courts', which work with offenders from conviction through sentence, to completion (or breach) of a community order with a Drug Rehabilitation Requirement (DRR) (Matrix Knowledge Group, 2008). It is highly likely that if you are working with offending service users who have problematic substance use that this will have been identified at some stage through the criminal justice system.

The Drug Intervention Programme (DIP)

The Drug Intervention Programme (DIP), a Home Office Initiative, began in 2003 to seek to offer 'offenders' a way 'out of crime and into treatment'. There have been a number of key developments under the DIP, including the 'Tough Choices' project. The DIP introduced a case-management approach to offer offenders treatment and support from the point of arrest to beyond sentencing. At the point of arrest, offenders who have been arrested for a trigger offence (an acquisitive crime linked to drug using, for example shoplifting or burglary) are required by law to submit to a drugs test. If offenders test positive for class A drugs, they are then required by law to submit to an assessment of their needs. This involves assessing their drug use, but also other aspects of their lives, for example mental health, housing arrangements, childcare, employment and physical health. At this stage, a package of care can be recommended to the individual and links to other services set up as part of their sentencing (Drug Rehabilitation Requirement (DRR) of a Community Order), or on release from custody. They may also be denied bail unless they agree to engage in relevant treatment – this is known as 'Restrictions on Bail' (RoB). Often, this assessed information is shared quite widely with the police, courts, probation, prison services, 'substance misuse' services and social services. Sharing information and working in partnership are key components of the DIP, and this partnership working aims to provide drug-using offenders with a seamless pathway into treatment. While the DIP may be seen as coercing people into treatment and raises several ethical and effectiveness issues for some practitioners, it does seem to be having a positive effect on getting more people with problematic drug use into treatment, and reducing crime. Concerns have been raised, however, that targeting drug users in the criminal justice system has had a negative effect on the provision of alcohol treatment services, which appear to have been neglected since the DIP's conception (Luty and Rao, 2008). There are also concerns that it is easier for service users with problematic substance use to access treatment for their problems via the criminal justice system as opposed to via health care services, and that this has created a 'two-tiered system'. It is true that there has been a significant amount of money spent on the DIP since its conception and that offenders will be offered and/or compelled to undertake treatment on numerous occasions throughout their offending career. This is in comparison with other service users who may have to request treatment numerous times and remain on long waiting lists prior to receiving it.

> Compared to traditional criminal justice sanctions, mandatory substance user treatment holds the promise of providing an efficacious and cost-effective way of rehabilitating substance-user offenders. However, the legitimacy of enforced drug and alcohol user treatment represents a hotly debated issue in the addiction field. (Klag et al., 2005: 1786)

If you are working with offenders, it is essential that you are aware of the possibility that your service user has problematic drug use. If working with offenders is not your speciality, but you have come across a number of people involved in the criminal justice system in your own social work practice (wherever that may be), it is also worth thinking about problematic substance use as a potential reason for offending.

Social care versus social control

In a variety of social work practices there is a constant bind between social care and social control. Social workers seek to empower service users and offer them choices on the one hand, while managing risk and performing 'social control' on the other hand. This is also typical when working with offenders. The criminal justice system is primarily concerned with social control and protection of the public, while social workers working with a variety of service users are concerned primarily with the needs of their service users and their families and can sometimes view the criminal justice process as disruptive and callous. Conversely for some social workers, it may be difficult to work in an anti-discriminatory way with offenders when it is easy to dislike them and their behaviours. This fine line between social care and social control is a difficult one to walk, especially if you do not reflect on your own values and ethics and clearly identify to yourself and your service users exactly what your role in their life means and where your responsibilities lie. How to work in an anti-discriminatory way while not condoning criminal behaviour is a difficult skill to master.

As a social worker, you may walk this fine line with service users being aware of the importance of managing the risk of their behaviours versus the long-term benefit of engaging them in a useful relationship and potentially getting them into specialised treatment for their problematic substance use. How you manage this potential dilemma is paramount and will be the difference potentially between long-term gain and engagement, and the risk that may result as a consequence of the loss of therapeutic trust. This is not, however, an unusual position for a social worker to find themselves in, with similar dilemmas faced in mental health and safeguarding social work on an almost daily basis. The key then is awareness, self-reflection, honesty with your service user and thorough risk assessment and management (ongoing and unobtrusive). This dilemma is summed up well by Waine et al. (2005: 23):

> When social workers are expected to play a role in the state control of citizens they are obliged to clarify the ethical implications of this role and to what extent this role is acceptable in relation to the basic ethical principles of social work.

Effective social work practice with offenders

Offenders still deserve your help and support regardless of their behaviours because not only is this anti-discriminatory practice, but we also know that this sort of engagement is likely in the long run to reduce the harm to the individual, their family and community. Offenders – especially those who have been in custody – are vulnerable to mental health problems, homelessness, isolation, discrimination and unemployment on release from prison (Littlechild and Smith, 2008). None of these vulnerabilities does anything to increase the likelihood of ongoing abstinence from offending or problematic substance use. Being aware of these vulnerabilities, and working to resolve them, will be in the best interests of all concerned. Social work approaches that value the individual while not condoning their behaviour are important, highly valued by the service users themselves and seem to engender a sense of personal loyalty and accountability (Littlechild and Smith, 2008; McNeill, 2006). 'A positive relationship between the worker and offender supports desistance from crime' (Gregory, 2006: 57). Social work practice with offenders should be needs-based and problem-solving focused as well as biopsychosocial, addressing the needs of the offender in their current context and environment. Helping offending service users find employment and mend family relationships will also provide them with a better sense of community. After all, 'social circumstances and relationships with others are both the object of the intervention and the medium through which ... change can be achieved' (Farrall, 2002: 212, cited in McNeill, 2006: 3).

We know that offenders tend to come from less advantaged communities and have reduced access to a variety of 'social capital' (Gregory, 2006). A focus on building strengths, extending the time between reoffending and relapse prevention (of offending behaviour) are potential solutions. Their offending is just one element of their environment, behaviour and character, and their needs are likely to be complex. It is important to instil a sense of self-responsibility in relation to these needs and work alongside the offender, rather than do things to them or for them, which may be tempting while juggling the potential risk that their behaviours can pose. The offending should not be ignored, however, and all issues surrounding their offending also need to be addressed, including an acknowledgement of the effects on the victims of the offending. If they have problematic substance use, it is likely that this does relate to their offending (perhaps they offend to get money to buy substances). Working with offenders on reducing or giving up their substance use will not only reduce the harm to them, but will reduce the harm caused to society because of their offending. All of the models outlined in Part 3 of this book are potentially relevant ways of working with offenders to reduce the harm caused by their substance use and associated offending behaviour.

Summary

There is a well-evidenced link between offending behaviour and substance use, although the exact nature of this relationship is complex. Offering and/or coercing substance-using offenders into treatment via the criminal justice system has been a pragmatic response to this complex relationship, with programmes such as the DIP focusing on offering offenders a way 'out of crime and into treatment', and legislation providing Drug Rehabilitation Requirements (DRRs) as part of sentencing options. Programmes like the DIP and sentencing options such as DRRs acknowledge that a reduction in substance use is, in turn, likely to reduce offending behaviour. If you work with offenders, it is important to be aware that substance use could potentially be linked to their offending. If you work with offenders, and/or their families whom you know have problematic substance use, it is important for you to be aware of how the criminal justice system works and what your service user will be offered by way of treatment. Being able to engage substance-using offenders in an anti-discriminatory way while not condoning their behaviours will be paramount if you are to reduce substance-related behaviours and offending long term. Walking the fine line between social care and social control will be a key skill to have when working with this specialist population, weighing up potential risk to the public with the long-term gains that can be achieved with ongoing engagement and therapeutic trust. Using these key skills alongside the models outlined in Part 3 of this book, will ensure that you offer substance-using offenders the best possible service, which in the long term is likely to reduce substance-related offending and lessen harm to individuals, families and communities.

Reflections

How well do you think that you work with offenders? Are you able to work in an anti-discriminatory way with them while not condoning their offending behaviours?

What do you think about coercing people to undergo treatment for their problematic substance use?

How well do you think that you 'juggle' social care vs social control?

Further readings

Dugmore, P. and Pickford, J. (2006) *Youth Justice and Social Work*. Exeter: Learning Matters.

Gregory, M. (2006) 'The offender as citizen: Socially inclusive strategies for working with offenders within the community', in K. Gorman, M. Gregory, M. Hayles and N. Parton (eds), *Constructive Work with Offenders*. London: Jessica Kingsley, pp. 49–65.

Website

For more information about the Drug Intervention Programme (DIP) see: http://www.nta.nhs.uk/community-based.aspx.

7

Problematic Substance Use in Black and Minority Ethnic (BME) Communities

Clear consideration needs to be given to addressing the specific needs of black and minority ethnic (BME) communities (including refugees and asylum seekers) with problematic substance use. Historically, research that has focused on drug and alcohol use in UK BME communities has largely been ad hoc and has lacked academic rigour. However, recent research by Fountain (2009a, 2009b, 2009c, 2009d, 2009e) has helped further our understanding of some specific BME communities in England. (Please see further readings at the end of this chapter for references to this work.) What we do know is that while some risk factors for problematic substance use that centre around social exclusion and deprivation may mean that some people from BME communities are put at increased risk of developing problematic substance use, it appears that generally speaking substance use in BME communities is not dissimilar to that of the general population in the UK. Problems for people in BME communities appear to arise because there are barriers to accessing appropriate services. Some of these barriers include a lack of information in appropriate languages, a lack of workers who speak appropriate languages, a lack of interpreter services and the shame that may be attributed to problematic substance use within some BME communities.

Before we go further, it is useful to consider the term 'black and minority ethnic' that is being used throughout this chapter. It is a reasonably good way to describe both people who identify with the term 'black' in a political sense and define themselves as different from others on the basis of skin colour, as well as the variety of ethnicities and cultures that exist within this wide-ranging grouping. Included in this group of people are also white ethnic minorities. This way of describing a minority community based around colour and ethnicity, while useful, is complex because it includes such a huge variety of people, nationalities, cultures, languages and religions that it can be difficult to make generalisations. With this in mind, however, this chapter does attempt to help you to think about the special issues that relate to BME communities who may experience problematic substance use.

Vulnerabilities to problematic substance use

It is probably a perception, rather than a reality, that black and minority ethnic communities have more problematic substance use. 'Assumptions about black people and drugs in Britain are generally underpinned by stereotypes, over-generalisations and racist posturing, rather than evidence, making this a risky area for research' (Awiah et al., 1990: 14).

It appears that some people from BME communities are more likely to be profiled and stopped and searched for drugs than people in the predominantly white majority population and that they are likely to receive harsher penalties for drug- and alcohol-related offending when they appear before the courts (Kalunta-Crumpton, 2003). The myth that BME communities have more problems with drugs and alcohol appears to stem from racist media and inaccurate public perceptions based on this type of institutional racism.

The reality is that lifetime prevalence rates for illegal drug use have been found to be highest among white adults over the age of 16, followed next by black ethnic groups, with the lowest rates among Asian populations (McCambridge and Strang, 2005). It appears that in reality, BME communities have very similar if not reduced levels of drug use compared to the mainstream UK population. There are some interesting differences in patterns of drug use among different BME communities, however. For example, fewer Black African, South Asian and Kurdish, Turkish and Cypriot women use illegal substances compared to the majority population (Fountain, 2009a, 2009d, 2009e) and khat use is the stimulant of choice among Somalis and Ethiopians (Fountain, 2009a). BME substance users are less likely to inject drugs than the white population and while crack, heroin and 'dance drugs' are used by BME communities, it is to a lesser extent than in the white population (NTA and Centre for Ethnicity and Health, 2003). For all BME communities as well as the majority white population, cannabis is the most widely used drug. There can be a lot of shame and stigma attached to problematic substance use in some BME communities, especially if culture or religion expressly prohibits its use. The relative lack of awareness and knowledge about substance use among the older generation of some BME groups also appears to mean that any resulting problems remain hidden. According to the NTA and Centre for Ethnicity and Health (2003), BME communities are more likely to deal with any problems related to substance use by sending family members home to countries of origin, paying for private treatment or 'enforcing' home detoxification.

Alcohol use does seem to affect some BME communities (white Irish men) more so than the general population, or more so when they are in the UK as opposed to their country of origin (for example, South Asian (Sikh) male migrants to the UK) (Rao, 2006). According to some research, rates of heavy drinking among BME communities are at least as high as national figures as a whole for the general population (Orford et al., 2004: 27).

Vulnerabilities to problematic substance use in BME communities may not be dissimilar to those in the majority white population. However, BME communities may be more vulnerable because they are more likely to experience social exclusion and depravation. Vulnerabilities, including exclusion, depravation and poverty can mean that some BME communities are put at more risk of problematic substance use, especially if they have come from particularly difficult backgrounds (for example, refugees and asylum seekers). Exclusion from accessing appropriate health and social care services, whether in subtle (lack of interpreter services and/or lack of understanding about BME communities) or more obvious ways (institutional racism) coupled with a sense of shame and/or stigma can make it extremely difficult for people in some BME communities to access help and support for problematic substances use:

> Studies have also indicated that drug users' experience of racism in other services and in the wider context of everyday life creates an expectation that approaching drug services would be unrewarding and possibly unpleasant. (Perera et al., 1993; Khan, 1999, cited in NTA, 2002: 127)

Other barriers to accessing services include a lack of awareness by BME communities of what services can offer and fears about breaches of confidentiality (NTA and Centre for Ethnicity and Health, 2003). According to the NTA (2002), other barriers to service utilisation include the fact that historically there has been a focus on treatment for opiate use at the expense of other drugs such as cannabis and crack cocaine, which may be more likely to be used by BME communities.

As a social worker who is not a specialist in the area of problematic substance use but who may have access to a variety of BME communities in the work that you do, it is vital to think about the nature and extent of any substances used in the communities you work with. Research shows that members of ethnic communities, especially older people, are more likely to access help for substance use from religious or community organisations (Orford et al., 2004), so for some your service may be the first and only place people come with issues relating to problematic substance use.

Asylum seekers and refugees

For many asylum seekers and refugees, problems of poverty and social exclusion alongside difficult and traumatic experiences in their countries of origin are profound and make them particularly vulnerable to developing problematic substance use (GLA, 2004):

> Refugees may have experienced traumatic events such as detention, torture and/or the death of loved ones, and once in the UK refugees and asylum seekers often face poverty and acute anxiety about their legal status. They also experience racism, social exclusion and isolation, all of which is compounded by language barriers and the absence of existing social networks. (Social Care Institute for Excellence (SCIE), 2006: 8)

The terms 'refugee' and 'asylum seeker', while sometime used interchangeably, are terms that describe people who legally have different sets of rights, although they may very well come from similar countries and have experienced the same trauma. 'Refugee' is the term used to describe individuals who have been offered sanctuary and protection by the British government (or any foreign government offering protection in their homeland), to live and work in the UK. Refugees achieve refugee status because of a humanitarian need, and will be granted humanitarian protection in the UK for up to five years, or discretionary leave of up to three years. To be offered this protection, refugees will have been assessed as having a humanitarian need based on a well-founded fear of persecution in their country of origin due to race, religion, nationality, political opinion or membership of a particular social group (UN Refugee Agency, 2007). After their initial term of protection finishes, their cases are reassessed and reviewed. Refugees have the right to access health and social care services and to work. 'Asylum seekers' are people who have applied for refugee status but are still having their cases reviewed. While they await the decision, they are excluded from many mainstream services and benefits, and are unable to work.

Asylum seekers who have been refused refugee status usually face removal from the UK. However, this is not always possible (for example, due to ill health or lack of appropriate documentation). Refused asylum seekers are entitled to extremely limited, if any, welfare, health or social care services. Unaccompanied children and families with children are exceptions to this rule and continue to be eligible for support until they can be returned to their country of origin (SCIE, 2006). As you can see, therefore, the terms used to describe a similar demographic of people are very different in terms of legal rights and access to appropriate services and support. Refugees and particularly asylum seekers and failed asylum seekers are some of the most traumatised, isolated and poverty-stricken people in the UK. Their trauma comes not only from their experiences in their countries of origin, but in the way that they are treated when they finally manage to get to the UK and seek protection.

Generally, there is a lack of knowledge and sound research about problematic substance use within asylum seeking and refugee communities. It appears that most asylum seekers and refugees who enter the UK do not tend to have problems with substance use. According to McCormack and Walker's (2005) literature review, the most serious problem for asylum seekers and refugees is their experience of other people's use of alcohol and drugs and how it is often implicated in the violence and abuse they face from the public. One study found that the alcohol and drug use of those around them was something that refugees and asylum seekers regarded as one of the worst aspects of living in their new home (Save the Children and Glasgow Greater Council, 2002: 18).

There are, however, a number of refugees and asylum seekers who do come into the country with problematic substance use, as well as a number who develop problems once they are in the UK due to a variety of vulnerabilities. For example, Brako and Saleh (2001) report that young asylum seekers from Sierra Leone who were soldiers in that country's civil war continue their use of heroin once in the UK. During the war, child soldiers were supplied with opiates in order to encourage co-operation, but in the UK it is continued because they are opiate dependent and may use drugs as a coping strategy to deal with their past experiences and new stressors (McCormack and Walker, 2005: 15). As well as past trauma, asylum seekers are often exposed to a number of vulnerabilities on their arrival in the UK that may mean that they are more likely to begin to experiment with substances, or continue to use them if they already do. These include exposure to or experience of poverty, homelessness, unemployment, lack of education, social exclusion, crime, poor physical health and mental health issues, which are all risk factors associated with problematic substance use. A vulnerability that is especially important to be aware of is that of mental health problems. Because of the trauma that they have experienced in their counties of origin and the difficult journey that they may have had to get to the UK, asylum seekers and refugees are very vulnerable to mental health issues such as post-traumatic stress disorder (PTSD), depression and anxiety. Mental health problems, in turn, are a risk factor associated with developing problematic substance use.

Khat

Khat has been identified as one of the leading substances of use among some African refugee and asylum-seeking communities and it has been shown to exacerbate many mental and physical health problems (Havell, 2004). Khat (Catha edulis) is a leaf that is chewed over a number of hours, used widely in Somalia, Yemen, Eritrea and Ethiopia as a stimulant. It is legal in the UK but illegal in many other countries around the world, including the US. While historically and traditionally used by older men for social interactions and in discussing business transactions, there is some evidence that when used in the UK, it is more likely also to be used by younger men and women (Havell, 2004). Due to this more common non-traditional use in the UK, khat is being blamed in some asylum-seeking and refugee communities for a number of social issues and health concerns (McCormack and Walker, 2005).

Khat use is the largest drug problem within the Somali community in the UK. Health concerns include sleeping difficulties, loss of appetite, depression, anxiety, hallucinations, oral infections and mouth cancer, impotence and exacerbation of mental health problems. Social problems that can be related to khat use include domestic violence and family and financial problems. Users of khat can experience a slight physical dependence on it (similar to caffeine) and also report some psychological dependence (Patel, 2008).

Any interventions for problematic khat use offered to individuals and families in the community will need to include consideration for the cultural and social aspects of the use of this drug if they are to be effective. Interventions will also need to include consideration for the huge number of barriers that asylum seekers and refugees face in accessing services. If you are a social worker working with asylum seekers and refugees, it will be important to understand khat in this context and know that the use of it may be common, that it is legal, but that it may cause some problems to individuals, their families and the community.

Effective social work practice with BME communities, including refugees and asylum seekers

Many people from BME communities have problematic substance use, but their uptake of specialised substance misuse services does not always reflect this reality and people from BME communities are underrepresented in treatment services. More than other communities, asylum seekers and refugees have a reason to hide their problematic substance use. They may not want anyone to be aware that they may have a problem as they may think that this will influence their refugee status or their application for protection. Given this, and coupled with what we do know about how BME communities access services, we need to think about how we can make all of our social work services not just substance misuse services, more appropriate for use by BME communities. It is likely that people from BME communities will come into contact with other health and social care services before or instead of specialised substance misuse services. If this is the case, we need to make sure that our services are welcoming, anti-racist, reflect the diverse nature of the communities they serve and are well equipped to work with people who may present with problematic substance use in the context of broader advice, assistance and support. It is vital that social work services are adept at multi-agency working, family work, outreach work (if possible) and community engagement initiatives if they are to foster environments and services that BME communities are both aware of and feel comfortable using.

According to Fountain (2009a), what is needed is the ability of organisations and individuals within these organisations to be 'culturally competent'. Fountain (2009a) discusses cultural competence in relation to specialised substance misuse services. However, some of the things she covers in relation to a variety of different BME communities also relates very well to a variety of other social work services (Fountain, 2009a, 2009b, 2009c, 2009d, 2009e). While exactly what cultural competence is and how it is measured is hotly debated, the literature suggests that it is being applied differently in different localities (Bhui et al., 2007: 14, cited in Fountain, 2009a).

> Individual cultural competence is skills-based and relates to individual practitioners' professional practice in working with diverse communities and individuals. Organisational competence, on the other hand, is defined by the level of maturity in the organisation for addressing equality and diversity across the full range of its functions and policies. (Fountain, 2009a: 28)

Both individual and organisational cultural competence is required for effective work with people from BME communities and all diverse cultures. Neither individuals nor organisations can function effectively without support from one another. Individual competence involves practitioners acquiring skills that acknowledge, accept and value difference between cultures. This includes developing skills that improve their local knowledge of the diverse cultures in their own communities (languages, religious practices, health and social care needs and cultural norms), as well as developing skills for engaging and communicating with people whose first language is not English (this will include developing competence at working with interpreters). Coupled with this, a clear focus on reflective practice is required that acknowledges the limitations of practitioner knowledge as well as their own prejudice and how this may affect relationships with people from diverse backgrounds (Fountain, 2009a).

Organisational cultural competence is shown through a clear commitment to valuing and working effectively with diversity. This is done by embedding proactive policies that focus on equality and diversity throughout the structure of the organisation. A commitment to equality and valuing diversity must be clearly articulated in the aims of the organisation and be practically implemented with the provision of appropriate training programmes for staff at all levels within the organisation and a clearly defined management performance-monitoring system. These policies and systems should be developed alongside local communities, engagement with whom is paramount if services are to reflect honestly the local communities that they serve (Fountain, 2009a). According to Fountain (2009a), taking a 'maturity' approach to developing cultural competence recognises that there are stages that individuals and organisations must pass through on their way to being culturally competent, and that it can be a slow process.

Fountain's work has been pivotal in indentifying a number of key issues that are important to recognise and bear in mind when developing cultural competence for working with specific BME communities. For the communities her research covered (Black African, Black Caribbean, Chinese and Vietnamese, Kurdish, Turkish Cypriot, Turkish and South Asian), there were a number of key issues that were identified:

- **Diversity** – It is important to recognise diversity not only within the BME community, but also within each BME community.
- **Language** – For many BME communities, it appears that language differences and difficulties communicating with services is a huge barrier to accessing services. The use of interpreter services and targeted literature where appropriate is essential.
- **Generic or specific services** – There is always a debate regarding the most effective way to work with BME communities and whether generic services should be more culturally competent or whether specialised services should be available.
- **Ethnicity of staff** – It is widely accepted that for most BME communities, having staff at services that are from a similar community as the service user can effectively engage people from BME communities.
- **Stigma and taboo** – In many BME communities, problematic substance use is a taboo and people who require services to assist with their problem are highly stigmatised, which tends to mean that problems remain secret and people do not ask for help.

- **Religious beliefs** – In many BME communities, substance use is prohibited, which makes identifying problems and/or seeking help for them very difficult.
- **Confidentiality** – Issues around confidentiality need to be addressed with BME communities. They need to be aware of the ability of services to offer confidentiality and what this means in reality for small communities.
- **Open access services** – According to Fountain (2009e), many BME communities, especially refugees and asylum seekers, would feel more comfortable accessing low-threshold services where they can walk in off the street, rather than engaging in a long assessment process with services that are perceived as 'government' related.
- **Women only services** – Some BME communities may require specialised women only services.
- **Engaging communities** – Working with and engaging local BME communities in the continuing development of services is paramount if services are to work effectively with those in their local communities.

These areas for consideration when working with BME communities relate differently to different communities. Readers are encouraged to read all of the Fountain documents mentioned in the Further reading section of this chapter in order to see how they relate to specific BME communities.

Summary

Problematic substance use in BME communities is concerning because while there are differing patterns of use in a variety of BME communities, substance use generally is reasonably similar to that of the mainstream population; however, people from BME communities are less likely to access services. There are a variety of reasons why people from BME communities tend not to access services as well as a number of identified barriers. These include stigma and shame, services not providing literature in appropriate languages, a lack of diversity amongst staff, a lack of interpreter services, a lack of specialised services and social exclusion. Asylum seekers and refugees are some of the most widely stigmatised, marginalised and traumatised people in our communities. They may have experienced torture, persecution and witnessed war, rape and murder in their country of origin. They may have had an extremely difficult journey to get to the UK, and on their arrival may face detention, poverty, homelessness, discrimination and social exclusion. All of these things mean that while they are actually less likely than the general population to have problematic substance use, they are vulnerable to continuing or developing problematic substance use once they arrive in the UK. This may include the use of khat, which is particularly common in some asylum-seeking and refugee communities (Somalia, Yemen, Eritrea and Ethiopia).

When working towards cultural competence as an individual, there are a number of issues to consider in your developmental journey. These include specific skill acquisition such as learning to communicate with people who do not speak English, learning to work with an interpreter, seeking to understand cultures and communities in your local area and reflective practice. This skill development should be supported by an organisation that is equally committed to developing cultural competence by embedding appropriate policies within its fabric. Fountain (2009a, 2009b, 2009c, 2009d, 2009e) has identified a number of key issues that are relevant for people and organisations to consider as they work towards gaining cultural competence to work with a variety of BME communities. As social workers, it is vital that you and your organisation consider these issues and work towards cultural competence and anti-racist practice so that you are aptly able to serve the communities with whom you work. Most of the models outlined in Part 3 of this book are appropriate to use when working with BME communities. Motivational approaches are particularly useful and have been shown to work effectively with a variety of different cultures around the world. Communication and cultural differences may mean that they will be more difficult to implement. However, developing cultural competence in working across languages and with interpreters is a skill well worth developing.

Reflections

How well do you think that you and your service or practice learning placement work with people from black and ethnic minorities? What do you do well? What could you do better?

Do you have good access to appropriate translation and interpreting services? If not, is this something you can work towards?

How do you feel about working with asylum seekers and refugees? Are you confident?

Further readings

Dominelli, L. (2008) *Anti-racist Social Work*. 3rd edn. Basingstoke: Palgrave Macmillan.

Social Care Institute for Excellence (SCIE) (2006) *The Social Care Needs of Refugees and Asylum Seekers*. London: SCIE.

Website

The Professor Jane Fountain series can be found at: http://www.nta.nhs.uk/publications.aspx?category=Equality+and+Diversity&section=Healthcare.

8

Problematic Substance Use in Lesbian, Gay, Bisexual and Transgendered (LGBT) Communities

Research suggests that people in lesbian, gay and bisexual (LGB) communities are more likely to have problematic substance use than those in the heterosexual population and evidence about problematic substance use in the transgendered community suggests extremely high rates (Substance Abuse and Mental Health Services Administration (SAMHSA)/Center for Substance Abuse Treatment (CSAT), 2001). Historically, much of the research on LGBT communities has been criticised for having methodological flaws and so it is difficult to determine the exact extent and nature of the problem. Nevertheless, an understanding of the specific issues relating to problematic substance use in LGBT communities is important for social workers in a variety of settings, or when working specifically with this service user group.

Before embarking on the rest of this chapter, it is necessary to cover some brief definitions of some of the terms used throughout. The acronym 'LGB' is used to talk about lesbian, gay and bisexual people, so it is the term used to describe minority sexual orientations. 'Sexual orientation' is the term used to describe the nature and direction of a person's sexual attractions, and can also be referred to as 'sexual identity' or 'sexual preference' (Bywater and Jones, 2007: 4). While LGB will be used throughout this chapter to describe a group of people that may have similar experiences, it is a somewhat controversial way of describing sexual identity. It is controversial because it categorises people, and some (for example, queer theorists) believe that sexual orientation is not so simple to define. For example, there are people who might describe themselves as heterosexual but who have sex with people of the same sex (for example, men who have sex with men). Being of a particular sexual orientation is not just about the sexual act. People who may be celibate can still feel sexual attraction, and be LGB. What is important to note here then is that there is a difference between sexual behaviour, sexual attraction and sexual identity. For the sake of this chapter, we use

LGB to cover people who define themselves as such (sexual identity) but also to cover LGB sexual attraction and homosexual behaviour. As you will recognise, not only is the term LGB a very overly simplified way of defining a group of people, but it also defines a very diverse group of people who may also come from different ethnicities, religions, ages, classes and/or other diverse lived experiences. Given this, it can be difficult to make generalisations. There are, however, some common experiences within this group of people that it is important to be aware of, especially in regards to offering appropriate support and services. Some of the similarities of experience are discussed throughout this chapter to help inform your practice.

Sometimes transgendered people are also covered by research and/or writing about LGB people. This is because some transgendered people have felt comfortable being seen alongside people with minority sexual orientation. However, it is important to note that being transgendered has nothing to do with sexual orientation but rather with gender identity and it is not always appropriate to group transgendered people under the LGB umbrella:

> 'Transgender' and 'Trans' are broader terms that refer to people who live part or all of their lives in their preferred gender role. This includes people who may cross-dress or undergo some hormone treatment, but not necessarily full gender reassignment, as well as transsexual people. (Commission for Social Care Inspection (CSCI), 2008: 8)

Transgendered people may be heterosexual, lesbian, gay or bisexual. Their gender identity is separate and independent from their sexual orientation. For this reason then, this chapter may sometimes refer to this group of service users as LGB and at other times as LGBT (to include people in the transgendered community), depending on whether the point is relevant to all of these groups of people. It does this, however, with full recognition of the differences between these groups.

Vulnerabilities to problematic substance use

As yet, there are no official figures regarding how many LGB people there are in the UK because up until recently sexual identity was not asked about in official government surveys. In 2009, the Office for National Statistics (ONS) published new guidance on how best to measure sexual identity in social surveys and a question on sexual identity was introduced in all ONS social surveys in January 2009 (ONS, 2009). At present, it is estimated that LGBT people make up approximately 7 per cent of the UK population (Home Office, 2006).

People in the LGBT community often experience negative reactions from others in society, some of whom see these minorities as 'sexually deviant' or 'unnatural'. People in the LGBT community may experience 'homophobia' or 'transphobia', which are a fear, loathing, irrational hatred and/or intolerance of LGBT people. These attitudes can lead people in the LGBT community to experience violence and extremely negative attitudes towards them. These behaviours and beliefs are extremely dangerous, discriminatory and illegal. People in the LGBT community can also experience heterosexism:

heterosexism is more subtle. It refers to a belief that heterosexuality is normative and superior to homosexuality and can be manifested among people who would not be considered homophobic. (Brownlee et al., 2005: 486)

Heterosexism occurs when people assume that being heterosexual (being attracted to people of the opposite sex) is normal, right and natural. Heterosexism helps support these heterosexual norms and behaviours to remain dominant in our society and can foster homophobia. Heterosexism manifests in everyday living and certainly can manifest in social work practice if social workers are not aware of it. Assuming people are in heterosexual relationships happens all the time. Think about the assumptions you make when you ask someone if they are 'married' (which usually implies to someone of the opposite sex), or when you ask a woman whether she has a husband. This assumes that they are heterosexual and is a form of heterosexism. This is similar to heteronormativity, which is described as the overt, covert and implied reinforcement of heterosexuality by social institutions (Pega and MacEwan, 2010). Heterosexism is extremely common and as a social worker at the very least you should be aware that you are not heterosexist in the way you practise. Ask people about their 'partners', not whether they are single or married (although LGB people can be in civil unions), and do not assume that these partners will be of the opposite sex. Do not assume that because a person has children that they must be heterosexual.

Because of these both overt and obvious (homophobia, transphobia) and more subtle (heterosexism) forms of discrimination, people in the LGBT community face different stresses and pressures than heterosexual people. They may also have internalised some of this discrimination and feel unease and shame about their own sexual or gender identity. This can make the process of 'coming out' and forming and expressing their sexual or gender identity very difficult. LGBT people have disproportionately poor mental health, suicidality, self-harm and problematic substance use (Dodds et al., 2005), and it is thought that this is probably related to some of the discrimination they face throughout their lifetimes. People in the LGBT community often deal with these issues in isolation, especially if family or religious support systems have broken down due to their 'coming out' and expressing their sexual orientation or gender identity. LGBT people are seen as more vulnerable to problematic substance use as it is thought that using substances may help alleviate these negative feelings and block out the pressures and stressors that they may feel.

Another risk factor for LGBT people is that they may be used to socialising in clubs and bars, as 'gay' bars and clubs have historically and traditionally been seen as 'protected' places for people in the LGBT community. The LGBT community has long been associated (rightly or wrongly) with socialising, partying, drinking alcohol and taking drugs. None more so than gay men. Recent research (Keogh et al., 2009) concluded that for gay, bisexual and other men who have sex with men and who are concerned about their substance use, the use of substances is often integral to many aspects of their lives, including their social life, their work life and their intimate and sexual relationships. For example, drugs like methamphetamine and other stimulants, as well as amyl nitrate (known as 'poppers'), are commonly used by gay men and other men who have sex with men to enhance sexual experiences. The men interviewed in this research described a gay culture that was immersed in substances: 'Substance use was bound up with gay identity in many ways' (Keogh et al., 2009: 44). While generalisations cannot be made about all LGBT communities, it is true to say that bars and clubs are often seen as 'safe havens' for LGBT people. Regular attendance at bars and clubs to help achieve a sense of community, can mean that LGBT people are more vulnerable to problematic substance use because they may have more regular access to alcohol and other drugs in these situations.

For these reasons, it is imperative that if you work with people in the LGBT community that you are aware of the stigma and discrimination they may feel, coupled with their more ready access to alcohol and other drugs in bars and clubs, if they find a sense of community in these places. All of this may make them quite vulnerable to developing problematic substance use.

Effective social work practice with LGBT people

Under UK law, it is illegal to discriminate on the basis of sexual orientation. The Equality Act (Sexual Orientation) Regulations 2007 prohibits discrimination on the basis of a person's sexual orientation in England, Scotland and Wales. Northern Ireland has its own, but similar, regulations. The Civil Partnership Act 2004 allows civil partners to enjoy the same rights as married heterosexual couples and the Gender Recognition Act 2004 gives transgender people the right to change their gender on their birth certificate and marry and adopt a child with someone of the opposite sex. Social workers have a duty to uphold the law and provide anti-discriminatory services to people from all minority sexual orientations and transgendered people. For some social workers who have certain beliefs about LGBT people that may be based on their own religious or moral views, this can sometimes be difficult. There is no doubt, however, that if you chose social work as a profession and you are a registered social worker then it is your duty to grapple with these personal beliefs and any conflicts that may arise, until you are comfortable working with LGBT people in an anti-discriminatory way that not only supports their lifestyle choices but actively calls into question those who do discriminate against them. As a service user quoted in the Commission for Social Care Inspection (CSCI) (2008) puts it:

> I am not sure that they really understand the need for staff to be comfortable (as opposed to vaguely tolerant, or trying not to mind!) with my being a lesbian. (CSCI, 2008: 18)

Unfortunately, LBGT people do often face discrimination when they access health and social care services, if not in the form of homophobia, then often in the form of heterosexism. If they do access services, there is evidence to suggest that because of the fear of discrimination, LGB people tend not to disclose their sexual orientation to health and social care professionals (Dodds et al., 2005). Furthermore, a Commission for Social Care Inspection survey (2008) found that 45 per cent of LGB people surveyed had faced some sort of discrimination whilst using services.

This is not satisfactory and every effort should be made within services and by each individual health and social care professional to change this reality. When working with LGBT people, social workers need to have an awareness of the specific issues that may affect this service user group and understand why they may be more susceptible to developing problematic substance use (as discussed above). Asking about sexual orientation in a respectful, positive and open way is important in 'normalising' all sexual orientations. Be aware of the need to reiterate confidentiality policies if people appear apprehensive about disclosing their sexual orientation. Creating LGBT friendly spaces and services that openly reflect the diverse range of service users that may attend is vital.

Social workers should be genuine, non-judgemental, open and tolerant and have respect for the values, beliefs, diversity of experience and lifestyles of those they work for (service users). In order to maintain this level of anti-discriminatory work, self-reflective practice is paramount because it can be all too easy to act in heterosexist ways. Assessing your own attitudes, assumptions and prejudice allows you to work on changing these if necessary and helps raise awareness of how they will impact on the work you do with your service users. Coupled with this, it is very important that you don't make assumptions about sexual orientation because of the service user group you work with:

> Sometimes people assume that older people and disabled people are not interested in sex, whether they are lesbian, gay, bisexual or heterosexual. Firstly, this is not true. Secondly, being lesbian, gay or bisexual is not just about sex, it is about identity and community. (CSCI, 2008: 11)

There will be LGB people in most social work services. Do not assume that there are no LGB service users attending your service. Also, remember that people will experience their sexuality differently, depending on their own lived experience (race, class, gender and age), and that while LGBT people may have some similar experiences they may also be very different and just as with any other service user will require an individualised approach. All of the key skills and models outlined in Part 3 of this book are appropriate to use when working with LGBT people. Read Part 3 of this book with special consideration of the key issues outlined in this chapter if you do work with LGBT service users who have problematic substance use.

Summary

People in the LGBT community have disproportionately poor mental health, suicidality, self-harm and problematic substance use. This appears to be because people in LGBT communities experience greater amounts of stress relating to sexuality and identity confusion, homophobia, transphobia and heterosexism, which leads to low self-esteem and low self-worth (CSCI, 2008). People in the LGBT community may also have more frequent and ready access to alcohol and other drugs when the pub or club scene is used to provide a sense of community. Service users from LGBT communities tend not to reveal their sexual or gender identities when accessing health and social care services and a number of them report facing discrimination when they do. Discrimination from the general public that is mirrored in health and social care services can take the form of homophobia, transphobia or heterosexism.

Social workers can make sure that their social work services are LGBT friendly by respectfully asking about sexual orientation and not assuming heterosexuality, providing LGBT friendly spaces, being genuine, non-judgemental, open and tolerant. It is vital that social workers examine their own attitudes, beliefs and prejudice toward people in the LGBT community by remaining reflective on their practice. LGB people are probably attending your social work service wherever you work. Do not assume that they are not. When working with LGBT people with experiences of problematic substance use you can chose to use any of the models outlined in Part 3 of this book. Do so in conjunction with an understanding of the key issues outlined in this chapter so as to provide inclusive and anti-discriminatory practice with this diverse group of people.

Reflections

How do you feel about people in the LGBT community?

How well do you believe you and your service, or practice learning placement, work with people from LGBT communities?

What steps could your service or practice learning placement take to be more LGBT friendly?

Further readings

Brownlee, K., Spakes, A., Saini, M., O'Hare, R., Kortes-Miller, K. and Graham, J. (2005) 'Heterosexism among social work students', *Social Work Education*, 24: 485–94.

Bywater, J. and Jones, R. (2007) *Sexuality and Social Work*. Exeter: Learning Matters.

Fish, J. (2009) 'Invisible no more? Including lesbian, gay and bisexual people in social work and social care', *Practice: Social Work in Action*, 21(1): 47–64.

Part 3

Concepts and Models for Social Work Practice

Part 3 of this book covers some key concepts and models of practice for working with service users with problematic substance use in social work practice.[1] All too often, social workers do not conceive of asking their service users about problematic substance use. This denial to engage people in a discussion about problematic substance use, whether because of a lack of knowledge, training or fear, is doing service users a disservice. If we do not begin to engage all of our service users around the possibility of problematic substance use, we are potentially leaving individuals, families and communities open to the harms associated with unrecognised problematic substance use (Bliss and Pecukonis, 2009).

The concepts and models in Part 3 of this book have been chosen because of their ease of use and perceived transferability to social work practice settings. However, how social workers are able to work with service users who have problematic substance use will depend on their agency's policies and procedures. While there is limited research about the use of these models in non-specialist social work practice, it is reasonable to present them as offering a range of strategies and ideas that may be useful as part of the social work intervention toolkit. Further reading and/or training in relation to these models, skills and strategies is recommended. Further research into their effectiveness in social work practice settings is also required and recommended.

Chapter 9, 'Screening assessments', overviews a variety of screening assessments that would be appropriate to use in a variety of social work settings in order to explore potential problematic substance use, and provide some evidence for ongoing referral to specialist services if required. Chapter 10, 'Harm reduction, abstinence and "recovery"', provides an overview of each of these three key concepts that are essential to be aware of in relation to the field of problematic substance use. Chapter 11 overviews the 'Motivational approaches'

---

[1] There are a large number of other models of practice used by 'substance misuse' specialists but it is not the intention of this part of the book to cover all of these models.

based on Motivational Interviewing, one of the best evidenced models for work with service users who may have problematic substance use. The motivational approach is used by specialists and non-specialists in a variety of allied health and social care sectors for a variety of behavioural problems. Chapter 12 covers 'Relapse prevention', a practical way of working on goal-setting for people who are motivated to make and maintain behaviour change with a focus on reflecting on potential triggers that might 'trip' them up along the way. Chapter 13 overviews 'Brief interventions', another well-evidenced model of effective practice used by a variety of allied health and social care professionals, based on making the most of opportunistic meetings with service users who may present with problematic substance use.

Part 3 of this text assumes that the reader has some basic communication and micro-counselling skills as required for all social work practice. Prior to reading the chapters in this part of the book, please note that Hohman et al. (2006) identified three key factors that can affect how social workers work with services users who may have problematic substance use. These were:

- Attitudes.
- Worker–service user relationship skills.
- Lack of knowledge about problematic substance use.

The importance of social worker 'attitude' was discussed in Chapter 2. It is of the utmost importance that social workers are anti-discriminatory in their attitude towards people with problematic substance use, and must be able to build sound therapeutic alliances with the people they work.

9

Screening Assessments

This chapter aims to provide any social worker, regardless of where they work or with whom, the ability to screen for problematic substance use. Problematic substance use permeates all of the service user populations that social workers serve; therefore, the ability to screen for a potential problem is extremely useful. Screening is not necessarily designed to establish the nature and extent of problematic substance use, and may merely provide evidence that further specialised assessment is required. When thinking about and implementing screening for problematic substance use, remember to be non-judgemental and use your client-centred skills to ask the necessary questions in an appropriate manner. If your agency already uses a problematic substance use screening tool, it is important that you continue to use this.

Risk

It is important that you continue to consider and monitor risk in an ongoing assessment of your service user and those around them. Screening for problematic substance use does not negate the need for ongoing evaluation of risk. In regards to specific risks relating to substance use, please consider the short- and long-term effects as well as overdose potential and withdrawal symptoms of substances as outlined in Chapter 3. You may also find it useful to have information in pamphlet or leaflet form about risks relating to various types of substance use that you can refer to and/or give to your service users. Always make sure that there is no imminent risk from intoxication and/or overdose. If you believe your service user to be at high and imminent risk to themselves or others, make this your priority and call emergency services if necessary.

Screening assessments

Before undertaking an initial substance use assessment or screen, you should be aware of your own agency's policy on working with problematic substance use. Coupled with this, you should be aware of local 'substance misuse' agencies and peer-led services in your area, what they can offer and how you can refer to them if necessary. Preferably, you should have visited the agencies that you may need to refer on to, know their referral process and specific things such as if they have a waiting list and how long it is. It may be that you suspect problematic substance use and in your social work role you feel confident enough to work with this issue following an initial screening of the problem. Or it may be that the screening assessment provides you with the information you need to know that a referral to a specialist service is required. If this is necessary, these screening assessments will also provide you with most of the necessary information you need to make a referral.

If you are going to complete a screening assessment with your service user, it is likely that you already know them, have completed a comprehensive social work assessment in line with legislation and your agency protocols and are working with them on a regular basis. If this is the case, then it is assumed that you already have an established working relationship with the service user(s) and their family, and have built a suitable rapport with them. This will provide you with a perfect platform from which to begin your discussions about possible problematic substance use, and potentially will enable you to do the screening assessments. We know that a positive, empowering, honest and empathic relationship between a social worker and their service user(s) is extremely beneficial. If you have only just met the service user(s) and are assessing them for the first time, a screening assessment may be used alongside the more comprehensive assessment you already do, which should anyway include some evaluation of the potential for problematic substance use. If your agency's social work assessment does not already screen for problematic substance use in some way, then adding a simple question about this can be a great place to start. More will be discussed about how this can be done later in this chapter. Remember, however, that service users are probably more likely to be honest about substance use once you have already established a suitable rapport, so this issue may need revisiting. It is also useful to remember that it is much less threatening to ask questions about drinking rather than drug use at first, as more people drink and it is legal (Straussner, 2004). Either way, remaining anti-oppressive and non-judgemental in your stance towards those who may have problematic substance use will be the best way of engaging them on this issue.

The National Treatment Agency for Substance Misuse (NTA) (2006) has identified that a screening assessment is a brief process that aims to establish whether an individual has a drug and/or alcohol problem, whether there is a need to refer to a specialist service and whether there is any immediate risk for the client. Screening assessments can be used in any social work setting, and should become a part of the social workers' intervention toolkit. Before screening for problematic substance use problems, however, you should be clear about the purpose of the screen and discuss the possible implications of the screen with your service user. The screening assessment should identify those who require referral to specialised treatment services and the urgency of the referral. If the screen indicates that further assessment is required, a triage or comprehensive assessment can be carried out at a specialist 'substance misuse' treatment service. Screening assessments, which may also include an element of brief intervention, can also help to engage and prepare the service user for further specialist intervention or treatment.

There are several screening tools that may be of benefit for you to be aware of and you may feel comfortable administering these questionnaires, or getting the service user to complete their own. Use of any formal screening tool will probably require the approval of your manager. Alternatively, you may feel more comfortable doing this screening in a more informal manner by asking a few simple questions. The important thing is to find the right way, in your own context, to get useful and accurate information. People are more likely to be open and honest with you about their substance use if you have already developed a good rapport with them, if you have been open and honest with them about why you are asking about their substance use and the limits to the confidentiality you can provide. In essence, there is nothing too complicated about screening for substance use and you certainly do not need to be a 'substance misuse specialist' to do it. Do not be afraid of the process. If you choose a less formal approach to screening in a social work context, the best approach is probably a person-centred enquiry into the way substance use fits into someone's life, coupled with some specific questions about quantity and frequency of consumption. This will begin the process of the service user identifying their own concerns about their substance use (NTA, 2004).

What you are likely to want to know is:

- What substances are used.
- How often they are using them. Going back over the last week can be a useful and reasonably accurate way of determining this.
- Whether they or others are at any risk when they take substances. For example, driving while under the influence (DUI).
- Whether substance use has ever interfered with work, family life or relationships.
- Whether they have any physical/medical or mental health problem that may be exacerbated by substance use.
- Whether their friends or family have concerns about their substance use.
- Whether their substance use has ever led to any legal problems, for example acquisitive crime to pay for drug use, or arrest for DUI.
- Whether they want to do anything about their substance use.

The answers that are received from this line of questioning can lead to further questioning if required. Further questioning may revolve around whether the service user would like to give up or cut down, how difficult they feel this may be for them and whether they would like any further support. If you feel that the problematic substance use does not require specialist intervention, you may feel comfortable proceeding with a form of brief intervention (Chapter 13), using a motivational approach (Chapter 11) or providing harm reduction education (Chapter 10) about the use of substances. In cases where you have serious concerns about someone's substance use, you may be required to refer to a specialist service for a more in-depth assessment of their needs (NTA, 2004). If you are unsure about your own skill level, always seek supervision, and if in doubt make a referral to a specialised service.

If you would rather use an assessment screening tool to gather this information instead of an informal questioning approach, that is also fine. The important thing is that you are asking the right questions to determine if there may be a problem, rather than ignoring it completely or panicking and 'referring them on' when this may not be necessary. There are a variety of screening tools to choose from, but for the purposes of this chapter three specific screening tools will be discussed. The first screening tool discussed is very simple to use and covers both alcohol and drugs (CAGE-AID). Also included is a screening tool that is somewhat more in-depth and only covers alcohol (AUDIT), and one more in-depth drug screening tool (DAST-10).

CAGE-AID (Brown and Rounds, 1995) – A simple tool to screen for problematic substance use

According to Bliss and Pecukonis (2009), CAGE-AID (Brown and Rounds, 1995) provides social workers in non-substance use specialist roles with a simple way of screening for problematic substance use. The CAGE-Adapted to Involve Drugs (CAGE-AID) is adapted from the CAGE (Ewing, 1984) alcohol screening tool. The CAGE-AID has been shown to be 70.9 per cent sensitive and 75.7 per cent specific for substance 'abuse' disorders. Nevertheless, it is a very simple and easy to use tool that could be a starting point for social workers to screen for an issue. It will not necessarily negate the need for social workers to ask further questions about problematic substance use, but can be an easy-to-use screening tool to begin a discussion about problematic substance use. The CAGE-AID is an acronym that reminds you of the four easy questions to ask regarding problematic substance use. These are:

- Have you ever felt that you ought to **CUT** down on your drinking or drug use?
- Have people **ANNOYED** you by criticising your drinking or drug use?
- Have you ever felt bad or **GUILTY** about your drinking or drug use?
- Have you ever had a drink or used drugs first thing in the morning to steady your nerves or get rid of a hangover? (**EYEOPENER**). (Brown and Rounds, 1995: 137)

Each affirmative answer scores 1 point. A score of 1 or more points indicates that a further assessment or more probing about problematic substance use is required. The higher the score the more likelihood of more severe problematic substance use.

According to Bliss and Pecukonis (2009), some of these questions (especially question 1) can be added into comprehensive biopsychosocial social work assessments if service users answer in the affirmative regarding the use of alcohol or drugs. In this way, the screening tool is integrated into the general social work assessment. It can also be used in already established social work relationships with service users to explore further concerns about problematic substance use. If the service user is only an alcohol user or only a drug user, then the four questions can be easily adapted to include only the substance that the service user uses. If after further probing, the service user is found to have some problematic substance use then the social worker can intervene with harm reduction education, brief interventions or use a motivational approach to influence behaviour change (see Chapters 10, 11 and 13). Alternatively, they can refer on to a specialist or peer-led service.

More comprehensive screening tools

Alcohol screening assessment tools

There are a range of structured and quick screening questionnaires available for use with users of alcohol. They screen for different things, so before using an assessment tool, it is important to understand what a positive screen tells you (NTA, 2004). Only initiate using a screening assessment when you are clear about who to use it with and when to use it, and with the express consent of your manager and the service user.

Standard drinks

First, you will need to be able to explain to your service user what a 'standard alcoholic drink/unit' is, as most of the alcohol screening tools ask questions about the amount consumed by 'standard drink/unit'. While this is measured in grams of pure ethanol, it is easier to explain to the service user how much this is in the form of standard glasses of alcohol that they may drink. In the UK, the standard unit is 10 mls or 8 grams of pure alcohol but it is easier to explain that this is the equivalent of a small standard glass of wine, half a pint of standard strength beer or a single 'shot' of spirits. How many units of alcohol are in a drink depend on how strong it is and how much of it there is. As a guideline, a standard 125 ml glass of 9 per cent wine is 1 unit; however, realistically most wine is on average 13 per cent and is served in a 175 ml glass, thus making 1 'standard' glass of wine approximately 2.3 standard drinks/units. Half a pint of 3.5 per cent beer or cider is 1 standard drink/unit. Realistically, many beers and ciders are in excess of this and can be anywhere from 3.5 per cent to 9 per cent alcohol, and are usually drunk by the pint. Thus, a pint could easily be 2.8 or 3 standard drinks/units. A 25 ml shot of 40 per cent spirit is 1 standard drink/unit. Some pubs measure 35 ml for a 'shot' and will often serve doubles, so that a spirit drink can potentially be 2.8 standard drinks/units. If this sounds confusing, it can be. You don't need to confuse your service user, however. If you have a general idea about what constitutes a standard drink/unit, then you can ask them to explain to you how big their glasses are and what percentage of alcohol it is that they are drinking. They will usually know. Then you can work it out for yourself. The equation is volume (in ml) times alcohol per volume (or the percentage of alcohol) divided by 1,000. There is an excellent calculator to add up standard drinks/ units available at: http://www.drinkaware.co.uk/tips-and-tools/drink-diary (this website also has some very good information about alcohol that may be useful for you and your service user to know). Don't worry too much as it will get easier to get a realistic idea of how much someone is drinking by the unit the more times that you do this screening assessment.

Coupled with this knowledge, you also need to be aware of the recommended 'safer drinking limits'. In the UK, it is recommended that women drink no more than 14 units of alcohol in a week, and men no more than 21 units. Women should drink no more than 2–3 units per day, and men no more than 3–4 units per day, and everyone should have a number of alcohol-free days in the week. Drinking more than this can cause serious health risks. This information becomes critical for you to know when you feedback to your service user about the level of their drinking. Giving this information and feedback to the service user is a form of brief intervention (see Chapter 13 for more information about brief intervention).

The Alcohol Use Disorders Identification Test (AUDIT)

For the purposes of this part of the chapter, we will concentrate on the use of the Alcohol Use Disorders Identification Test (AUDIT) questionnaire, which assesses 'hazardous and harmful as well as dependent drinking', and was developed by the World Health Organization in 1989 (Babor et al., 2001). The AUDIT provides a framework in which to begin looking at reducing alcohol-related harm in individuals who are experiencing problems. The questions take a couple of minutes to complete. It has been validated across age, gender, in various cultures, in six countries and in a range of community and hospital settings (Babor et al., 2001; NTA, 2004). The AUDIT screening tool was originally developed for use in the primary care setting, but can easily be used by other health and social care professionals and is appropriate for social workers to administer. The screening tool is particularly beneficial for certain groups that are statistically more likely to develop alcohol-related problems. These include middle-aged males, adolescents, and people in certain occupations for example business executives, sex workers and publicans (Babor et al., 2001). According to Babor et al. (2001), it is also beneficial to use the screening tool with people who have physical health problems that are known to be related to alcohol use, people who have depression and/or suicidality, as well as other people with mental health problems, patients attending casualty and emergency, homeless people, prisoners and offenders (Babor et al., 2001). It is therefore very well suited to a number of social work settings and service user groups.

The AUDIT screens for recent hazardous, harmful and dependent drinking. According to the AUDIT criteria:

Hazardous drinking is a pattern of alcohol consumption that increases the risk of harmful consequences to the user or others ... **Harmful use** refers to alcohol consumption that results in consequences to physical and mental health. Some would also consider social consequences among the harms caused by alcohol. **Alcohol Dependence** is a cluster of behavioural, cognitive and physiological phenomena that may develop after repeated alcohol use. Typically, these phenomena include a strong desire to consume alcohol, impaired control over its use, persistent drinking despite harmful consequences, a higher priority given to drinking than to other activities and obligations, increased alcohol tolerance, and a physical withdrawal reaction when alcohol use is discontinued. (Babor et al., 2001: 6)

If you do choose to use the AUDIT, it is paramount that you explain to your service user what you are going to do and why. This opportunity should always have followed a discussion about alcohol-related concerns and you should have the service user's permission to use the screen. It may be necessary to be extra cautious and reassuring to the service user when discussing alcohol consumption with people who may be prohibited to drink by law or by their culture or religion, for example if they are under the age to drink legally or are Muslim. You need to let them know that it is important that they answer the questions as accurately as possible. Try not to use the screen if the service user is intoxicated. You will need to think about whether you ask the questions yourself, or whether you get the service user to self-administer the screen. This will depend on the circumstances at the time, the service user's ability to fill in the screen and the service users' preference. There are copies in the appendices of both the self-administered questionnaire (Appendix A1) and the AUDIT (Appendix A2), which you can use to interview the service user.

If you choose to use the interview type AUDIT, then according to Babor et al. (2001), it is really important that you read the questions as they are written in the AUDIT and give the service user the list of options for their answer. This is because the screening tool has been identified as valid and reliable if used in this way. You can, however, probe and clarify to make sure that the service user has given the most accurate answer it or explain the question if they appear reluctant to answer it or if you think this is necessary. It may sometimes be difficult to work out what a 'typical' drinking session is, if this is the case ask the service user to respond at a time when their drinking was at its heaviest. Record the answers on the AUDIT carefully, but do also make other notes or observations if you feel this is necessary. If you decide to let the service user fill out the AUDIT as a questionnaire, it will still be important to tell them about standard drinks/units. You may like to go over the questionnaire with them so that you have the opportunity to clarify anything you may want to.

Scoring on the AUDIT is relatively easy. Each of the questions has a set of responses to choose from, and each response has a score ranging from 0 to 4. In the interview format (Appendix A2), the interviewer enters the score (the number within parentheses) corresponding to the service user's response in the box beside each question. In the self-report questionnaire format (Appendix A1), the number in the column of each response checked by the service users should be entered by the scorer in the extreme right-hand column. All the response scores should then be added and recorded in the box labelled 'Total' (Babor et al., 2001: 19). If a service user scores 8 or above, this is seen as an indicator of hazardous and harmful drinking and could be considered dependent drinking. For people over the age of 65, this may be decreased to a score of 7. The higher the score, the more likelihood of hazardous, harmful or dependent drinking. A more detailed analysis of the score can be made by checking which questions the service user scored the most points on:

> A score of 1 or more on Question 2 or Question 3 indicates consumption at a hazardous level. Points scored above 0 on questions 4–6 (especially daily or weekly symptoms) imply the presence or incipience of alcohol dependence. Points scored on questions 7–10 indicate that alcohol related harm is already being experienced. The total score, consumption levels, signs of dependence, and present harm should all play a role in determining how to manage a [service user]. (Babor et al., 2001:19)

In general, the following can be implied:

• Scores between 8 and 15 are most appropriate for simple advice focused on reducing hazardous drinking.
• Scores between 16 and 19 indicate the need for brief counselling and continued monitoring.
• Scores of 20 or above clearly require further assessment for alcohol dependence.

Depending on your level of confidence, training and experience, you may be comfortable working with scores of up to 19. If you are not comfortable offering brief intervention for people with a score of between 16 and 19, you may want to refer these people to an appropriate service. Unless you are a specialist 'substance misuse' social worker, you will refer people with a score of 20 or above to a more specialist service. Remember that if a service user is drinking large amounts on a daily basis, it may be very dangerous for them just to stop drinking, as they are likely to need some form of medical detoxification.

Most social workers should be able to offer harm reduction education in the form of brief intervention to service users with a score of between 8 and 15. Brief intervention can involve presenting the screening results, pointing out possible risks and consequences associated with their alcohol use, further advice, encouragement and goal-setting around reduction or abstinence of alcohol use (more will be discussed regarding what this actually involves in Chapter 10). People who score under 8 can be positively encouraged and reminded of the risks associated with hazardous drinking. At the very least, all service users should know the recommended 'safer drinking limits'. You may also like to remind them that it is recommended that they do not drink when operating heavy machinery, including a car, when they are pregnant, when they have a contraindicated medical condition and when they have taken some types of medication. Giving this information to service users is a form of brief intervention.

Regardless of the AUDIT scores, if you have other serious concerns about risk relating to the service user or others, you may need to refer on or seek advice and support. This may include times when a parent's drinking is putting their children at risk or when a service user has exacerbating mental health problems. You will need to undertake your normal ongoing risk assessment procedures in line with relevant legislation and your agencies policies. Remember that the AUDIT does not replace your social work skills; it is merely another instrument in your toolkit.

Drug screening assessment tools

The NTA's *Models of Care* document (2002) outlines the framework for the commissioning of treatment for all adult drug 'misusers' in England. *Models of Care* provides a tiered framework whereby each tier offers various types of assessment, intervention and services. According to *Models of Care*, tier 1 services, which include services offered by a range of professionals including GPs, social workers, teachers and probation officers to name but a few, should, with the right knowledge and training, all be able to undertake initial drug screening assessments. They should also be able to provide brief intervention and refer on if necessary. The other three tiers provide more specialist services for drug users, from outpatient drop-in services through to residential rehabilitation and detox. At a tier 1 level, social workers will work with a variety of service users who may never encounter or need to encounter drug services, and therefore are in the perfect position to screen for problematic drug use and possibly engage people who would otherwise be missed by specialty services. According to *Models of Care*, an initial drug screening by tier 1 services should include information about:

- Whether there is a drug problem.
- Whether there are any co-existing physical, social or psychological problems.
- Identification of any risk, including self-harm and risk to others.
- An assessment of the urgency of the referral if one is necessary. (NTA, 2002: 32)

This suggests a slightly more in-depth screen than the CAGE-AID can give. The NTA recommends that screening assessments be agreed locally to meet local needs, be straightforward to apply as well as able to meet targets and standards. Because of this, the NTA has not recommended a specific screening tool that should be used by all tier 1 services.

There are, however, a number of valid and reliable screening tools that have been developed for the screening of drug use. Remember, however, you should be cautious about using these screening tools in your role as a social worker unless you have had further training. For the purposes of this part of the chapter, we will focus on a drug screening tool called DAST-10.

Drug Use Inventory-10 (DAST-10)

Remember to discuss with your service user the implications of the discussions or screenings you undertake and be aware of the agencies in your area that could further support your service user if a referral is necessary. Remain non-judgemental and person-centred in your approach towards the service user when undertaking any form of screening assessment.

The original Drug Abuse Screening Test (DAST) was a 20-item screening test designed by Skinner (1971), and based on the Michigan Alcoholism Screening Test (Selzer, 1971). The original DAST has excellent internal consistency reliability, and the shorter 10-item DAST-10 correlates very highly with the original 20-item DAST. Subsequent research has evaluated the DAST with various populations and in various settings, including with mental health service users, prisoners and people with problematic substance use, in primary care and in the workplace (Carson DeWitt, 2009). The DAST-10 is an easy-to-administer screening tool that provides an index of drug-related problems in a variety of settings. It can be self-administered, used in a questionnaire format or even administered online. (Please find a copy of the DAST-10 in Appendix B.) The DAST-10 should not be administered when the service user is under the influence of drugs or withdrawing from the use of drugs. The drug use that the DAST-10 refers to includes all substances except alcohol and tobacco, but does include prescription medication used in excess of the directions or for non-medical purposes. When using the DAST-10, score 1 point for each 'YES' answer, except for question 3 where a 'NO' receives 1 point. (The scoring system is explained in the DAST-10, which is available in Appendix B.) To interpret the scores, follow the guidelines below:

- Scores of 0 indicate no problem, and require no further action at this time.
- Scores of 1–2 indicate a low-level problem that requires monitoring, possible brief intervention education and re-screening at a later date.
- Scores of 3–5 indicate a moderate problem that requires further investigation and possible brief invention and/or harm reduction education using a motivational approach if a more substantial problem is not discovered on further investigation.
- Scores of 6–8 indicate a substantial problem and requires referral for further specialised comprehensive assessment.
- Scores of 9–10 indicate a severe problem that also requires referral for further specialised comprehensive assessment.

Giving feedback to your service user about their score is an intervention in itself and can be a great way to explore further their drug use. Give feedback to them about what the scores may indicate and offer to provide information about the drugs that they are using in pamphlet form or by suggesting an appropriate website, if they would like to know more. Use the information provided in Chapter 3 of this book to help with some of the basic information around the effects of drug use and tolerance and dependence potential. Where the service user scores 6 or above, tell them that you are quite concerned about their drug use and explain their options for referral to a more specialised service. Depending on your level of training and confidence in problematic substance use, you may feel comfortable working with service users who score up to 5 on the DAST-10 by offering brief intervention and/or harm reduction education using a motivational approach (see Chapters 10, 11 and 13). Remember that if in doubt do consult your supervisor and always refer on if necessary. Regardless of the DAST-10 scores, if you have other serious concerns about risk relating to the service user or others, you may need to refer on or seek advice and support. This may include times when a parent's drug use is putting their children at risk or when a service user has exacerbating mental health problems. You will need to undertake your normal ongoing risk assessment procedures in line with relevant legislation and your agencies policies. Remember that the DAST-10 does not replace your social work skills; it is merely another instrument in your toolkit.

Remember, too, that if you are not comfortable using formal screening tools, a more 'informal' discussion or screening, as outlined at the beginning of this chapter, can also be appropriate if you are concerned about your service users' substance use.

Summary

Prior to screening for problematic substance use, it is useful for social workers to be aware of the variety of specialised substance 'misuse' agencies and services (including peer-led) that may be available in their area. It is also ideal to have visited the agencies or services and know the referral process and the length of the waiting list, if there is one. Using screening assessments to check problematic substance use can be a useful way for social workers to engage their service users in meaningful discussions about potential problematic substance use. Whether using a screening assessment tool such as the CAGE-AID, AUDIT or DAST-10 or by screening more informally, a social worker can make an initial assessment about whether a service user has a problem. To gather the most accurate and useful information, a non-judgemental person-centred approach should be taken when talking with service users about these issues. Remember that offering screening is a form of brief intervention in itself. Depending on the seriousness of the problem, social workers may be able to work with the issue themselves by offering harm reduction education, further brief intervention and/or use a motivational approach to elicit behaviour change. Initially, this can be done by offering feedback about the outcome of the screening and giving service users information about drug use, standard drinks and 'safer drinking levels'. If the problem is more serious, the screening assessment will often have provided the social worker with the necessary information to refer on to a local specialised 'substance misuse' agency or service.

Any use of screening assessments should be done in accordance with the social work agency protocol and with the full knowledge of the service user after a discussion about the implications of the outcome of the assessment. How social workers are able to work with service users who have problematic substance use will depend on their agency's policies and procedures. A screening assessment does not replace ongoing assessment and risk assessment and any concern regarding high risk and imminent danger for the safety of the service user or others should be dealt with immediately in the appropriate manner.

Reflections

Why is it relevant to you in your social work setting to screen for possible problematic substance use?

Does your agency or your placement agency have a policy or protocol for working with service users who have/may have problematic substance use? Do you ask about substance use as part of the assessment you do?

Do you like the idea of a screening tool? Or are you more comfortable asking these types of questions in a more informal way?

Further readings

Bliss, D. and Pecukonis, E. (2009) 'Screening and brief intervention practice model for social workers in non-substance-abuse practice settings', *Journal of Social Work Practice in Addictions*, 9(1): 21–40.

Petersen, T. and McBride, A. (2002) 'Client assessment' in *Working with Substance Misusers: A Guide to Theory and Practice*. London: Routledge, pp. 75–91.

Websites

For information about alcohol and standard drinks/units see: http://www.drinkaware.co.uk/tips-and-tools/drink-diary; and: http://www.nhs.uk/chq/Pages/846.aspx?CategoryID=87&SubCategoryID=87.

10

Harm Reduction, Abstinence and 'Recovery'

Some key concepts that it will be necessary for you to understand in your work with people who may have problematic substance use, are the ideas of 'recovery', abstinence and harm reduction. Abstinence (meaning to refrain from the use of all substances) is firmly advocated within disease concepts of problematic substance use and being abstinent is usually a requirement for 'recovery'. While this has historically been the case, there have been recent calls to widen the definition of 'recovery'. For example, the UK Drug Policy Commission (UKDPC) (2008) suggests that: 'The process of recovery from problematic substance use is characterised by voluntarily-sustained control over substance use which maximises health and wellbeing and participation in the rights, roles and responsibilities of society' (p. 6). This understanding of recovery recognises that in order to be in 'recovery', people must maximise their full potential to be healthy and well, as well as have sustained control of their substance use. It does not require abstinence, but it does require a healthy lifestyle and participation in society. This is a relatively new understanding of what 'recovery' might be and is quite different to how the term has been used historically in the 'substance misuse' field.

'Harm reduction', as the name suggests, includes interventions that seek to reduce the harm to people who may choose to continue to use substances. Being abstinent may not always be practical, appropriate or the service user's personal goal. Harm reduction acknowledges that some people may not be ready to give up their substance use completely. This reality means having to work with service users to reduce the harm caused by this continued substance use. Interventions to reduce drug-related harm may include needle exchange programmes and substitution therapy such as prescribing methadone, for example.

Abstinence and recovery

In theory, to be abstinent from substances would mean that you no longer have a problem with the use of substances. Abstinence therefore has historically been the only way of 'beating' problematic substance use, and this seems to make sense. Merely giving up substances does not always equate to being 'in recovery', however. Problematic substance use includes a pattern of unhealthy thinking and behaviour which includes, but is not limited to, the use of substances.

In the 1940s and 1950s, three residential treatment centres opened up in Minnesota in the US, that incorporated the Alcoholics Anonymous (AA) 12-step programme within a disease approach to addiction (Petersen and McBride, 2002). The 'disease' model perceives 'addiction' to be the behavioural consequence of pre-existing and permanent physical vulnerability that 'addicts' have to substances (Barber, 2002). The model used in these three centres became known as the 'Minnesota Model' and is probably the most well-known model associated with the disease and abstinence approach to 'addiction'. This model of treatment centre went on to become one of the most popular and well-known ways of treating 'addiction' in a residential setting.

Twelve-step programmes (also see Appendix C)

The 12-step programme developed out of the original Alcoholics Anonymous (AA), a self-help organisation founded in the 1930s (Williams, 2004). The 12-step programme has made a huge contribution to the lives of millions of substance users around the world. Twelve-step meetings, which are anonymous self-help support groups, are now run in communities in 134 countries around the world. There are also 12-step meetings for drug users (Narcotic Anonymous, NA), gamblers (Gamblers Anonymous, GA), people with eating disorders (Eating Disorders Anonymous, EDA) and families of people with alcohol and drug problems (Al-Anon and Families Anonymous), as well as the original Alcoholics Anonymous (AA).

Twelve-step programmes view 'addiction' as a loss of control due to vulnerabilities in the individual, coupled with the continued use of the substance(s), or the 'addictive' behaviour (Williams, 2004). This understanding relates directly to Step 1 of the 12 steps. That is: 'We admitted we were powerless over alcohol – that our lives had become unmanageable' (Alcoholics Anonymous, 2001). The 12-step programmes view 'addiction' as a lifelong condition from which you cannot be cured. Because of this understanding of 'addiction', the 12-step programme does not advocate harm reduction interventions, controlled or moderated use of substances and maintains that abstinence is the only viable route to 'recovery' (Williams, 2004). It does not, however, advocate any specific cause of 'addiction', and is consistent in supporting a 'multifactoral' understanding of causation of the 'disease'. Twelve-step programmes are spiritual programmes that, in supporting the disease concept of 'addiction', maintain that people should not feel guilt and shame for having the 'illness'. The 12-step programme does, however, advocate that people take responsibility for the consequences of their behaviour.

Twelve-step programmes view 'recovery' as not merely being 'clean and sober' (abstinent), but as being free of all 'addictive' behaviours and thinking (Borkman, 2008). In the 12-step programme, people may be abstinent from substances, but may still be acting in unhealthy ways towards others and themselves. They may still be exhibiting behaviours and thought patterns that are inconsistent with 'recovery'. In the 12-step programme, this is often called being a 'dry drunk'. Abstinence is achieved by giving up substances, but 'recovery' is achieved by 'working the 12-step programme', replacing negative thinking and painful emotions with positive, more healthy behaviours and attending regular meetings (Williams, 2004). Twelve-step meetings happen throughout the UK and are open to anyone who considers that they may have an 'addiction', coupled with a desire to change (stop using substances, or stop the addictive behaviour). Meetings usually last 1 to 2 hours and usually revolve around members 'sharing' their stories of 'addiction', or a discussion around a specific topic or 'step'. Sharing is central to the 12-step programme's philosophy. Members share their experiences of 'addiction' to help others see that they are not alone with their problems. Members are encouraged to stay in touch out of meeting times and develop a 'sponsorship' relationship. Sponsorship occurs when a member who has been in the fellowship for some time mentors a new member through the 12-step programme. The 12-step programme contains a great deal of literature that members are expected to read (Williams, 2004). Members are expected to adhere to the 12 traditions that are the principles of the 12-step programme but different from the actual 12 steps. Members are also supported by slogans that are used to motivate and encourage them. Some of the slogans include: 'One day at a time', 'Easy does it', 'Let go and let God' and 'Live in the now'.

The spiritual aspects of the programme are also important and as such are written into the steps themselves. For example, Step 3, 'Made a decision to turn our will and our lives over to the care of God as we understood Him' (Alcoholic Anonymous, 2001). The programme is clear that a 'higher power' may not necessarily be a 'traditional deity' (Williams, 2004: 141), but a more abstract understanding of a power outside oneself that may be able to support and guide members on their recovery journey. The terms 'God' or 'Higher Power' are used throughout the 12-step literature and can be a difficult thing for service users without a sense of spirituality or religiousness to grasp.

According to Williams (2004: 141), many features of the 12-step programme have theoretical aspects that parallel person-centred therapy (non-judgemental philosophy), cognitive behavioural therapy (use of slogans), social learning theory (sponsor as role model) and family and systemic approaches (use of social networks). Researching an anonymous 'addictions' support group and its impact on peoples' lives has, however, been notoriously difficult. According to the available research, 12-step programmes have proved to be as effective as cognitive behavioural therapy and motivational enhancement therapy in short-term therapy for people with problematic substance use (Project MATCH Research Group, 1997), and slightly more effective than these types of therapies in the long term (Miller, 1995). This longer-term effectiveness is potentially due to the ongoing support that can be received in the community via the 12-step fellowship meetings, which other forms of treatment may not offer post-completion of treatment. More recent research has shown a positive relationship between 12-step involvement and improvement on substance use outcomes for both users of alcohol and drugs over extended periods of time for up to 16 years (Donovan and Floyd, 2008). These are correlational findings, however, and the researchers were not able to prove a causal link. While there is research to support the effectiveness of 12-step programmes, and anecdotal testimony would suggest that the programme is effective at supporting people with problematic substance use in the community, there are a number of critiques of the programme.

Some people do find it difficult to grasp the spiritual aspect of the programme and given that this is a huge part of the 12-step programme, it can alienate some people with problematic substance use when they feel that they just don't 'get it'. There are also concerns that the notions of illness and disease create an 'all or nothing', 'submit or rebel' mentality for service users that could set them up to rebel through excessive use of substances if they are unable to remain abstinent. Service users may believe that they are incapable of controlled substance use and therefore their 'addiction' becomes a self-fulfilling prophecy. The disease concept of 'addiction' coupled with the importance of help from a 'higher power' can also potentially mean that people do not have to take responsibility for their behaviours, because they can blame the 'disease', or lack of support from their 'God'. There is also concern that some problematic substance users 'cross addict' to the 12-step movement, attend meetings compulsively and merely replace one 'addiction' with another. There is also suspicion from some that because of this possibility, the 12-step fellowship has a cult-like status for many vulnerable people.

A major concern about all abstinence-based approaches is the danger of death for service users who after a period of abstinence return to using substances and are very prone to overdose. This is because during the period of abstinence their tolerance for substances will have decreased, meaning that they will not be able to use as much of the substance as they used prior to treatment. Service users are particularly vulnerable to overdose upon completion of abstinence-based treatment services and after detoxification.

Both the 12-step programmes and the Minnesota Model continue to have a huge influence on residential rehabilitation services throughout the UK. If any of your service users were to require residential rehabilitation, it is very likely that they will encounter the 'disease' concept of 'addiction' as well as at least one of the 12-step programmes, and be required to be 'abstinent' from all mind-altering substances. This is in contrast to services offered in the community which generally tend to have a 'harm reduction' focus. It is a relatively new notion that an abstinence-based treatment service would incorporate harm reduction approaches. However, this does happen in some residential services primarily in response to the problem of HIV and Hepatitis C transmission (World Health Organization (WHO), 2006). Many abstinence-based services that have incorporated harm reduction approaches into their services have found the conflict between the two less complex than they envisaged, because both approaches have the service user as their number one priority, and agree that abstinence is the best way to avoid substance-related harm (WHO, 2006). This useful way of understanding these two orientations will be further discussed later in this chapter.

Harm reduction

Harm reduction has come about partly in response to the 'one size fits all' attitude of abstinence approaches to problematic substance use, but is primarily a policy-driven, evidence-based approach to reducing the substance-related harm caused to individuals, families and communities. It is primarily concerned with preventing blood-borne diseases, particularly HIV and hepatitis, and preventing overdose and substance-related death (NTA, 2008a), as well as focusing on public safety. At a social level, for example, we can see harm reduction strategies embedded in much of the legislation and policies regarding alcohol use. There are laws around who can sell alcohol, who can buy alcohol, who can drink alcohol and where it can be drunk. There are public education campaigns raising awareness about 'binge drinking' and 'safer' drinking limits, and restrictions on where and when alcohol can be advertised. All of these things are in recognition that people are going to use alcohol and that given this, individuals should be aware of how to drink safely to limit the harms that can be caused by excessive use and binge drinking.

Similar harm reduction strategies are apparent where illicit drugs are concerned, but these have attracted much more negative attention. Harm reduction strategies for drug use include needle exchange programmes, advice and support on safer injecting practices and preventing infections, and advice and support on preventing overdose. These strategies are highly contentious and opponents of harm reduction strategies believe that such interventions only seek to encourage drugs users to continue using drugs. Although controversial, the retention rates and overall success of harm reduction interventions are very good (Farrell et al., 2005; Hunt et al., 2006; Marlatt, 1996; Tatarsky, 2003).

Many substance users avoid seeking help with problematic substance use because they have no intention of 'giving up' and assume that they will be persuaded to do so by substance use treatment services (Tatarsky, 2003). They therefore neglect to seek help and continue to have problems related to their substance use. By accepting that not all people want to give up substance use, harm reduction opens the door for a variety of service users who would otherwise not be eligible for traditional abstinent-based treatment programmes. The number of theories that abound in explanation of problematic substance use are evidence of the variety of factors and variables that can potentially be involved when someone has problematic substance use. Harm reduction allows us to work with individuals and their families 'where they are at' and with what their goals are, rather than just requiring abstinence for all. Just as everyone's reasons for using substances may be different, so may be their goals. They may want to continue to use, cut down, use differently or give up. Harm reduction allows us to acknowledge that.

Abstinence versus harm reduction?

The concepts of harm reduction and abstinence have often been seen as 'either/ or' (Kellogg, 2003) orientations when working with problematic substance use.

However, it is probably more helpful to view these orientations as partners with a focus on similar objectives and with similar aspirations. Think about a substance use continuum that ranges from no use/abstinence, through to severe problematic use/dependence. Across this spectrum it is easy to recognise how there is room for both harm reduction and abstentionist interventions. The need for different types of interventions may be based on the severity of the problem (people with severe dependence may be less able to cut down), people's individual vulnerabilities and most importantly the service user's own choices and goals. Interventions can lay at any point on this continuum, with interventions aimed at harm reduction, abstinence and 'recovery' being part of the same overall solution, as abstinence obviously causes the least harm. Harm reduction strategies and interventions do not have to neglect attempts at abstinence. In other words, abstentionist interventions can be seen as a form of harm reduction. In this way, the two approaches arguably become more than merely partners but coalesce, united by their mutual goals and objectives. Abstinence is seen as the ultimate harm reduction goal. This way of conceptualising harm reduction and abstinence allows the social worker to work in partnership with the service user at any point along the continuum rather than having an 'either/or' approach: 'harm reduction may be considered an umbrella concept that encompasses the broad spectrum of treatment modalities that can be matched to the needs of this diverse group of problem users' (Tatarsky, 2003: 250). When it comes to problematic substance use, 'one size does not fit all'. Abstinence-based interventions are not realistic or appropriate for all substance users, and in and of themselves do not account for personal choice. Seen as a type of harm reduction intervention, however, an abstinence-based intervention is seen as one choice in a range of many, while harm reduction as an orientation comes to include that which causes the least harm – abstinence. A focus on the importance of understanding these concepts and the substance use continuum in the context of individualised care is vital to all social workers who seek to work effectively with their service users. The key is to be able to work with service users 'where they are at' to reduce substance-related harm, and to believe that recovery is possible and that abstinence is an achievable goal.

There have always been difficulties with getting the general public and those not able or willing to understand the issues around problematic substance use to accept the idea behind harm reduction. It is difficult, for example, to get your head around educating someone about how to use drugs more safely, when it is clear that any use of drugs can be detrimental. It has taken some time for health and social care professionals to feel comfortable with this way of working, and for some it is never easy. Depending on the social work role and the context in which they work, acknowledging the illegal use of drugs by service users can also have very serious ethical and legal implications. Staunch advocates of abstinence models of treatment often disagree with the entire approach, fearing that people will be encouraged to continue to use when clearly they need to 'just give up'. Such advocates might find it extremely difficult to agree that abstinence-based interventions can be seen as part of the harm reduction approach.

This argument was never clearer than when media attention was drawn to NTA figures regarding treatment success and retention in 2006/7 (NTA, 2008b). These outlined that only 3 per cent of drug users leaving treatment had left 'free from all drugs' (Ashton, 2007). To an unknowing public this probably looked absurd, but to people working in the field this was seen as unsurprising given that these figure included people undertaking harm reduction focused treatment, on methadone maintenance and other types of substitution therapy. Due to the types of treatment on offer, there has always been difficulty in measuring treatment 'success'. What constitutes success in one case may not in another, and certainly within the 'substance misuse field' abstinence is not the only measure of success. The majority of treatment services in the UK are harm reduction orientated, with only a few service users being offered abstinence-based treatment. In the minds of many 'substance misuse' workers and their service users, those who reduce the harms associated with their substance use and/or are being maintained on substitution therapy are being successful. To the media and an unknowing public, however, this way of thinking is difficult to understand because their assumption is that abstinence is the only gauge of success.

The 'substance misuse' treatment field in the UK took the opportunity this media frenzy created to debate the issues. In 2008, DrugScope supported 'The Great Debate' event around the country to hear from stakeholders their ideas about harm reduction, abstinence and recovery. The outcome of these events culminated in the publication of *Drug Treatment at the Crossroads* (DrugScope, 2009). This document provides some key messages to policy-makers and the field in general. One of the key concerns raised at the event was that the 'treatment' field may have used harm reduction interventions to the detriment of supporting service users to believe that they can achieve abstinence. There were no clear conclusions about the accuracy of this concern; however, it certainly raised awareness of its possibility. Some of the key messages that a majority of people at 'The Great Debate' agreed on were:

- Drug treatment is important.
- Choice in treatment should be supported – Treatment services should support both abstinence and harm reduction approaches.
- The system should put people first.
- Relationships matter – The values, competencies and attitudes of people who work with service users is as important as any intervention they are delivering.
- We should be aiming higher – An increased emphasis on recovery and social (re)integration is necessary.
- Families and communities need support, too. (DrugScope, 2009: 2)

This debate, perhaps long overdue, provided a number of stakeholders with the opportunity to reflect on the state of the 'substance misuse' treatment field and hear from others their experiences of being offered either/or treatment options (either abstinence-based or harm reduction interventions). It was generally reflected that perhaps the field does need to increase belief in the possibility of 'recovery' and incorporate abstinence as a legitimate end goal, even if this may appear to be at times a long hard road for many services users.

Harm reduction – giving information and advice

With these issues in mind then, giving harm reduction information and advice, including supporting abstinence as a real option, may be something you would feel comfortable using in your social work practice. Harm reduction in its simplest and most effective form is about educating substance users about the risks associated with substance use and helping them take responsibility for the choices they make.

There is a huge range of harm reduction literature available. Some of the areas that you need to make sure you are aware of are:

- Standard drink/units.
- Safer drinking levels.
- Substitute therapy (methadone, buprenorphine).
- Needle exchange programmes.
- Safer drug using practices, e.g. smoking drugs instead of injecting, not sharing needles or pipes.
- Safer injection principles, e.g. wound management, cleaning of syringes, sharps bins.
- Mixing drugs, e.g. dangers associated with mixing drugs, including with prescribed medications.
- Preventing overdose. Dose limits and what to do if someone overdoses.
- Keeping others safe, e.g. not driving or looking after children when using substances and keeping drugs away from children.
- First aid knowledge.
- Legal implications of being caught in possession.
- Safer sex and condom use.

A good start with users of alcohol would be to educate them about standard drinks/units and recommended safer drinking limits (information about these things can be found in Chapter 9). There are pamphlets and fact sheets about this and other information about how to drink safely available from a variety of sources, including Alcohol Concern (http://www.alcoholconcern.org.uk/servlets/home), Alcohol Focus Scotland (http://www.alcohol-focus-scotland.org.uk) and Drink Aware (http://www.drinkaware.co.uk/). Giving non-judgemental feedback to your service user if they are drinking more than is recommended is a good start. Generally, people are unaware that they may be drinking at hazardous levels and this information may be enough to get them to consider cutting down. It is also worth contacting local 'substance misuse' and peer-led services to see if they have any literature that you could collect to have on hand when working with service users who have problematic substance use.

Helpful sources of literature and educational information about substances can be found on the internet but it is important that you use reputable websites for information about alcohol and drugs as there are many websites that exaggerate, understate or provide inaccurate information about the effects of substance use. Chapter 3 of this book is also a good source of general information about a variety of substances.

Always check with the service user how much they already know as they may know more than you! Please make the information you give to your service users relevant to them and aim it 'where they are at'. It obviously makes no sense to give a user of alcohol information on safer injection principles. Make sure that you have read the information yourself and understand the information you are giving out. Information should be given in small 'chunks' and repeated at a later date if necessary. Make sure that the service user understands what you have been talking about by asking them if they do, and by being clear and straightforward in the way you speak and the language you use. There may be some topics that you feel better able to discuss than others. For example, you may be happy to talk about 'avoiding sharing needles' as opposed to 'how to clean syringes'. You may feel more comfortable discussing keeping drugs out of the reach of children than you do 'safer injection practices', but whatever you do is infinitely better than doing nothing, and if more information is required this can always be given in written form or via DVD (available from the various websites listed in the Further reading section) or by referring someone to a drop-in 'substance misuse' service in their local area who will be able to answer any more specific questions. For you to be aware of harm reduction information does not require you to be an expert in all of these areas, but it is important that you have the information to hand to be able to give to service users as required and that you are prepared to answer questions about it. Make sure that you are aware of local services that you could refer to if you are unable to answer any questions.

Remember that the key is to provide service users with information 'where they are at'. Do not try to use this information to scare and force service users to give up. If there are negative consequences of their substance use, they will be well aware of them and will not need you to tell them to 'just say no' or 'just stop'. Yes, using substances can be extremely dangerous, but people choose to use them for a number of reasons, not least because at some point they have enjoyed using them. The way you present them with this information is vital. You are not giving them the information to convince them to change but to make them aware of accurate information, in a non-judgemental manner, about the substance(s) they chose to use. Of course, you can show concern or tell them you are concerned; however, pushing them in a direction they are not yet ready for can often have the opposite effect. Service users can feel 'backed into a corner' and in turn they may defend their use of substances and their lifestyle choices, as any of us would if we felt that we were being judged. The only exception to this is if you are concerned about imminent and immediate danger for your service user or those around them, for example if you are concerned that they may be over-dosing. In this case, do as you would for any other medical emergency and call the emergency services.

The key then is to offer the information in a neutral way, coupled with a brief expression of personal concern (if necessary), and tell the service user that they can approach you if they require any support to make lifestyle changes (including cutting down and/or giving up) as a result of this information. You will find that in this way, service users are much more likely to stay engaged with you and to return to seek support. This engagement may mean that at some point they will allow you to make a referral to a specialised substance use agency if this is necessary. Giving information in this way to seek to reduce the harm associated with substance use is also considered a 'brief intervention'. Brief intervention is covered in more depth in Chapter 13.

Summary

While historically 'abstinence' and 'harm reduction' initiatives have been seen as very different approaches to helping with problematic substance use, this chapter outlines how they can fit together to support service users in achieving their goals. Social workers may find offering harm reduction information and talking about some harm reduction strategies difficult. Alongside an understanding of their effectiveness (Farrell et al., 2005; Hunt et al., 2006; Marlatt, 1996; Tatarsky, 2003), however, and within a clear anti-discriminatory framework, the harm reduction approach, including the potential for abstinence, provides social workers with an excellent opportunity to work with service users and engage them in discussions around problematic substance use. Just because you are discussing substance use and harm reduction strategies does not mean you are continuing to support problematic substance use. It means that you are giving service users accurate information about their lifestyle choices and supporting them to make changes, including the ability to choose abstinence and 'recovery', by being non-judgemental and engaging with them 'where they are at'.

If abstinence is the service user's goal, then a 12-step programme (like AA or NA) operating in the community will support this aim. If reducing their use and/or reducing the harm it causes is their primary concern, then you may be able to intervene and offer some harm reduction education information. Depending on your level of knowledge and confidence, you may also feel comfortable working alongside them with some key motivational approaches and/or offering them other types of brief intervention (see Chapters 11 and 13) that will help them on their journey. Regardless of the service user's goal, they should always be offered the opportunity to be referred to a specialist 'substance misuse' service, which will be able to offer a much wider range of interventions and can refer directly into other specialised services such as abstinence-based residential services or opioid substitution therapy (OST) programmes, if required.

Reflections

How would you feel discussing 'safer drug-using practices' with a service user?

What if they have children? A mental health problem? Does this change the way you might deal with a substance user? If so, why?

How do you think that you would measure success with your service users? Would you expect them to be abstinent?

Further readings

DrugScope (2009) *Drug Treatment at the Crossroads: What it's for, Where it's at and How to Make it even Better*. London: DrugScope.

National Treatment Agency (NTA) (2004) *Promoting Safer Drinking: A Briefing Paper for Drug Workers*. London: NTA.

NTA (2008) *Good Practice in Harm Reduction*. London: NTA.

11

Motivational Approaches

Motivational interviewing is a well-known and significant model for working with people who have problematic substance use. The model was developed by William Miller in 1982 while he was supervising a group of psychologists who were working with people who had problematic substance use. He began to see the importance of motivation in the process of behaviour change and began thinking about how motivation could be enhanced by the practitioner and within the sessions that the psychologists were having with their service users (Davies and Petersen, 2002). There is now a vast array of evidence to suggest that this model is very useful when working with problematic substance use and with other service user populations.

> The evidence base for motivational interviewing is strong in the areas of addictive and health behaviours. Useful as a brief intervention in itself, Motivational Interviewing also appears to improve outcomes when added to other treatment approaches. (Hettema et al., 2005: 109) (Also see http://motivationalinterview org/library/biblio.html for an extensive bibliography of the evidence base.)

While it is used primarily in the 'substance misuse' sector it has also more recently been used in mental health settings, domestic/interpersonal violence settings, sexual health services, for HIV risk reduction, diabetes control and medication compliance, health promotion and chronic disease prevention (Davies and Petersen, 2002; Wahab, 2005).

Motivational interviewing is a directive, client-centred counselling style for eliciting behaviour change by helping clients to explore and resolve ambivalence (Hettema et al., 2005). This model is especially useful for when service users may be unsure as to whether they really want to change their behaviour, that is, when they are ambivalent. The idea behind the model is to get service users themselves to explore this ambivalence and to reach their own decisions about potential behaviour change. The model was developed in direct response to the more aggressive confrontational styles that were historically used in the treatment of alcohol and drug problems. In these types of treatments, service users were often described as being unmotivated, resistant or in denial about their problematic substance use if they failed to change their behaviours. These types of treatment often had high relapse and dropout rates and generally poor treatment outcomes. Motivational interviewing was developed in response to this. This model supposes that if service users are not engaging with services and if they are going back to using substances and dropping out, then the professionals working with them need to do something differently. While not confrontational in an obvious sense like some of the more traditional models for working with problematic substance use (e.g. the Minnesota Model), motivational interviewing is focused and goal directed, with attention directed at exploring ambivalence and increasing readiness to change.

The spirit of motivational interviewing

Motivational interviewing is a blend of principles and techniques from a range of theories and interventions, including social psychology, motivational psychology, stages of change (which we will discuss further later in this chapter), cognitive dissonance and Rogers person-centred counselling. It is primarily a communication style that is intended to help service users feel safe, to enhance rapport and resolve ambivalence. According to Rollnick and Miller (1995) understanding the spirit of motivational interviewing is just as important as knowing the skills and strategies used in the approach. They outline seven key points to convey this spirit:

1 Motivation to change is elicited from the service user, and not imposed from outside the individual. Motivational interviewing relies on identifying and activating the service user's intrinsic values and goals to stimulate behaviour change and not on coercion, threats or bribes.

2 It is the service user's task, not the practitioner's, to articulate and resolve his or her ambivalence. The practitioner's task is to facilitate expression of both sides of the ambivalence impasse, and guide the service user toward an acceptable resolution that triggers change. Many service users have not been allowed to articulate both sides of their ambivalence, and exploring both without fear is hugely beneficial.

3 Direct persuasion is not an effective method for resolving ambivalence, as these tactics generally increase service user resistance and diminish the probability of change.

4 The counselling/communication style is generally a quiet and eliciting one. Direct persuasion, aggressive confrontation, and argumentation are the conceptual opposite of motivational interviewing and are explicitly proscribed in this approach. If you are accustomed to giving advice and confronting issues you may find this way of approaching problems somewhat uncomfortable.

5 The practitioner is directive in helping the client to examine and resolve ambivalence. The specific strategies of motivational interviewing are designed to elicit, clarify, and resolve ambivalence in a client-centred and respectful atmosphere. Once the service user has resolved to change their behaviour then other models and methods will be necessary, for example

cognitive behavioural approaches that then go on to teach service users new behavioural coping skills.

6   Readiness to change is not a service user trait, but a fluctuating product of interpersonal interaction. Resistance and 'denial' are seen not as service user traits, but as feedback regarding the practitioner's behaviour, that is, that they need to do something differently.

7   The therapeutic relationship is more of a partnership than that of expert/ recipient roles. The practitioner respects the client's autonomy and freedom of choice (and consequences) regarding his or her own behaviour. (Rollnick and Miller, 1995: 326)

The motivational interviewing philosophy also emphasises the importance of the service user's self-efficacy. Both the practitioner and the service user must believe that they can change, and that 'recovery' is possible.

The principles of motivational interviewing

Coupled with the 'spirit' of motivational interviewing there are four general principles behind the model. The four principles are:

- Express empathy
- Develop discrepancy
- Roll with resistance
- Support self-efficacy (Miller and Rollnick, 2002: 36).

Express empathy

Building a rapport, reflective listening, showing empathy (using empathic responses such as paraphrasing and reflecting) and accepting the person, are the key skills on which motivational interviewing is built. Ambivalence is seen as normal, as is problematic substance use. The practitioner neither condones nor agrees with the behaviour, but they do accept it. Empathy is shown by using some of the basic key micro-skills of asking open-ended questions, paraphrasing, reflecting, probing and summarising (for further information about these key micro-skills in the social work context see Moss, 2008). As we know, when service users feel like they have been heard and believe that you can see the world through their eyes, they are much more likely to open up to you and share their experiences. Service users are then more likely to be open to gentle challenging and less likely to defend their behaviour. An accurate understanding of the service user experience can facilitate change.

Develop discrepancy

'Motivation for change occurs when people perceive a discrepancy between where they are and where they want to be' (Miller et al., 1992: 8). Discrepancy or incongruence is developed in a person's life when there is a difference between where they are at and how they live their lives, and where they would like to be and how they would like to live their lives. In motivational interviewing, the practitioner needs to elicit these differences or inconsistencies in the service user's life, focus on them and develop them. For example, a service user may want to join a gym to get fit and healthy in their ideal world, but in reality they cannot afford to go to a gym as all their money is spent on alcohol which also causes them several physical health problems. In motivational interviewing, the practitioner gets the service user to discuss the differences between their current behaviour and their future goals. If clients perceive that their current behaviour is not supporting their future goals, they can become more motivated to change their behaviour.

Roll with resistance

At the heart of this principle is the reality that arguing increases resistance. Resistance from the service user can come in the form of argument, denial, excuses, blaming, interrupting, ignoring and changing the subject; it can be both passive and aggressive (Davies and Petersen, 2002). The idea then is not to challenge resistance from the service user, but rather use this 'momentum' to explore fully the service user's views. The service user will also be very surprised that you are not trying to convince them to change their behaviour, and it is unlikely that they will have been able to express themselves in this way before. They will be left with no option but to explore thoroughly their ambivalence. Strategies for rolling with resistance will be discussed later in this chapter.

Support self-efficacy

Service users must believe that they can make changes if they choose to do so. They should be supported to explore other times in their lives when they have been able to make changes, even if for very small things. In this way, the motivational interviewing practitioner can highlight the skills and strengths that the service user already has. They should be asked how important the change is to them and how confident they are that they can change. Motivational interviewing practitioners should let the service user know that there is no right way to make changes and that their way, whatever they may choose, is right for them. If their way does not work the first time, they should be encouraged to try again or to do something different.

Understanding 'stages of change'

The transtheoretical model of change was developed by DiClemente and Prochaska (1982) to describe the process of intentional behaviour change. This is a stages of change model, each stage representing a point through which individuals pass on their way to changing their behaviour. Change is seen as a progression

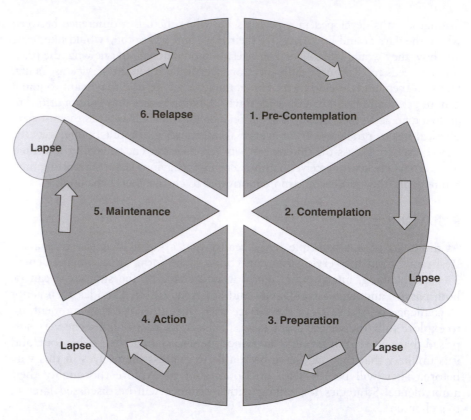

Figure 11.1   The transtheoretical cycle of change model

Source: Adfam, 2010. Reproduced courtesy of Adfam. For more information on families, drugs and alcohol visit: http://www.adfam.org.nz

through 'pre-contemplation', where individuals are not considering behaviour change; to 'contemplation', where individuals seriously contemplate change, and weigh up the pros and cons; to 'preparation', where planning to change and a commitment to this is made; to 'action', where the individual makes the behaviour change; to 'maintenance', where the individual works to maintain their behaviour change (Miller and Rollnick, 2002: 201). Please see Figure 11.1 for a visual representation of an adaptation of this model. Each of these stages will be discussed in more depth a bit later in this chapter. This is a circular model that is also referred to as the 'wheel of change' or the 'cycle of change', indicating that change is not linear and that people can enter or exit their process or 'cycle' of change at any time. It is also indicative of the fact that even if people do make changes, they can readily 'slip back to' or 'relapse into' their old behaviours and start once again anywhere on this cycle of change. This is because permanent behaviour change can be very difficult and may take several attempts. This is particularly true for people wanting to make changes to their substance-using behaviour.

As you will have noticed, this wheel in Figure 11.1 has an extra stage to that of the original model created by DiClemente and Prochaska in 1982. Over the years there have been several adaptations of this model to help us to understand better the process of change. This Adfam adaptation, one of the more simple yet useful adaptations, adds a sixth stage called 'relapse'. 'Slipping back' or 'relapsing' into old behaviours is relatively common, and in reality behaviour change may take several attempts before change is permanent. This stage is not supposed to encourage relapse, but normalise relapse and prevent the service user from becoming demoralised. You will also see that this adaptation includes the term 'lapse' at various places in the cycle. This indicates that it can be likely that people may lapse into their old behaviours from time to time on their way to permanent behaviour change. Adding 'relapse ' and 'lapse' to the cycle of change helps service users see these things as a normal part of the process of change and encourages them to get back on the 'cycle of change' more promptly if they do 'lapse' or 'relapse'. The terms 'lapse' and 'relapse' will be explored further in Chapter 12 on relapse prevention.

Differing motivational interviewing techniques and strategies can be used to suit people where they are at on their cycle of change. As a practitioner, it is important for you to think about and reflect on where a service user might be at in regards to their readiness to change with whatever model of social work you use. In regards to motivational interviewing, however, it is very important to be able to assess a service user's change stage and readiness to change in order to choose the appropriate motivational interviewing strategy.

Pre-contemplation

If a service user is at 'pre-contemplation' on the 'cycle of change', this means that they do not consider that they have a problem and do not want to change their behaviour. Perhaps others have seen the problem that their substance use has created, but they do not see it (Miller and Rollnick, 2002). Usually, these types of service users come to services for help because they have been convinced to go by someone else, or have been sent involuntarily by a social service or criminal justice agency. They will commonly be referred to as 'resistant' or 'in denial' about their problematic substance use. In order to avoid further resistance or rebellion, it is necessary not to be too confrontational with a service user at this stage on the cycle of change. Trying to convince or coerce them to change by bribing, threatening or advising them will usually only result in further resistance. Service users at this stage on the cycle do not think that they have a problem, and so are not likely to be convinced by you of their need to change. Practitioners working with service users at this stage on the cycle should focus on rapport building, listening to their story (even if it is about the fact that they don't think they have a problem) and finding out what motivation they do have. If they are sitting with you discussing the topic, then there is some level of motivation and it is up to the practitioner to nurture what little motivation there may be. The key for practitioners working with service users at the pre-contemplation stage is not to alienate them, and engage them sufficiently so that they might come back to see you. This may be the best possible outcome for a service user at this stage on the 'cycle of change'. This stage can take some people a long time to move through, but the longer you are able to work with service users at this stage, the stronger the therapeutic relationship you will create and the more likely they will be to move on to the next stage in the cycle of change.

Contemplation

Service users at the 'contemplation' stage in the cycle of change can recognise that they have some negative (or less good) consequences as a result of their substance use, but they are still ambivalent about doing anything about making any changes to their behaviour. Service users at this stage are open to being able to resolve their ambivalence and this is the task of the practitioner at this stage. Services users can be supported to explore their ambivalence by looking at the 'good things' and 'less good things' about their substance use and reflecting on how their behaviours might be in conflict with their own values, beliefs or hopes for the future. Service users are also supported to explore what their future holds if they were to change their behaviour and what it would be like if they do not. At this stage, it is hoped that service users come to their own conclusions about wanting to change their behaviour by exploring these areas.

Preparation

At the 'preparation' stage of the cycle of change service users have 'tipped the decisional balance' and decided that they need to change their behaviour. Their ambivalence has for the most part been resolved; however, their actual behaviour has not yet changed. The role of the practitioner when service users are at this stage is to support the service user's self-efficacy and to help them believe that they are capable of making the necessary change. At this stage, the practitioner should assess the skills and strengths that the service user already has, and also prepare them to employ a range of new coping skills as necessary to enact the required change. A plan of action should be prepared before the service user moves onto the next stage of change.

Action

At the 'action' stage, as the name suggests, the changes are being made. Service users are often highly motivated and ready and willing to change their behaviour. It is at this stage that people wanting to give up alcohol tip all their drinks down the sink, drug users enter treatment programmes and service users start to employ the coping skills that you will have been teaching them when they were preparing for this change. This is the stage where they implement the plan that they may have been preparing for some time. The practitioner role at this stage is to support the service user with any hurdles they may face during this time as well as offer ongoing encouragement and positive feed-back about how well they are doing. For behaviour change to be permanent people have to believe that they can do it. Enhancing self-efficacy at this stage is imperative.

Maintenance

The 'maintenance' stage continues the change process with an emphasis on assimilating and integrating the new skills that have been learnt and are being used. The goal is continued change while keeping the possibility of relapse, or going back to old behaviours, at bay. It is at this stage that 'reality' sets in for service users that have been so highly motivated at the action stage. Service users will continue to experience the highs and lows of life at this stage, but without their preferred coping mechanism (substance use). They are usually inexperienced at practising their new-found coping behaviours and can find this maintenance stage extremely unforgiving. Having made the commitment to change, and having enacted the change, they are faced with the reality that life is still sometimes difficult. This stage may begin while the service user still sees you as the practitioner, but much of this stage will occur once the service user has stopped seeing a practitioner or left their formal treatment. At this stage, the service user is often out there on their own, having to practise what they have so recently learned. This does place a huge amount of pressure on a service user who has just recently changed their behaviour, and it does make them vulnerable to relapse or a return to their old behaviours. If, however, they do make it through the maintenance stage, they may exit the cycle of change and continue to maintain their behaviour change.

Relapse

Suspending or stopping maintenance strategies will usually signal the onset of 'relapse' or a return to old behaviours. Relapse is not a one-off event (that of the actual return to the old behaviour, e.g. substance use), but a process. The process is thought to be cognitive, behavioural and affective, that is, involving the person's thoughts, behaviours and actions. In Chapter 12, we will discuss 'Relapse Prevention' which is one model for understanding this process. Though incredibly difficult to deal with for a service user who has tried so hard, relapse can be seen as part of the change process and also something from which the service user can learn. Next time the service user attempts change, they will need to reflect on what went wrong the last time and alter their goals and actions accordingly. Service users must know that if relapse occurs they can re-enter the cycle of change and try again.

The following motivational strategies are relatively simple ones that can be used as part of the social worker toolkit. According to Miller and Moyers (2006), practitioners should be able to switch flexibly between motivational approaches and other intervention styles. These strategies should also be used in conjunction with an understanding of the spirit and principles of motivational interviewing, and alongside the transtheoretical model of change. These strategies alone do not make up the entire Motivational Interviewing model. They have been selected for use in this text because they are thought to be the most useful within a social work context. For more information about the model in its entirety, please see the recommended reading section at the end of this chapter.

Motivational approaches and strategies for social work practice

For use in the social work context it is useful to think about the spirit and principles of motivational interviewing, and taking a 'motivational approach' with service users, rather than expecting to implement the pure model in your work. This chapter provides a relatively brief introduction to motivational interviewing and if you decide to use some of the ideas and skills from this model it is likely (depending on your experience and skill level) that you will require further training, or will need to read more widely on the model. That is not to say, however, that some of the skills and strategies that are part of this approach cannot be used to enhance your social work practice. Most of the strategies discussed here are for use primarily with service users who are at the pre-contemplative or contemplative stages in the 'cycle of change'. This is where the motivational approach can offer the social worker something a little different from other models they might be used to using. You may feel comfortable using some of the following skills and strategies immediately as they are not so very different from basic skills and principles of social work practice. Others that will be covered, however, may seem very 'unusual' and 'uncomfortable' to you, especially if you are used to advising and confronting. Hopefully you will see the value of the ideas behind them and think about using them the next time you are working with an ambivalent or 'resistant' service user.

OARS

Motivational interviewing has at its foundation some very basic micro-counselling and communication skills that all social workers should know well and use on a daily basis. Some of these, as already discussed, include rapport building, listening and giving empathic responses. Literature about motivational interviewing reminds us of the importance of these key skills by the use of the acronym OARS. This is a very useful way of remembering: (1) Open-ended questions; (2) Affirmations; (3) Reflective listening; and (4) Summaries.

As you will know, open-ended questions are questions that cannot be answered with a 'yes', 'no' or short answer. They encourage the service user to be descriptive and explore their own thoughts. While it is often necessary to ask closed-ended questions, motivational interviewing advocates the use of open-ended questions to help explore the service user's ambivalence. Affirmations fit with the 'support self-efficacy' principle of motivational interviewing and focus on giving positive feedback to the service user about their strengths. It is important that affirmations are genuine and sincere (Miller and Rollnick, 2002). Reflective listening involves giving service users empathic responses. These show that you have heard what the service user is saying and know what they mean by it. Empathic responses show service users that you are listening, and include reflections (focusing on feeling) and paraphrases (focusing on content). Using a motivational approach, reflections and paraphrases focus more directly on the positive than on the negative. In a sense, in motivational interviewing practitioners are guiding the 'change talk'. Change talk happens when the service user comes up with their own reasons to change. Miller and Rollnick (2002: 24) have identified that there are four types of 'change talk' that practitioners should listen out for. First, when the service user mentions the 'disadvantage of the status quo'; second, when the service user mentions the 'advantages of change'; third, when the service user expresses 'optimism for change'; and fourth, when the service user mentions an 'intention to change'. These types of change talk should be noted, picked up on, explored and worked with by the practitioner.

According to Miller and Rollnick (2002), as a guide it is a good idea to give three reflections and/or paraphrases for every question asked to encourage the 'change momentum'. 'Summarising' is another type of reflective listening that summarises and feeds back to the service user what has been said. Summarising can help show empathy, build rapport with your service user and clarify that you have heard what it is that they have been saying. Summaries can also be used to shift direction or attention if necessary, and are also an excellent way to conclude the session and/or start a new session (e.g. by summarising what was discussed the last time you met). You would usually begin the summary by stating that you are going to summarise what has been discussed and make sure that the service user is aware that they can correct anything you may have got wrong along the way.

The practitioner can use OARS wherever their service user is at on the 'cycle of change'. Please see Moss (2008) for further information regarding open-ended questions, affirmations, reflective listening and summaries that are all relevant core social work skills.

Motivational reflections and rolling with resistance

Motivational reflections and rolling with resistance work best with people who are at the pre-contemplation and contemplation stages of the 'cycle of change'. They can, however, be used whenever necessary. The motivational approach uses the basic micro-skill of reflection in a very clever way.

An *amplified reflection* means that rather than just simply repeating back what the service user has said to you, you amplify or exaggerate a piece of the reflection so that the service user might disagree with it and reason the other side of the argument (this is what you want them to do). For example:

> *Service User:*   But I can't quit drinking. I mean, I've always been a drinker!
> *MI Practitioner:*   Oh, I see. So you really couldn't quit drinking even if you tried.
> *Service User:*   Well ... no I'm not saying that. (Miller & Rollnick, 2002: 101)

As you can see from this simple example, the service user has moved away from saying they can't quit drinking, and this has occurred with one amplified reflection from the practitioner. From here the practitioner could explore this further with the service user and build on any change talk to increase motivation to change.

Double-sided reflections are another type of motivational reflection that require the practitioner to both reflect what the person has said, while also adding to their ambivalence. The first part of the reflection acknowledges what the person has said in the form of a simple reflection but then adds to this by using information the person has previously given them that will develop discrepancy. This has to be something they have previously said that appears to be in direct contrast to the more recent statement. For example:

> *Service User:*   But I can't quit drinking. I mean, I've always been a drinker!
> *MI Practitioner:*   So it would be difficult to give up drinking, and at the same time you have managed to do it in the past.
> *Service User:*   Yeah, I know but it wasn't easy. (Miller and Rollnick, 2002: 102)

As you can see this service user has gone from saying that they cannot give up drinking to acknowledging that even though it was difficult they have done it in the past. With these reflective skills it is important that they are done with expertise and so that the service user does not feel patronised or mocked. They also need to be used with recognition that they will only work with ambivalent service users who do have some ability to see the other side of the argument. If a service user really has no inclination to give up using substances (if they are at the pre-contemplation stage on the 'cycle' of change), then some of these skills may be counterproductive. In saying that however we must remember that clients are showing some level of motivation if they are turning up to see us, even if they have been coerced in some way. It is up to us to make the most of this motivation.

Shifting focus is another key tool of the motivational approach. Simply put this means not going down the resistance road but taking a step back and re-directing the conversation away from the resistance. For example (using the same statement):

> *Service User:*   But I can't quit drinking. I mean, I've always been a drinker!
> *MI Practitioner:*   You're getting way ahead of things here. I'm not talking about your quitting drinking here, and I don't think you should get stuck on that concern right now. Let's just talk through the issues – and

later on we can worry about what, if anything, you want to do about it.

Service User: Well I just wanted you to know. (Miller and Rollnick, 2002: 102–103)

As you can see the practitioner has deflected the resistance by redirecting it at this stage. It is likely that there is some way to go before this service user is ready to think more about giving up their drinking. When they do think further about it, it will be of their own volition after they have fully explored their ambivalence with their practitioner and are much less 'resistant'.

Reviewing a typical day

Reviewing a typical day is a good strategy to use with people who are at the pre-contemplative stage of the cycle of change so as to help build rapport and get to know the service user better. While this strategy is useful at all stages of the cycle of change, it is usually used at the beginning of the therapeutic relationship. 'Reviewing a typical day' is a simple motivational approach that helps the practitioner to engage with their service user and see how their use of substances fits into their day-to-day living. It allows you as the practitioner to hear about the service user's use of substances in a way that avoids any judgement because the service user is just telling you about a 'typical day'. When using this strategy, the practitioner will ask the service user to think about and reflect on what they might be thinking and feeling when they use substances and whether or not certain things in their everyday life are acting as triggers for them to use substances. You can get the service user to start telling you about their day, starting from when they get up in the morning. Get them to describe their daily habits and rituals and ask them to tell you how they are feeling when they have their first substance of the day, and what is going through their mind. Then you would encourage them to continue describing their day. What happens after 10 a.m., at lunchtime, throughout the afternoon, when the children come home from school, throughout the evening and then what time they usually go to bed. At each stage during the day, the focus should be on the thoughts and feelings that they might be able to associate with their use of substances. Remember that at no point should you judge their substance use. It may be appropriate to provide feedback or ask open-ended questions about certain things, for example if you feel that the service user or anyone else is at risk of harm to themselves or others, then you must take the appropriate course of action to ensure their safety. Use this strategy to build rapport and to get to know how the service user's use of substances fits into their everyday living. Use it alongside some of the other motivational approaches as well as your other social work skills.

Looking back and looking forward

Looking back and looking forward are two strategies that are best used when service users are in the pre-contemplative stage of the cycle of change. Although different, these two motivational approaches are similar. *Looking back* requires the service user to look back on their life and think about and remember what it was like before they began using substances and/or starting using substances problematically. The practitioner asks what life was like back then and what hopes and dreams they had for the future. This strategy is not about eliciting information about difficult backgrounds and trying to resolve underlying issues – it is about getting the service user to reflect on what life was like before substances came into their lives. For some service users this may require that they think back a long way, especially if substances have been in their life for a long time. As a practitioner, you should focus on picking up on anything that the service user says about 'things being better back then' or 'things have not turned out the way I hoped'. Exploring how the service user's life went from one of having hopes and dreams (if indeed it did), to that of having problematic substance use, can help the service user to reflect on the role that substance use may have played in creating the difficulties that they now find themselves with. At the very least it will probably help them to further explore their ambivalence about changing their substance-using behaviour. Use the looking back technique until you feel that you have fully explored the issues and supported the service user to reflect on how things have changed.

Looking forward is another simple yet effective technique that involves the service user imagining what their future might be like in five or ten years time if they continue using substances. Ask them what they see for themselves, where they see themselves living and with whom, what employment they may have, if any, what friends and family they may have in their lives and so on. The idea behind this strategy is to get the service user to reflect on what life will be like in the future if they do not make any behaviour changes. Following this, you ask the service user to imagine what life might be like if they do make some changes to their lifestyle. As a practitioner, your job is not to compare or judge the two different futures but merely to get the service user to explore these two prospects.

Good things/less good things and decisional balance

These two strategies are best used with service users in the pre-contemplative or contemplative stage of the cycle of change as they help them explore the issues and resolve their ambivalence. 'Good and less good things' is an essential motivational technique to have in your social work toolkit, and like many of the others can work very well in a variety of social work settings, particularly where service users are ambivalent. Essentially, with this technique, the practitioner gets the service user to explore the 'good and less good things' about their substance use. Always start with getting the service user to describe all the 'good things' about using substances. Remember that there are a lot of 'good things' about substance use, otherwise people would never use them. Allow them to explore everything they like about substances, how they help them, what they do for them and how they make them feel. Once they have done this, reflect back to them and summarise. Let them know that you have heard that there are good things about their substance use. The main reasons for this type of enquiry is that often service users will be so surprised that you are asking them about the 'good things' about their substance use, that they will be disarmed and are likely to be less resistant when you ask them about the 'less good things'. Next let them discuss with you the 'less good things' about their substance use, again until the subject appears to be exhausted. Once you have heard from the service user about all the 'less good things', focus your attention on exploring these in more detail. Once you feel that you have elicited the maximum amount of 'change talk' possible, summarise and ask the service user to give their perspective on the discussion. The idea is that their ambivalence about behaviour change will be resolving from their own exploration of their use of substances. The use of the term 'less good things', while sounding somewhat awkward, is thought to be necessary as it purposefully avoids labelling the substance use as a problem. That is, it avoids labelling the behaviour as 'bad'. While 'less good things' is the favoured language, people have been known to use phrases such as 'pros and cons' or 'good and not so good things'. The key though is to try and avoid labelling the substance use as a problem if the service user has first not done so themselves.

The decisional balance strategy is similar to the 'good and less good things' strategy but with a focus on future behaviour. The practitioner gets the service user to look at the pros and cons of not changing behaviour and the pros and cons of changing behaviour, while finally asking the service user what their preference is based on the decisional balance. It is a good idea to do the decisional balance on a piece of paper and it may even be something that your service user can do outside of your time with them, as a sort of homework.

Summary

Motivational interviewing recognises the importance of motivation in the formula for behaviour change. It seeks to provide practitioners with an understanding of how they can enhance the service user's motivation to change by supporting service users to resolve their ambivalence. It is a non-directive model that purposefully avoids direct confrontation and argument, and seeks to help the service user come to their own conclusions about changing their behaviour. It has four key principles: express empathy, develop discrepancy, roll with resistance and support self-efficacy, which are supported by a number of key strategies. The motivational approach should be used alongside the transtheoretical model of change, also known as the 'cycle' or 'wheel' of change. This model describes change as a cyclical process involving six key stages. It is useful to assess where the service user you are working with is at in regards to the process of change, by working out where they are in the cycle. This can help you to identify what strategies to use when working with the service user. This chapter has covered some of the strategies that are most useful when service users are at the pre-contemplative and contemplative stages on the 'cycle of change'. It is expected that social workers could use these strategies where appropriate as extra tools in their social work toolkit, and be able to switch flexibly between them and other interventions as required. As a pure model, motivational interviewing provides a number of other strategies that may complement your social work practice. It is recommended that you read more widely if you wish to incorporate these into your practice. While motivational interviewing started out as a model for working with people who have problematic substance use, it is now being used widely in a variety of areas in which social workers work. It could be argued that if done well, taking a motivational approach could be used in most social work settings where we work with people on change journeys and/or who may be ambivalent about this change.

Reflections

How do you think you would feel attempting some of the motivational approaches outlined in this chapter?

Would you feel uncomfortable asking a service user what is 'good' about their substance use?

Would you have the opportunity to use the idea of the 'cycle of change' in your everyday work with service users?

Further readings

Miller, W. and Rollnick, S. (2002) *Motivational Interviewing: Preparing People for Change*, 2nd edn. New York: Guilford Press.

Moss, B. (2008) *Communication Skills for Health and Social Care*. London: Sage.

Wahab, S. (2005) 'Motivational interviewing and social work practice', *Journal of Social Work*, 5 (1): 51–60.

12

Relapse Prevention

'Relapse prevention' is a cognitive-behavioural model primarily used when working with people who have problematic substance use and who have already made a commitment to behaviour change. A large body of research has been conducted to support its efficacy for use with problematic substance use (Gossop, 2002). There is also evidence to support its use with specialised populations, including youth, older people, offenders and black and ethnic minorities (Witkiewitz and Marlatt, 2007). It is likely that seeing 'relapse' as a dynamic and complex process requiring an assortment of coping strategies and interventions is useful in a variety of social work settings where service users are attempting behaviour change.

> Relapse prevention is a collection of techniques that increase the client's ability to control cravings and urges, and enhance coping skills for handling high-risk situations where lapse or relapse is a possibility. By combining the learning of specific skills with lifestyle changes, these interventions assist clients to manage lapses and prevent relapses. (Turning Point Alcohol and Drug Centre, 2000: 1)

The term 'relapse' originates from the 'disease' notion of 'addiction', and indicates a return to the disease state after a period of remission (Marlatt and Witkiewitz, 2005). These days, however, it is used to describe the return of old substance-using behaviours. A 'lapse' (or slip) indicates a one-off or short-term return to old behaviours, but not a complete return to old behaviours (relapse). Most of us can probably recognise the difference between a 'lapse' and a 'relapse' if we consider a time in our lives when we attempted to change our behaviours (go on a diet, give up smoking, and/or start exercising). At times we may have a lapse in our behaviour change (eat chocolate, have a cigarette or miss our daily jog), but the following day we get back on track and maintain our behaviour change. This is a lapse (also sometimes called a 'slip'). A relapse would be a full return to previous behaviour (eating anything we liked, starting smoking again and no longer exercising). It is a reasonably normal part of any behaviour change that we have 'lapses' and even 'relapse'. The idea behind models of relapse prevention, however, is to make sure that these lapses do not turn into full-blown 'relapses'. How to maintain change is at the heart of relapse prevention.

Relapse prevention models, which will be discussed further later in this chapter, have primarily been used alongside abstinence models of problematic substance-use treatment. However, while the ultimate goal may be abstinence of all substance use, relapse within this model can also be understood to mean a 'relapse' of old behaviours. Behaviour change may include a reduction in substance use or safer substance use, and 'relapse' may include a return to heavy or unsafe substance use. 'Relapse prevention is equally relevant for those pursuing abstinence or moderation goals' (Jarvis et al., 2005: 221).

Marlatt and Gordon's (1985) Relapse Prevention model

According to Hill et al. (n.d.), the original Relapse Prevention model (Marlatt and Gordon, 1985) integrated classical and operant conditioning, social learning theory, social psychology, cognitive psychology and Buddhist philosophy. Interventions were aimed at increasing awareness of the possibility and even likelihood of lapse and relapse, and awareness of self. The model saw relapse as a process that could be identified and resisted. There was a focus on building an enhanced collection of coping skills and supporting lifestyle balance in the lives of service users. The model sought to walk the 'middle ground' with service users and moved away from the 'all-or-nothing' (abstinence or relapse) thinking that many models of working with problematic substance use had historically advocated. Introducing the reality of 'lapses' and 'relapse' meant that these notions were 'demystified' for service users, and feelings of guilt, shame and overwhelming failure after a lapse or relapse could be reduced. If these feelings can be limited, then it is much more likely that service users will re-engage with services and use experiences of lapse and relapse as learning for future efforts at behaviour change.

The model had two parts. The first part of Marlatt and Gordon's relapse prevention model (1985) describes the relapse process (see Figure 12.1). This identifies that once service users have made a change in their behaviour, then maintenance of this change continues until the service user encounters a 'High Risk Situation' (HRS). HRSs are any situations or mood states in which a service user might be 'triggered' to return to old behaviours. These HRSs might relate to 'people, places, feelings, thoughts and things' that are likely to cause some stress to the service user. Research suggests that relapse more commonly occurs in response to negative emotional states; interpersonal conflicts and social isolation; social pressures; and cravings and urges (Jarvis et al., 2005). For example, HRSs might include being around other people who are using substances, being in an environment that reminds you of substance use (walking past the pub), feeling low and/or depressed or physically unwell, and seeing old substance-using paraphernalia (needles, pipes, bottles of alcohol). These are just a few simple examples. Every service user will have different examples of what puts them at risk and it will be up to the individual service user to identify these for themselves. Identifying in detail as much as possible the 'where, when, with whom, doing what and feeling what' of situations that are high risk for them, will help identify situations to avoid and to be wary of. Identifying these things will also help the service user to identify relevant coping skills that they can put in place for when these HRSs arise. This may involve looking at the strengths and coping skills that the service user already utilises, but will also include the practitioner teaching them new coping skills. For example, you may teach the service user self-monitoring, problem solving, relaxation techniques, time and/or anger management strategies, provide a list of telephone helplines or appropriate people to call when stressed and/or get them to supply a list of other things that they could do to distract themselves in the HRS (read a book, bake a cake, do some gardening, go for a walk). Some useful coping skills to use when working with behaviour change and relapse prevention are discussed later on in this chapter. It can also be a good idea for the service user to write a relapse prevention plan at this stage, in which they can identify these coping strategies. Having a written plan means that when they feel triggered to use substances, they can consult their plan and implement the coping skills outlined in it. Increasing self-efficacy is fundamental at this stage. If people believe that they can change and maintain the change, there is a decreased probability of relapse (Marlatt and Gordon, 1985).

Failure to cope with these HRSs can lead to a lack of self-efficacy and Positive Outcome Expectancies (POE) (refer to Figure 12.1). According to Marlatt and Gordon (1985), POEs are the positive expectations that the service user has about using substances. These are likely to materialise if the service user fails to cope with an HRS. That is, the service user might believe that going back to old behaviours is likely to make them feel better and relieve the stress of the HRS.

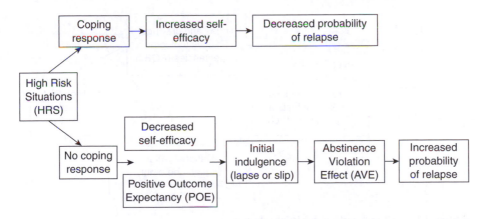

Figure 12.1   Cognitive behavioural model of the relapse process

Source: Marlatt and Gordon, 1985, p. 38. Reproduced with permission from Guilford Publications

According to this model, POEs coupled with decreased self-efficacy put the service user at risk of 'lapse' and 'relapse'. If a lapse does occur, then it is highly likely that the service user may feel guilt and shame associated with this. This is described in the model as 'Abstinence Violation Effect' (AVE). If these feelings are not addressed then they are likely to influence a full return to old behaviours (a relapse).

The second part of Marlatt and Gordon's (1985) model describes covert antecedents of relapse (see Figure 12.2) and relates more to long-term maintenance of behaviour change. Covert antecedents are things that are likely to lead to relapse that may be less obvious than HRSs. This part of the model primarily emphasises the importance of maintaining a balanced lifestyle. This might mean having a good balance between work and family life, sleeping well, eating healthily and exercising regularly to be able to cope as much as possible with everyday stressors. According to the model, service users should focus on maintaining a balanced lifestyle and be aware when their lifestyle is becoming unbalanced. If service users can recognise when their life is unbalanced, then they can work to correct this balance before their ability to cope with an HRS is jeopardised. According to this part of the model, if lifestyle becomes unbalanced not only can it lead to relapse in the future, but to a number of precursors to relapse. These precursors have been identified within this model as the Problem of Instant Gratification (PIG), Positive Outcome Expectancies (which we covered earlier), rationalisation, denial and Seemingly Irrelevant Decisions (SIDs). The Problem of Instant Gratification (PIG) or the 'desire to indulge' may manifest as urges or cravings to return to old behaviours if the service user's lifestyle becomes unbalanced. Seemingly Irrelevant Decisions (SIDs) are decisions that are made by the service user that on the surface appear irrelevant, but with insight and reflection it may be obvious that they have put the service user at some risk. Practitioners should encourage service users to be consciously

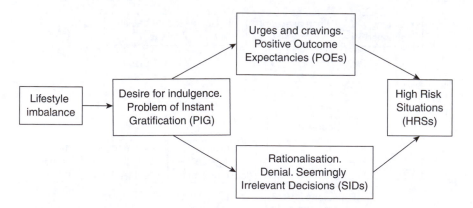

Figure 12.2   Covert antecedents of relapse

Source: Marlatt and Gordon, 1985, p.48. Reproduced with permission from Guilford Publications

aware of all the decisions they make and how they may impinge on their continued behaviour change. In this part of the model, PIG, coupled with denial, rationalisation and SIDs can lead to the service user putting themselves in a High Risk Situation (HRS).

Useful coping skills

Regardless of the complex nature of the relapse process, in practical terms practitioners should, to the best of their ability, support service users to put in place a number of coping strategies to limit the likelihood of complete relapse. A useful and practical model for working with service users is outlined in Figure 12.3; this is an adapted and simplified version of the original Marlatt and Gordon (1985) Relapse Prevention model with a focus on coping skills and strategies. Based on this model, you may find the following coping skills useful to teach your service user when they are looking at relapse prevention.

When getting your service user to look at lifestyle balance it will be valuable to get the service user to think about such things as work/life balance, getting at least 8 hours of sleep a night, eating a healthy diet and exercising. It may also be useful to talk to your service user about taking up meditation, attending a place of worship, joining a local community group or taking up other recreational activities. Leading a balanced lifestyle will be different for different people but the key thing here is that whatever they are doing, they are doing it in moderation and looking after themselves.

For dealing with urges and cravings to use substances, it is suggested that you should encourage your service user to get rid of all their substances and the paraphernalia associated with it. This is likely to decrease some of the urges to use substances that may occur when they are presented with, or see, a visual cue that reminds them of their substance of choice. These are referred to as 'stimulus control techniques', and may also include staying away from places and people that may also remind service users of old behaviours (Larimer et al., 1999). At this point, it may also be useful to teach service users visualisation and self-talk techniques to help them overcome urges at a specific point in time when they are tempted to use substances or go back to their old behaviours. While these visualisations or self-talk may be different for different people, the key is to 'ride the urge' or concentrate on something else until the craving dissipates.

Relapse roadmaps can be useful as part of the relapse prevention plan. These involve working with the service user to identify possible HRSs in advance of them happening and then making a list of the possible coping strategies that can be implemented at this time, or a 'map' of the available choices. This means that the service user can attempt to consider an array of potential situations in which they may be tempted to revert to old behaviours, and have a plan of action in place to prevent this 'lapse' or 'relapse' from occurring. It is also very useful at

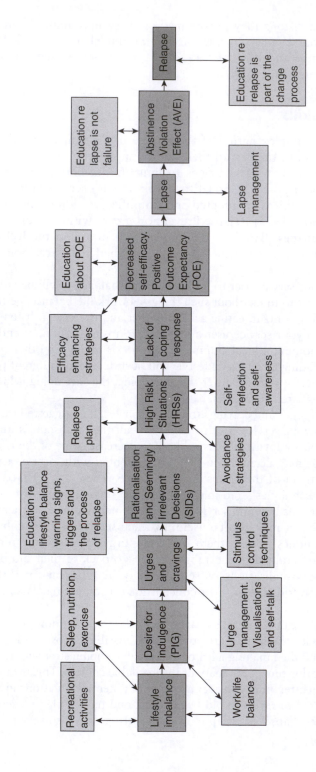

Figure 12.3 Specific and global self-control strategies

Source: Adapted from Marlatt and Gordon, 1985, p. 61. Reproduced with permission from Guilford Publications

this stage to reflect on past lapses and relapses and learn from them. Practitioners should also encourage service users to be consciously aware of all the decisions they make (SIDs) and how they may impinge on their continued behaviour change.

An array of coping skills such as relaxation techniques, anger and stress management and assertiveness training can also be very useful to maintain lifestyle balance, as well as for when the service user recognises that they are in an HRS. These can be taught to the service user, who will then need to go away and practise them for themselves. This practice can be supported by offering the service user written literature (if appropriate) about the skill that they are learning. The idea behind learning and practising some of these types of coping skills is that a 'lapse' can be prevented and 'practise makes perfect'. If the array of coping skills, relapse prevention plans and self-reflections do not manage to arrest the relapse process and a lapse does occur, there is still the chance to stop the process in its tracks.

Coping with a lapse

Relapse Prevention models accept that having a 'lapse' or 'slip' can be part of the process of behaviour change (see Chapter 11 for information about the 'cycle of change' model). They also recognise that a 'lapse' or 'slip' is usually part of the process of relapse. If having a lapse is likely on the way to permanent behaviour change, then there are several coping strategies that can be identified and implemented to stop further lapse, and halt the process of relapse. These should be discussed with your service user as part of their relapse prevention plan. They need to identify High Risk Situations and triggers that may lead to a lapse, and put in place coping mechanisms to prevent it occurring. However, they will also need a contingency plan if they do lapse. Service users will need to learn when to put this contingency plan into action and be aware that they need to learn to reflect on their thoughts, feelings and actions as much as possible throughout the relapse prevention process. According to Witkiewitz and Marlatt (2007: 12), the first skill that the service user should be encouraged to utilise if a lapse occurs is 'Stop, look and listen'. This involves stopping the potential ongoing events, and making themselves aware of the situation around them. Second, the service user needs to know that they should keep calm. A lapse is not a catastrophe and it does not mean that they have failed. Service users should be taught to recognise that they can stop the process of relapse in its tracks at this point. Following the lapse, their motivation needs to be restored and a recommitment made to continued behaviour change. This can be very difficult if the service user feels deflated and pessimistic about their future. If, however, they are able to get over this motivational hurdle, then they will need to reflect on what happened leading up to their lapse, and how they could respond differently next time. If the service user can stop the relapse process and learn something from their lapse, then the experience can be a very useful one for the future. The practitioner should take time to remind the service user that they have not failed, and to encourage and motivate them. Self-efficacy may not be high at this time, so it will be important to rebuild this.

In the later stages of implementing the relapse prevention model, the service user will have at their disposal a huge number of skills and supports that they can implement to halt the relapse process. Whether or not they chose to use these skills when HRSs or lapses occur will be down to them and will depend on a variety of variables (as explored by Witkiewitz and Marlatt, 2004). If the service user you are working with does take several attempts at maintaining their behaviour change, it can be frustrating for you and the service user. It is crucial that no matter how frustrated you may feel, you remain open to the service user re-engaging. Do not judge the 'relapse' and maintain the mantra 'never give up'. It is likely to take some time for most of your service users to maintain their behaviour change, but this is part of the process and to a certain extent should be expected.

Relapse prevention strategies work nicely alongside other interventions that you may be familiar with in your social work practice. Do explore your service user's social networks and supports. Involve family and significant others in your service user's world. Encourage them to participate in self-help groups such as Alcoholics Anonymous (AA) and/or Narcotics Anonymous (NA), and/or become involved in recreational activities in their communities (Jarvis et al., 2005). Replacing their favourite hobby (using substances) for something equally pleasant and enjoyable, but with less negative consequences will be very important if behaviour change is going to be permanent. Focusing on these areas will increase the likelihood of the relapse prevention strategies you use being effective and is generally good social work practice.

Dynamic Model of Relapse (Witkiewitz and Marlatt, 2004)

Over the years since the original relapse prevention model was established there have been a number of criticisms of it. The Dynamic Model of Relapse (Witkiewitz and Marlatt, 2004) conceptualises relapse as a 'fluid process of behaviour change' and adds to the original model by putting 'emphasis on timing and interrelatedness of events' (Witkiewitz and Marlatt, 2007: 19). This model takes into consideration that some service users may feel more or less vulnerable to HRSs depending on a number of things. For example, under usual circumstances a particular situation may not really be high risk for a service user; however, if they have not slept well the night before, if they are feeling depressed and/or highly anxious, then the situation becomes more high risk. Witkiewitz and Marlatt's (2004) model allows for these variables and in turn the model requires that service users and practitioners also reflect on these realities. What this model recognises then is that some factors or variables in the relapse process are always there, while others come and go and put more or less pressure on the service user depending on a number of variables. The model helps us to see that relapse is not a linear process that can be accurately mapped out, but a much more complex entity that is very difficult for both practitioners and service users to make sense of. What it helps us to further understand is the very difficult nature of sustained behaviour change.

Summary

Relapse prevention provides the practitioner with a useful way of understanding the dynamic process of relapse. Relapse is a return to old behaviours when attempting to maintain behaviour change. Relapsing is seen as a relatively normal part of the process of behaviour change, but one that can be identified and stopped in its tracks if service users are supported to become self-aware and implement necessary coping strategies. Coping strategies that may be necessary for service users to learn, practise and implement might include problem solving, relaxation, visualisation and/or meditation techniques, time, stress and/or anger management strategies and assertiveness training. Practitioners can also help service users compile a list of telephone helplines or appropriate people to call in an emergency and/or get them to recognise a number of other things they could do to distract themselves in HRSs, or when they may be triggered to 'lapse' (e.g. read a book, bake a cake, do some gardening, go for a walk). Relapse prevention has a good evidence-base for working with problematic substance use and in a variety of other settings (Gossop, 2002; Witkiewitz and Marlatt, 2007). The idea of relapse prevention can be a useful one for social workers who may be dealing with people with problematic substance use, or with service users who are attempting behaviour change of any type, and is another implement for their ever-increasing interventions toolkit.

Reflections

How do you feel when you find it difficult to maintain your own behaviour change?

Has thinking about the process of relapse prevention helped you to view your own behaviour change differently? If so, in what ways?

Can you imagine using the idea of 'relapse prevention' in your social work practice?

Further readings

Jarvis, T., Tebbutt, J., Mattick, R. and Shand, F. (eds) (2005) *Treatment Approaches for Alcohol and Drug Dependence*, 2nd edn. Chichester: John Wiley & Sons.

(Continued)

(Continued)

Marlatt, G. and Gordon, J. (eds) (1985) *Relapse Prevention: Maintenance Strategies in the Treatment of Addictive Behaviours.* New York: Guilford Press.

Witkiewitz, K. and Marlatt, G. (eds) (2007) *Therapist's Guide to Evidence-Based Relapse Prevention.* Toronto, Canada: Elsevier.

13

Brief Interventions

Brief interventions are time limited, self help, and preventative strategies to promote reductions in substance use in nondependent clients and, in the case of dependent clients, to facilitate their referral to specialised treatment programmes. (Zweben and Fleming,1999: 253)

Brief interventions, sometimes also referred to as 'brief opportunistic interventions' and/or 'early interventions', aim to detect, screen and intervene with service users before substance dependence develops (Jarvis et al., 2005). They are usually short in duration but can range from between 5 minutes, where service users are briefly asked about their level of consumption and given feedback about this, to several sessions of a model such as motivational interviewing. Brief interventions can be carried out at specialist substance misuse services, especially open access services that are more likely to see people with problematic substance use that is less severe. They are also effectively used in specialist substance misuse services that work with community sentenced offenders over short durations of time. However, they are mainly used by non-specialists in a variety of different settings. Two key aspects of these types of interventions then are that they are often used by people other than substance use professionals, and they are usually used with people who are not necessarily dependent (Bliss and Pecukonis, 2009). The goal of a brief intervention is to encourage people to change problematic substance-using behaviour, or to motivate them to consider this behaviour change. Practitioners using brief interventions do this by:

- Screening for and detecting risky substance use.
- Offering clear concise information to service users to help them reduce their risky use of substances.
- Referring service users that appear to have more severe problematic substance use to specialist services.
- Following up on service users' progress and offering ongoing support if necessary. (Jarvis et al., 2005: 80)

Historically, brief interventions have been used in primary health care settings with alcohol users. For example, screening (see Chapter 9) and brief interventions are often offered at GP surgeries and accident and emergency departments. Service users do not usually attend their GP or local accident and emergency department for a substance-related problem directly; however, they may attend for illness or injury as a direct or indirect result of their substance use. They may not necessarily be alcohol or drug dependent, but they may use substances problematically. They may not even be aware that they may have any substance-related issues and would be unlikely to attend specialised alcohol and drug services at this stage. If primary health or other non-specialist practitioners can perform a brief intervention at this point, it may be very useful in reducing substance-related harm and decreasing the likelihood of the service user developing a more severe problem in the future. 'Brief interventions should be conducted routinely in settings where: (a) the number of risky drinkers is likely to be highest; and (b) where the impact of detection and advice to cut down will have the greatest effect' (Jarvis et al., 2005: 81). It is likely that many social work settings offer the perfect opportunity to offer a brief intervention. Coupled with this natural opportunity, the ability to motivate and empower service users to change and demonstrate a respect for service user self-determination, which are important brief intervention principles, are an extremely good fit with social work values.

There have been a number of studies and meta-analyses of the effectiveness of brief interventions and they have been shown to be very effective in changing alcohol consumption levels (Heather, 1998; Watson, 1999; Wilk et al., 1997), reducing alcohol-related problems (Richmond et al., 1995), and reducing drug-related problems (Baker et al., 2001; Stephens et al., 2000). Wherever and with whomever social workers work it is likely that their service users could experience some problematic substance use. Brief interventions provide a model for which to work briefly and very effectively with these service users in a time-limited fashion. Given the difficult job that social workers have, and the number of tasks that they have to complete in a short space of time, it is likely that performing a brief intervention may be all that the scope of their role allows. Brief interventions also provide a useful framework for which to facilitate referral to more specialised treatment if this is necessary (Babor and Higgins-Biddle, 2001). Many of the approaches previously outlined in this section of the book have the possibility to be used as a form of brief intervention. Using a motivational approach or providing harm-reduction education and even offering a screen or brief assessment of problematic substance use, can all be considered a form of brief intervention.

Whether or not you decide to use a brief intervention will depend on the situation and the motivation of the service user. Brief interventions are most useful if you are unsure if you will see the service user again and need to make the most of the time you do have together. Brief interventions should also be implemented with some awareness and understanding of the transtheoretical model or 'cycle of change', which was discussed in some depth in Chapter 11. It is useful to understand this model of behaviour change as the service users most likely to benefit from brief interventions are those that are at pre-contemplation or contemplation (showing ambivalence) in the 'cycle of change'. As well as using some of the key skills outlined in the previous chapters to provide brief interventions, there are other useful brief intervention models that could make a significant impact on your everyday social work practice. Two of these will be discussed here.

FRAMES

As mentioned above, aspects of the other models previously covered in this part of the book can be used as brief interventions. A brief intervention based on increasing the service user's motivation and readiness to change is often referred to as 'brief motivational counselling'. Based on this premise, Miller and Sanchez (1993) suggested the acronym FRAMES to describe six key ingredients of motivationally based brief interventions. FRAMES stands for:

Feedback is given to the individual about personal risk or impairment
Responsibility for change is placed on the service user
Advice to change is given by the practitioner
Menu of options for change is given
Empathy is expressed
Self-efficacy or optimistic empowerment is stimulated in the service user.

These elements are not unknown to the social work practitioner and could fit well within their everyday social work practice. Asking the service user about their substance use and whether they are concerned about it in a non-judgemental and empathic way is a start (Empathy). This might be followed by the practitioner letting them know whether or not they think that this use is problematic (Feedback and Advice) and letting the service user know that if they did want to change anything about their substance-using behaviour then this would be entirely in their hands (Responsibility). Following this, a range of possible options for change could be discussed, ranging from harm-reduction education, self-help groups, counselling and/or more intensive treatment options if appropriate (Menu). Finally, the practitioner could focus on instilling optimism and Self-efficacy in the service user. This type of brief intervention, done well, could take no more than 30 minutes, but leave the service user thinking about behaviour change and with a raft of potential choices for further help if they deem it necessary. This is something that could be done alongside a full and comprehensive assessment, or when meeting service users in almost any social work setting. All it requires is some basic key social work skills, some knowledge of the effects of alcohol and/or drugs and some information about referral and treatment options available in the area.

The use of the FRAMES acronym to remember key tasks when implementing a brief intervention, is a useful and practical tool for the social worker, no matter where or with whom they work. An even simpler model that has been suggested specifically for social workers in a 'non-substance-misuse' practice setting is outlined below.

Screening and Brief Intervention
Practice model (SBIP model)

The SBIP model for screening and brief intervention is a social work model for non-'substance misuse' practice settings and has been suggested by Bliss and Pecukonis (2009). This model suggests that social workers first use the CAGE (Ewing, 1984) or CAGE-AID (Brown and Rounds, 1995) screening tool to briefly screen for problematic substance use. Please refer to Chapter 9 for an overview of the CAGE-AID screening tool that is suggested for use with the SBIP model.

While the SBIP model suggests use of the CAGE or CAGE-AID, it can be used alongside any other screening tool, as long as some screening is completed. The idea is that the brief interventions that would be offered to the service user are based on conclusions made from the screening tool, that is, the level of potential problematic substance use. This model suggests that to keep it very simple, social workers categorise problematic substance use along a 3-point continuum, ranging from *'no problematic substance use'* to *'possible problematic substance use'* through to *'likely problematic substance use'*, based on the screen that they have completed (Bliss and Pecukonis, 2009). The type of brief intervention offered will depend on which point on the continuum the service user is thought to be at. Using the results from the CAGE as an example, the brief interventions that match each of the 3 points are explored below; however, remember that with some thought, any screening tool results could be applied to this 3-point continuum.

No problematic substance use. A score of 0 on the CAGE would indicate 'no problematic substance use'. A brief intervention for service users at this point on the continuum would entail positive reinforcement of substance-using behaviour (including abstinence), and affirmation about the current choices they are making about substance use (including abstinence). 'The power of positively reinforcing these kinds of healthy behaviours should not be minimized, as they can become the basis for helping clients improve their functioning in other biopsychosocial domains' (Bliss and Pecukonis, 2009: 34).

Possible problematic substance use. A score of at least 1 on the CAGE would indicate possible problematic substance use. According to the CAGE, this indicates that there may be a need for further screening or more in-depth assessment. Given this, the brief intervention offered at this stage on the continuum would be feedback about the screening result, further additional information about substances and potential options for further help. This might include brochures and fact sheets, books or website addresses. It might also involve the social worker explaining types of treatment options, including self-help groups (like Alcoholics Anonymous and/or Narcotics Anonymous), counselling, day programmes and residential rehabilitation. This is seen as non-confrontational brief intervention, which is primarily informative and educational in nature.

Likely problematic substance use. Using the CAGE screen, this would be indicated by a score of 2 or more. In this case, it is likely that the brief intervention offered will include feedback about the results from the screen and a recommendation that the service user be referred to a more specialised service for further investigation of the substance use. This should also be done in a non-judgemental and empathic way, with clear advice to seek further assistance, but without pressure or confrontation.

Clearly, the SBIP model is a very simple guide that, while it may not address the complexities of most problematic substance use, does attempt to direct the social worker and help them makes sense, in practical terms, of the results of screening tests that they may have completed. It relies on sound judgement as well as the screening tool, and directs the social worker to refer on as appropriate. For social workers working in non-specialist practice settings, it is surely the very least that they can be expected to do. Given the prevalence of problematic substance use among social work service users and the ease with which brief interventions can be simply and effectively performed, social workers should make brief interventions for problematic substance use part of the everyday practice.

Summary

Brief interventions are simple, effective, practical strategies to screen, detect and reduce the harm associated with problematic substance use. They are often used by non-specialists in a variety of non-specialist settings to intervene with everyday service users who may have some problematic substance use. The acronym FRAMES reminds us of the importance of Feedback, Responsibility, Advice, Menu of options, Empathy and Self-efficacy. The SBIP Model (Bliss and Pecukonis, 2009) suggested for non-specialist social work practitioners incorporates a 3-point continuum for categorising the type of brief intervention to be offered to service users based on the results of screening tests. While the model recommends the simple CAGE and CAGE-AID screening tools, this 3-point continuum model can be used with the results from any screening tool. The 3 points on the continuum range from 'no problematic substance use' to 'possible problematic substance use' through to 'likely problematic substance use' and offers an example of an appropriate form of brief intervention at each point. People with no problematic substance use should be positively reinforced regarding their current behaviours, people with possible problematic substance use should be offered feedback about their screening result and further information about substances, while people with likely problematic substance use should be referred on to a specialist service for further assessment.

Given their effectiveness and ease of use, it is likely that brief interventions are both practical and useful to social workers in a variety of settings. Problematic substance use is common among the people who use the services of social workers and this often exacerbates other difficulties in their lives. If brief interventions can be effectively implemented into a variety of social work practice, it is likely that service users and their social workers will see consolidated positive change.

Reflections

Do you always ask about problematic substance use in your social work practice? If not, why not?

What would you find useful about brief interventions in your social work practice?

Why do you think models of brief intervention 'fit' with social work values?

Further readings

Babor, T. and Higgins-Biddle, J. (2001) *Brief Intervention for Hazardous and Harmful Drinking: A Manual for Use in Primary Care.* Geneva: World Health Organization.

Bliss, D. and Pecukonis, E. (2009) Screening and Brief Intervention: Practice model for social workers in non-substance-abuse practice settings', *Journal of Social Work Practice in Addictions*, 9(1): 21–40.

Part 4

Social Work Practice Settings

Part 4 has a focus on particular social work practice settings where social workers may come across service users with problematic substance use. This part assumes some general knowledge about these specialist practice settings and acknowledges that readers may currently work with or intend to work in these settings. Chapter 14 covers 'Working with problematic substance use in disability practice settings'. Chapter 15 covers 'Dual diagnosis – working with co-existing problems in mental health settings practice'. Chapter 16 has a focus on the importance of 'Parental problematic substance use and working with families'. The final chapter centres on 'Problematic substance use in health care settings – pain, HIV and HCV'.

14

Working with Problematic Substance Use in Disability Practice Settings

There is generally a lack of knowledge, information and research about problematic substance use among people with disabilities. There is very little understanding about rates of problematic substance use and generally a perception that perhaps people with disabilities do not use substances. This is of course inaccurate as it is just as likely that people with disabilities will use substances as anyone else might, if they have access to them. What evidence there is does seem to suggest that people with disabilities are less likely than those in the general population to have problematic substance use; however, this does appear to relate to and depend on the type of disability that the person has. For example, people with mental health problems are more likely to experience problematic substance use, as are those who take substances to alleviate pain that may be as a result of their disability, and those for whom their disability is as a direct result of their problematic substance use.

The Disability Discrimination Act 2005 defines disability as 'A physical or mental impairment which has a substantial and long-term adverse effect on a person's ability to carry out day-to-day activities.' For the purposes of this chapter disability is taken to cover physical, intellectual and learning disabilities, but does not cover mental health problems (except where specified) as this is covered in Chapter 15 on dual diagnosis, or use of substances to alleviate pain that results from a disability (except where specified) as this is covered in Chapter 17 when we overview physical health and pain.

Defining someone by their disability is limiting and not always helpful, because people who may have disabilities also have many more attributes to their character. It is also extremely difficult to make generalisations about this group of people because people with disabilities are as diverse as the types of disability or impairment that they may have and also come from a variety of backgrounds, cultures, ethnicities, ages, classes and sexual orientations (to name but a few diverse lived experiences). It is useful, however, to think about problematic substance use with people with disabilities as a whole, because there are some generalisations that can be inferred from our limited knowledge and it is necessary that social workers are aware of this information. This chapter aims to cover some of this information, but does so with caution.

It is useful to think about the idea of 'disability' as a social construct rather than assume people who may have impairments are disabled because of them. It is useful to recognise that often people who have disabilities are being disadvantaged because society does not always cater for their differing needs. For example, it is interesting to think about a wheelchair user. They are not necessarily disabled due to any impairment they may have, in this case their inability to walk, but by a society that limits their access to people, places and things by not providing wheelchair access. According to Clawson (2008), 'Disability is constructed by the way society is shaped rather than it being an inherent physical state' (p. 540). There are other ways of viewing disability that are also useful to reflect on, however, as not all disabilities can have society suitably adjust to completely alleviate all of the difficulties they may face. For example, if someone has depression, chronic pain or a life-threatening illness, these would still remain even if all disabling barriers no longer existed. In this case then, it is also useful to think about the idea that it is the actual disabilities and/or impairments that create difficulties in peoples' lives. Having an open-minded approach to understanding disability will allow for an acceptance of the variety of different ways in which people can view disability, and more importantly help you support your service users' own view of their disability. It is vital that, however we view disability, we are aware of both the difficulties that people with disabilities can face, and also see these beside the rest of the person in their entirety. People are more than just their disabilities and will have strengths, skills and character which should also be recognised and nurtured just as it would be with anyone else.

Problematic substance use in disability practice settings

It appears that generally speaking people with disabilities are less likely than those in the general population to have problematic substance use. Some authors surmise that there is an increased likelihood that people with disabilities will experiment, use and develop problems with substances since deinstitutionalisation. Deinstitutionalisation refers to the process whereby many more people are now being cared for in community settings as opposed to in residential centres or long stay hospitals. Now that people with disabilities have more access to substances than they have ever had before, it may be that this becomes an area for concern and that we see levels of problematic substance use increase in the future (Slayter, 2010). Potentially, people with disabilities could be seen as more vulnerable to problematic substance use due to the additional stress relating to the disability; the need for pain relief; disability occurring due to 'substance misuse' and the nature of the disability, for example learning disabilities and mental health (FRANK, 2005). If people with disabilities do use and experiment with substances, there is also some potential for them to be at more risk of the adverse effects of substances if they are currently taking medications (which have the potential for adverse cross reactions) and they may become vulnerable to assault or theft from others who may be likely to take advantage of them. These thoughts regarding vulnerability are merely supposition and anecdotal, however, because so little research has been done in the area, we really do not know. While it is important to bear in mind these potential vulnerabilities, it would be unfair and paternalistic to assume that any use of substances would be problematic for someone just because they had a disability. In light of this, later on in this chapter an overview of an alcohol awareness and controlled drinking programme used within a medium secure service for people with learning disabilities will be discussed.

Research is very scarce on the subject of problematic substance use and disabilities, and most of the research that has been done has focused on learning and intellectual disability and problematic substance use, or cannabis use by people with multiple sclerosis. According to a small piece of research that interviewed both 'substance misuse' practitioners and professionals who work with people who have intellectual disabilities, more people with intellectual disabilities are experimenting with illicit drugs than ever before (McLaughlin et al., 2007: 133). It is estimated that approximately 0.8 per cent of the intellectual disability population has 'hazardous substance use' (Taggart et al., 2006). The most widely used substance for people with an intellectual disability in this study was alcohol, but cannabis and ecstasy were also used, and some prescribed medications were overused (for example, diazepam) (McLaughlin et al., 2007). Concerns in this study centred on the unique challenges that problematic substance use by people with disabilities may pose, especially in relation to physical, emotional and social health (McLaughlin et al., 2007: 133).

> Despite this lower prevalence rate compared with the non-intellectually disabled population, the impact of such substance use reported was disturbing, such as poorer physical and mental health, greater exploitation, increased offending behaviour and more likelihood of being admitted to hospital. (McLaughlin et al., 2007: 134)

Other pieces of research have focused on people who have intellectual disabilities and serious mental health problems as well as problematic substance use. This was described by one author as 'triple diagnosis' (Slayter, 2010). People who experience mental health problems are more likely than the general population to use substances problematically. This will be discussed in more depth in the next chapter on dual diagnosis. If a 'dual diagnosis' is also coupled with an intellectual disability, then service users may be very unlikely to access specialised substance 'misuse' services, and specialised services may be quite unable to offer them an appropriate service. According to McLaughlin et al. (2007), most substance use professionals feel quite unprepared to work with people who have intellectual disabilities and are aware that they need further education and training in this area coupled with an ongoing awareness of, and communication with, local services for people with intellectual disabilities. Substance use workers may feel better able to work with people who have physical disabilities (as long as they can physically access the service) than they do people with intellectual or learning disability; however, this is anecdotal.

According to Ghaffer and Feinstein (2008), a number of studies show that between 8 and 18 per cent of people with multiple sclerosis (MS) living in the community admit to using cannabis in the last month. In one UK study (Chong et al., 2006), one third of the participants with MS had used cannabis at some stage to alleviate symptoms. This is despite the fact that it is illegal. Using cannabis in this way potentially to alleviate symptoms associated with MS does not necessarily mean, however, that use may become problematic. Given this possibility though, and given the research with people who have intellectual and/or learning disability and problematic substance use, it would seem apparent that if you are a social worker already specialising in working with people with disabilities you are in a great place to work with any of your service users on this issue. At the very least, some co-working with a 'substance misuse' specialist would be essential. Unfortunately, conclusions about how well substance use workers might work with different types of disability are limited because of the lack of research, but it is likely that if you are a disability specialist, your particular knowledge would be useful for co-work with any substance use practitioner.

Effective social work with people who have disabilities and problematic substance use

There is limited information about how social workers can effectively work with people who have disabilities and problematic substance use. From the limited research we do know a number of keys things, however, and these should be taken into consideration when working in this practice setting. We do know that many people with intellectual disabilities and problematic substance use are excluded from mainstream 'substance misuse' services because these services feel unable and unprepared to work with people who have intellectual disabilities (McLaughlin et al., 2007). We also know that many people who specialise in working with people with intellectual disability feel that they have a lack of understanding about substance use, its assessment, treatment and management.

> As a consequence of such fragmented and uncoordinated services, many people with intellectual disability who have substance-related problems, continue to 'fall through the cracks' in both services. (McLaughlin et al., 2007: 134)

Because of this reality, two strong themes emerged from the McLaughlin et al. (2007) study. First, it was clear that people who worked with those who had intellectual disabilities required education about problematic substance use, and 'substance misuse' workers required more education and training in how to work with people with intellectual disabilities. There is evidence to suggest that some talking therapies work well with people who have intellectual disabilities (Beail, 1995; Collins, 1999; Hollins and Sinason, 2000 cited in McLaughlin et al., 2007), so it is possible for this education and training to be had. The second strong theme to emerge from this research came out of this dilemma, which is that there needed to be more collaborative work between 'substance misuse' teams and intellectual disability teams, as well as a 'link' person who would be trained up in both areas in order to support and advise on casework with service users. Similarly, this study recommended that information about services and problematic substance use be made available in user-friendly formats whose development may require a joint approach from service users, 'substance misuse' specialists and intellectual disabilities services.

According to FRANK (2005), service users should be involved in the planning and decision-making processes within both specialist problematic substance use and disability services in order to provide more focused provisions. For disability services this would include involving service users with problematic substance use, and for 'substance misuse' services this would mean involving people with disabilities. Making sure that services are inclusive, non-judgemental and accessible is paramount.

According to Slayter (2010), those working with people who have problematic substance use and intellectual disability, as well as mental health problems, should concentrate on family education, harm reduction, social and communication skills development, and applied behaviour analysis to increase functional and appropriate skills (p. 50). Further research about what types of talking therapies or behaviour therapies might work well for people who have both problematic substance use and intellectual disability needs to occur. At present very few practitioners specialise in this area. According to Slayter (2010), however, social workers who specialise in working with people with intellectual disabilities are natural 'boundary spanners' who could easily adapt their skills to include becoming competent in working with problematic substance use. At the very least, social workers that practice in this setting could think about how to use the screening tools that are covered in this book (Chapter 9) in order to acknowledge and screen for potential problematic substance use within this practice setting.

Case study: A controlled drinking programme for people with learning disabilities

Although there may be several vulnerabilities that people with disabilities may have that make their substance use potentially more dangerous than it does to those in the general public (unknown results of mixing medications with illicit substances, exploitation), it would be wrong to think that just because people with disabilities use substances that this is in and of itself a problem. Obviously people with disabilities have the same rights as anyone else to enjoy an alcoholic drink in a social setting, for example. This part of the chapter overviews a controlled drinking programme developed in the UK for people with learning disabilities living in conditions of medium security (Brown and Coldwell, 2006). The development of this programme came about because it was recognised that some of the service users in this setting had previously had problems with the use of alcohol. In this medium secure setting the availability of alcohol depended on the service user's placement with the service, their legal status, whether or not they were taking any medication, their ability and level of independence, as well as the attitude of the support staff working at the service. It was hoped that educating people with learning disabilities about controlled alcohol use would allow them to take responsibility for their own drinking, and mean that they may be less likely to drink to excess or experience problematic alcohol use.

Initially, there was some concern from some of the staff that educating service users about the use of alcohol was potentially 'dangerous' and that they should not be encouraged to drink. This sort of attitude paralleled the debate that was had about people with learning disabilities having access to 'sex education'.

> Clearly these views whether regarding alcohol or sex, do not sit easily with the prevailing philosophy and values in wider LD services (e.g. Social Role Valorisation: Wolfensberger, 1998). Such values seek to enable clients with a LD to lead as ordinary and valued a lifestyle as any other person in society. (Brown and Coldwell, 2006: 89)

The programme that was developed considered the content of a mainstream 'alcohol awareness' course in terms of the service user's level of comprehension, concentration span, literacy skills, past/current alcohol use, underlying problems, patterns and triggers (Brown and Coldwell, 2006: 91). Initially, the course was offered in a group setting but was also followed up by individual sessions in order to monitor service user comprehension and allow for repetition. In this way the programme was tailored to suit the individual. The aims of the group were to raise awareness of the positive and negative aspects of using alcohol; provide a balanced view of its effects; provide factual knowledge and practical information through the group file, handouts and written information; and to promote sensible drinking and behavioural self-control methods. The content of these sessions included:

- Why people drink, and what are the triggers.
- Different types of drinks and their images.
- Concepts of units and safe limits.
- The effects of alcohol on the body.
- Attitudes to heavy drinkers, and an explanation of the continuum of alcohol use (service users are asked to place their current alcohol use on the continuum).
- The psychological effects of alcohol.
- Drink refusal skills.
- Practical exercise – a visit to a pub for a meal with support staff.

Three further group sessions using a motivational approach were also added to the programme that were focused on the work by Mendel and Hipkins (2002). A sustained focus on alcohol awareness also continued when service users were resettled in the community.

It may be that you feel it is appropriate to offer something like this to the service users you work with. If this is the case, please read more widely on the subject, beginning with the recommended reading section of this chapter. Brief motivational approaches similar to those described in Chapters 11 and 13 of this book have also been shown to be effective with people with learning disabilities (Mendel and Hipkins, 2002).

Summary

There is very little research that has focused on problematic substance use by people with disabilities. The research that has been done has tended to focus on people with learning or intellectual disability and the use of alcohol, or people who use cannabis to alleviate symptoms of MS, neither of which necessarily suggests problematic use. While there is evidence to suggest that people with disabilities are less likely than those in the general population to have problematic substance use, this does depend on the type of disability. There are higher rates of problematic substance use for those people who have mental health problems, who experience pain as a result of their disability, and for those whose disability is as a direct result of their substance use. While generally rates for problematic substance use may be low within this practice setting, when problems do occur people with disabilities are thought to be more vulnerable to problems associated with hazardous use of substances because of things such as the use of medication, and their vulnerability toward being exploited. That is not to say that all substance use by people with disabilities is problematic, but perhaps that more serious consideration may need to be given to harm-reduction measures for this service user population. The challenge for you if you are a specialist disability social worker or intend to be, is to acknowledge the possibility of substance use and screen for problematic substance use in your work.

Historically, 'substance misuse' services have not worked particularly well with people who have learning and/or intellectual disabilities even though there is evidence to suggest that a number of talking and behavioural therapies work well with people who have these types of disabilities. In the future it is vital that social workers who specialise in working in the disability setting co-work with specialist 'substance misuse' services so that service users get a more appropriate service for their problematic substance use. Social workers working in disability settings may also like to think about offering their service users 'user friendly' substance use information and/or controlled drinking-group programmes that have been written for this specialist setting.

Reflections

How would you feel about offering substance use education in a disability practice setting?

(Continued)

(Continued)

What do you think could be the main benefits of offering substance use education and/or problematic substance use services in a disability practice setting?

How would you deal with the issues of social care vs social control that could arise if you were aware of service users in a disability practice setting who were using substances?

Further reading

Brown, G. and Coldwell, B. (2006) 'Developing a controlled drinking programme for people with learning disabilities living in conditions of medium security'. *Addiction Research and Theory*, 14(1): 87–95.

15

Dual Diagnosis – Working with Co-Existing Problems in Mental Health Practice Settings

Social workers working or intending to work in the mental health sector need to be aware of the potential for problematic substance use among their service users. Co-existing problems and complex needs relating to mental health problems and problematic substance use (as well as other health and social care needs) are relatively common. Research suggests that approximately one third of people who use mental health services have problematic substance use (Department of Health (DoH), 2006a; Hawkings and Gilburt, 2004). Other documents suggest that this figure is much higher, at approximately 50 per cent (Department of Health, 2009). Similarly, approximately 50 per cent of people who use 'substance misuse' services have a mental health problem (most commonly depression and anxiety) (Hawkings and Gilburt, 2004). Some studies show that co-existing disorders (diagnosed) are just as common as disorders occurring on their own. For example, diagnosed substance abuse or dependence with anxiety or depression, is just as common as diagnosed substance abuse or dependence alone. Therefore the group of service users who experience co-existing problems and have complex needs are not particularly unique or exceptional, but are actually core business for both mental health and 'substance misuse' services. This is no surprise when we recognise that the same types of negative life events (including homelessness, poverty, abuse, neglect) and vulnerabilities that make people more susceptible to mental health issues are the same things that may also put them at risk of developing problematic substance use.

It is recognised that the term 'dual diagnosis' is not a particularly useful one (Hawkings and Gilburt, 2004; Watson and Hawkings, 2007). It assumes that a person has only two diagnoses or problems and does not clearly articulate the complex social needs that often coincide with having a diagnosis of problematic substance use and mental illness. There are a number of other terms that have been used in the literature to describe these sets of problems and these include co-morbidity, co-occurring/co-existing disorders and people with complex needs/ enhanced care needs. The term 'co-existing problems' will be used throughout most of this chapter, rather than the term 'dual diagnosis' (except where specified), which is more common in the UK, for two main reasons. First, the term 'dual diagnosis' is a highly medicalised term and one that, it has been argued, is not appropriate for use by social workers (Kvaternik and Grebenc, 2009). Kvaternik and Grebenc (2009) argue that while it is important for social workers to be aware of psychiatric diagnoses, this knowledge is only important in the context of the person's life, how the person experiences reality, what medication they are on and what obstacles they need to overcome in their everyday living. Further, they argue that the term 'dual diagnosis' assumes that complex problems are only medically based, which negates the importance of other related needs such as housing, employment, relationships and social isolation (Kvaternik and Grebenc, 2009: 510).

Second, where the term 'dual diagnosis' has been used to describe serious mental illness and more severe problematic substance use, it has also been used to exclude people (without clear diagnosis) from services. The term 'co-existing problems' is a recognition that significant problematic substance use can occur with mental health symptoms at levels that may not necessarily meet the criteria for a diagnosis of a disorder in their own right (Todd, 2010). Service users who present with problems that are not always severe enough to warrant diagnosis need to be included here because they make up the vast majority of people with complex needs that most 'substance misuse' services work with, and many of the people that present to mental health practice settings. The term 'co-existing problems' takes into consideration both people with severe and less severe problematic substance use and mental health problems. Given this then, it is important to note that co-existing problems comprise a heterogeneous set of issues that can be as diverse as the different combinations of mental health problems and types of substances used, for example alcohol use and depression or heroin use and bipolar disorder. Coupled with this, the people who may experience these problems can also be diverse and come from a variety of backgrounds and lived experiences because, as we know, both problematic substance use and mental health problems cut across race, ethnicity, religion and sexual orientation. Given this then, we must make any generalisations about working with this group of service users in the mental health practice setting with caution. The overview we can give, however, and that which is included in this chapter, is imperative for social workers working in mental health services to be aware of.

Key guidance and policy

There are now a number of key guidance and policy documents that focus on service provision for people with 'dual diagnosis' or co-existing problems. Most of these do focus on people who have co-existing problems at the more severe end of the scale. According to Watson and Hawkings (2007), local agencies need to work together to define what is meant by 'dual diagnosis' in their areas but they suggest that 'It should include major mental health and mood disorders, personality disorders and substance use' (p. 11). When it comes to commissioning and funding services, unfortunately, due to finite resources, local areas will probably need to define 'dual diagnosis' quite narrowly. That is not to say that both mental health services and 'substance misuse' services do not work with people with less severe problems, because they do.

New Horizons: A Shared Vision for Mental Health (Department of Health, 2009) is an across-government (England) programme of action intended to promote and improve mental health and well-being. It replaces the National Service Framework (NSF) for Mental Health and was effective from 1 January 2010. 'Dual diagnosis' is mentioned in *New Horizons* as one of the most challenging problems in mental health care. It recognises the need for:

- joint working, including referral pathways and specialist advice, between mental health and community alcohol and drug teams;
- training in the care of 'substance misuse' for mental health staff;
- priority for dual diagnosis under the Care Programme Approach and through drug and alcohol teams;
- clinical leadership (for example, consultant psychiatrists and nurses); and
- improved diagnostic practices with agreed risk and responsibility assessment between agencies and shared clinical action plans. (Department of Health, 2009: 61)

The aims set out for 'dual diagnosis' in *New Horizons* should be seen alongside some of the more specific guidance documents. These include *Dual Diagnosis Good Practice Guide* (Department of Health, 2002), in which it is recommended that people with a 'dual diagnosis' should be 'mainstreamed' into mental health services; *Dual Diagnosis in Mental Health Inpatient and Day Hospital Settings* (Department of Health, 2006a); *Closing the Gap* (Hughes, 2006), which outlines a capability framework for practitioners working with people with co-existing disorders in a variety of specialist and non-specialist settings; *Refocusing the Care Programme Approach: Policy and Positive Practice Guidance* (Department of Health, 2008); *Mind the Gaps – Meeting the Needs of People with Co-occurring Substance Misuse and Mental Health Problems* (Scottish Executive, 2003); *A Service Framework to Meet the Needs of People with a Co-occurring Substance Misuse and Mental Health Problems* (Welsh Assembly Government, 2007) ; and *Models of Care for the Treatment of Drug Misusers* (NTA, 2002). Unfortunately, it is not within the scope of this chapter to be able to cover each of these key documents in any depth, but they are referenced at the end of this text.

Problematic substance use in mental health practice settings

Research suggests that between approximately one third and half of all people who use mental health services use substances (Department of Health, 2006a, 2009; Hawkings and Gilburt, 2004). Given the nature of the relationship between mental health and substance use, it is likely that a high proportion of this substance use is problematic (exacerbation of symptoms, adverse unknown reactions between prescribed medication and other substances). There are many reasons why people with mental health problems might use substances. For example, to 'self-medicate' for symptoms of their mental health problem, to help promote social interaction, and/or to deal with the unpleasant side effects of any medication they may be taking (Owen et al., 2008). There are also a range of identified vulnerability factors for both the development of mental health problems and problematic substance use, and therefore co-existing problems. These vulnerabilities include genetic, environmental and behavioural vulnerabilities as well as triggers such a homelessness and bereavement, for example.

There have been four main relationships identified between problematic substance use and mental health problems, and while a definitive understanding of the relationship is not essential to work with and treat individual service users, an understanding of these relationships is important. The four relationships are: a primary psychiatric illness precipitates or leads to substance misuse; use of substances makes the mental health problem worse or alters its course; intoxication and/or substance dependence leads to psychological symptoms; substance misuse and/or withdrawal leads to psychiatric symptoms or illnesses (Department of Health, 2002). These relationships are further explained using examples in Figure 15.1.

Practitioners should be aware of these relationships, and while it may be important to hypothesise which of these relationships is relevant to the service users you work with, it is not necessary, indeed it is very difficult, to make any firm conclusions. These relationships or hypotheses about them should not be used as an excuse not to work with presenting service users. As you can see from

Severity of problematic substance misuse

	High
e.g. a dependent drinker who experiences increasing anxiety	e.g. an individual with schizophrenia who misuses cannabis on a daily basis to compensate for social isolation

Severity of mental illness

Low	**High**
e.g. a recreational misuser of 'dance drugs' who has begun to struggle with low mood after weekend use	e.g. an individual with bi-polar disorder whose occasional binge drinking and experimental misuse of other substances de-stabilises their mental health
	Low

Figure 15.1 The main relationships identified between problematic substance use and mental health problems

Source: Department of Health, 2002: 8

Figure 15.1, it is likely that mental health practitioners would work with service users situated in the right-hand quadrants, and that 'substance misuse' services would work with service users situated in the left-hand quadrants. That is not to say that service users should not be co-worked by two specialists wherever possible, or have specialist dual diagnosis services provided if they are available in your area.

Whatever the relationship between mental health problems and problematic substance use, the research shows that their co-existence is likely to worsen a range of outcomes for service users. These include:

- Increased rates of violence.
- Increased rates of suicide.
- Higher levels of mental health symptoms.
- Increased relapses, numbers of hospitalisations and time spent in hospital.
- Poorer general health, including increased rates of hepatitis C and HIV.
- Higher rates of offending and incarceration.
- Unstable housing and homelessness.
- Loss of family supports.
- Financial problems.
- Financial costs to treatment services.
- Poorer subjective well-being. (Drake, 2007 cited in Todd, 2010: 7–8)

Many of these outcomes relate directly to the areas of work that may be a focus for mental health social workers, so it is imperative that you are aware of these vulnerabilities.

Historically, there have been difficulties for people with co-existing problems accessing either substance use or mental health services, and being turned away because services have assessed that their need is primarily related to 'the other'. This has led many vulnerable service users in need of services being 'ping ponged' between services and pushed from 'pillar to post'.

> Dual diagnosis clients are everybody's business, but nobody's priority. Substance misuse and mental health are two parallel universes with totally different cultures and commissioning practices. (Clinician and researcher cited in Hawkings and Gilburt, 2004: 58)

Issues relating to the different cultures and ideologies of services, rigid professional boundaries, lack of training and education, lack of clarity around roles and responsibilities as well as pessimistic attitudes of staff towards people with co-existing problems have all added to this service user group having received a very raw deal in the past. With policy guidance indicting that people with a 'dual diagnosis' should be mainstreamed into mental health services (Department of Health, 2002), that there should be an emphasis on joint working of 'dual diagnosis' cases (Department of Health, 2009), and a capability framework that focuses on the attitudes of staff as well as knowledge and skills (Hughes, 2006), it is hoped that things will change in the future. Social workers working in mental health practice settings have a huge part to play in making sure that these positive changes are made in their own teams.

Effective social work with co-existing problems

While system issues can get in the way of working effectively with people who have co-existing problems, when you are able to, working with people who have co-existing problems is not so very different from working with other service users with complex needs in mental health practice settings. The key is to have a positive attitude and be non-judgemental. Having a belief that well-being and recovery are possible and recognising that change may take time is crucial. While this is essentially the case, there are some important assessment and treatment considerations to take in account over and above how you may already work with service users with complex needs. These include:

- Identifying emergencies or acute problems that may require immediate assistance (including acute intoxication and risk of overdose).
- Having assessments that cover risk, physical, social and mental health, alongside patterns of substance use.
- Consideration of the chronology and relationship between problematic substance use and mental health problems. See Figure 15.1 (while it is useful to hypothesise about this relationship it is not necessary to have made any firm conclusions before beginning to work with service users).
- Consideration of any likely interactions between medications and other substances.
- Assessment of knowledge regarding harm reduction for substance use (where service users are using substances and are unaware of ways to reduce the harm associated with this, you will need to discuss this with them at some stage. See Chapter 10 which overviews some harm reduction strategies).
- Consideration of mental health and problematic substance use treatment history.
- Both mental health and problematic substance use treatment options. (Department of Health, 2002)

Coupled with these extra assessment considerations it is also necessary to consider risk somewhat differently. When assessing risk in relation to service users with co-existing problems it is necessary to acknowledge that service users are more likely to pose a risk to themselves than to others, but that people with co-existing problems are also more likely to have histories of violence compared to mental health service users who do not use substances. You also need to be aware of risk in relation to the unknown and potentially adverse effects of mixing medication with other substances. Any risk management plans should include personalised relapse prevention initiatives for both deteriorating mental health and increasing or unmanageable substance use (see Chapter 12 on relapse prevention strategies for problematic substance use).

Hawkings and Gilburt (2004) outline one useful model for working with people who have co-existing problems. It outlines four key stages, which are: engagement, persuasion, active treatment and relapse prevention/management. Engagement, the importance of which has been discussed throughout this book, is imperative for this service user group when accessing mental health services. It is highly likely that service users with co-existing problems have been pushed from 'pillar to post' between services in the past and that they may be highly suspicious of professionals. Take the time to build a rapport with the service user and earn their trust. This will allow you to be able to work with them and per-suade them toward behaviour change, using a motivational approach (see Chapter 11). Special models of motivational interviewing have been designed for use with people who have co-existing disorders; however, you may feel comfortable using some of the motivational approaches mentioned in this book (Chapter 11). This stage may take some time and should not be rushed as this could lead to disengagement by the service user.

Once the service user is motivated to want to change their behaviour then the action phase of the work can begin. This will include goal-setting, preferably around giving up or cutting down on substance use (but may include goal-setting in relation to a number of other things, e.g. housing, employment), and it may be at this stage that you make a referral to a specialist 'substance misuse' service (if you have not already done so). That is not to say that you should discontinue working with the service user at this time, in fact co-working would be vital.

Following the action phase of treatment is the relapse prevention/management phase. Service users should be encouraged to identify triggers that may mean that they are more likely to have deteriorating mental health, or increased sub-stance use that becomes unmanageable. Coupled with this should be a plan about how to deal with this situation should it arise. The phases of work with someone who has co-existing problems are not entirely different from how you might work with any mental health service user, and can fit well alongside the Care Programme Approach. The key is to recognise that change may not happen overnight, but will require a long-term focus from both you and the service user.

Because of the complex needs of people with co-existing problems 'any door is the right door' should be the motto when it comes to their accessing services. Unfortunately, due to systems and operational issues this is not always the case and service users requiring help are often turned away from services because it is considered that 'the other' issue is the primary problem. While it is not within the scope of this chapter to discuss these systems issues in any depth, they are mentioned briefly here because they are of very genuine concern and create a barrier to people with co-existing problems accessing the services they desper-ately need and require. The main challenge for mental health social workers then is to make sure that they are able to work with people with co-existing disorders in a variety of mental health practice settings and challenge any systems that seek to use co-existing problems as a reason not to engage with people. With recent policy guidance indicating that systems changes need to be made to ensure that people with co-existing services are adequately catered for it is very much hoped that things will change for the better. The Turning Point *Dual Diagnosis Good Practice Handbook* (Watson and Hawkings, 2007) offers a variety of examples of how services and systems are already working together in the best interests of this service user group throughout the UK. This is referenced in the Further reading section of this chapter.

Case study – 'The Friday Group' (Watson and Hawkings, 2007)

'The Friday group' is a facilitated self-help group established by a local mental health trust to meet the unmet needs of people in their area with a dual diagnosis. It is now a joint project between Community Mental Health Teams (CMHTs) and 'substance misuse' services in the area, and the group is usually facilitated by someone from each of the services. It was funded initially through an innovations award (Queens Nursing Institute 'Innovations and Creative Practice' award), but more recently by the local Drug Alcohol Action Team (DAAT) and the mental health trust. Staffing costs are borne by the CMHTs and 'substance misuse' services.

The philosophy of the project team is that service users are experts in their own care and know what current services are missing for them. It is recognised that working with people with co-existing problems requires focused long-term engagement, and that services should be able to tolerate poor attendance, substance use and non-compliance with medication. The group membership was initially established by mental health workers outreach working with disengaged service users with co-existing problems, for whom it was recognised that services were not adequately meeting their needs. The three main components that were identified from this outreach work as being missing from current services were social and recreational activities, a shared meal and group discussions (Watson and Hawkings, 2007: 34). The self-help group therefore offers social and recreational activities, a shared meal, cultural activities, guest speakers and a discussion group. Members are not required to stop using substances or to commit to abstinence, although they are asked not to use substances prior to or during the group. 'The Friday group' is an open access group with a drop-in style, and members can come and go as they please. Members are sent weekly reminders in the form of newsletters about the group with an update of the following week's activities. Members are never discharged, unless they specifically ask to be so, and will continue to receive their weekly newsletter even if they have not attended for several months. The group members shape the group and decide on the activities, menu and guest speakers. They are also involved in shaping policy and informing the development of services. For example, the group made a submission to the 'Substance Misuse in Acute Inpatient Settings' policy consultation. Although only a small group, members have shown significant improvements in terms of service engagement, mental health, reduced substance use and housing stability (Watson and Hawkings, 2007: 34). Members' belief and trust in the 'system' has been improved through their engagement with this group, and they feel as though they have a say in how they are treated and what services offer them. A high level of peer/self-referral to the group means that the group is meeting the needs of the local dual diagnosis population (Watson and Hawkings, 2007: 34).

Summary

Social workers working in mental health practice settings should expect to work with service users with co-existing problems. Given that up to 50 per cent of people who access mental health services also use substances (often problematically), then working with co-existing problems is actually core business for mental health practitioners. There are many reasons why people with mental health problems might use substances. For example, to 'self-medicate' for symptoms of their mental health problem, to help promote social interaction, and/or to deal with the unpleasant side effects of any medication they may be taking. There are a number of specific considerations to take into account when working with people who have co-existing problems; however, for the most part the way in which you work with these service users will not be so very different from your work with other mental health service users with complex needs. There are four identified relationships between problematic substance use and mental health problems (a primary psychiatric illness precipitates or leads to substance misuse; use of substances makes the mental health problem worse or alters its course; intoxication and/or substance dependence leads to psychological symptoms; substance misuse and/or withdrawal leads to psychiatric symptoms or illnesses). While useful to hypothesise about these relationships it is not necessary to make firm conclusions before working with the service user. One model for working with people with co-existing problems involves engagement, persuasion, active treatment and relapse prevention/management (Hawkings and Gilburt, 2004). However, other key principles for working with people with co-existing problems have also been suggested (Todd, 2010). There are a number of key policy guidance documents for working with 'dual diagnosis'. These documents recognise the need for joint working, agreed referral pathways, further training, priority for dual diagnosis under the Care Programme Approach and through 'substance misuse' teams, mainstreaming of people with more severe co-existing problems into mental health services, and a capability framework that addresses knowledge and skills as well as attitudes of practitioners towards people with co-existing problems. Systems and operational issues continue to mean that sometimes people with co-existing problems are pushed from 'pillar to post' between services; however, with the policy guidance clearly in support of offering people with co-existing problems appropriate and effective services, it is hoped that agencies are becoming much more open to working with people who have co-existing problems.

Reflections

How do you feel about working with people who have co-existing problems?

If you work or have a placement in a mental health service, do you think that the service works well with people who have co-existing problems?

How do you think that the needs of people with co-existing problems are best met?

Further readings

Department of Health (2006) *Dual Diagnosis in Mental Health Inpatient and Day Hospital Settings: Guidance on the Assessment and Management of Patients in Mental Health Inpatient and Day Hospital Settings who have Mental Ill-Health and Substance Use Problems*. London: Department of Health.

Hawkings, C. and Gilburt, H. (2004) *Dual Diagnosis Toolkit: Mental Health and Substance Misuse*. London: Rethink and Turning Point.

Watson, S. and Hawkings, C. (2007) *Dual Diagnosis Good Practice Handbook*. London: Turning Point.

16

Parental Problematic Substance Use and Working with Families

Given that a number of qualified social workers work with children and their families, where their primarily role is safeguarding children, it is essential that they are aware of the potential for problematic substance use in these families. The term 'parental problematic substance use' used in this chapter includes problematic substance use by carers, guardians and close family that has the capacity to affect children adversely. It is estimated that between 780,000 and 1.3 million children in the UK are negatively affected by parental problematic alcohol use (Templeton et al., 2009), and that between 250,000 and 350,000 children are affected by parental drug use (Advisory Council on the Misuse of Drugs (ACMD), 2003). There are a number of ways in which parental problematic substance use can have a harmful effect on children (attachment, family dynamics, neglect, risk of violence); however, it is important to recognise that not all substance use is incompatible with being a good parent. The role of the social worker in this setting is to assess harm and potential harm caused by parental problematic substance use, not to judge simply on the basis of whether parents may use substances. *Hidden Harm: Responding to the Needs of Children of Problem Drug Users* (Advisory Council on the Misuse of Drugs (ACMD), 2003), a groundbreaking document on the subject of parental drug use, alerted health and social care services to the enormity of the problem. The authors reflected that:

> The effects of drugs are complex and vary enormously, depending on both the drug and user. While there is probably no drug that is entirely harmless in all circumstances, the Working Group accepts that not all drug use is incompatible with being a good parent. (ACMD, 2003: 7)

Social workers need to be able to recognise potential problematic substance use (including alcohol use) within the families they are working with in order to lessen the likelihood that the affects of it impact negatively on the children. Taking a whole family approach and recognising the potential adverse effects of parental problematic substance use will mean that child and family social workers will need to be able to screen for problematic substance use, offer brief interventions, refer to appropriate services and co-work with 'substance misuse' specialists.

Key guidance and policy

All current UK child and family policy and guidance, including The Children's Act 2004 and *Every Child Matters: Change for Children* (DfES, 2004), (or the equivalents in the three devolved governments) are relevant to families experiencing problematic substance use. This section details more specific guidance where it exists.

Hidden Harm (ACMD, 2003) has influenced much of the key guidance and policy development regarding parental problematic substance use in both children and adults services throughout the UK. The key messages from *Hidden Harm* were:

- Parental problem drug use can and does cause serious harm to children at every age from conception to adulthood.
- Reducing the harm to children from parental problem drug use should become a main objective of policy and practice.
- Effective treatment of the parent can have major benefits for the child.
- By working together, services can take many practical steps to protect and improve the health and well-being of affected children.
- The number of affected children is only likely to decrease when the number of problem drug users decreases. (ACMD, 2003: 3)

Hidden Harm made a number of recommendations (please see Further reading for a reference on this document) that covered a variety of areas, but at their heart lay a need for a coherent 'joined-up' approach across children, family and adult services. The document also recommended that 'all social care workers receive pre-qualification and in-service training that addresses the potential harm to children of parental substance misuse and what practical steps can be taken to reduce it' (ACMD, 2003: 16).

While this particular recommendation has not yet been fully addressed, most of the recommendations from *Hidden Harm* have been included in both guidance and policy relating to children and family services as well as specialist 'substance misuse' and other adult services. Initially, however, Scotland and Wales made better headway when it came to implementing these recommendations. At first, the response to *Hidden Harm* in England was one of 'mainstreaming' with the further promotion of the *Every Child Matters* agenda underpinned by the Common Assessment Framework (CAF): in essence, that the current arrangements already adequately addressed the issues raised in *Hidden Harm* (Homayoun et al., n.d.). Therefore while the review of *Hidden Harm* three years on (ACMD, 2007) was favourable towards the integrated Scottish and Welsh approaches to implementing the recommendations, and Northern Ireland's *New*

Strategic Direction for Alcohol and Drugs (Department of Health, Social Services and Public Policy, 2006), it effectively heavily criticised the English Drug Strategy of the time (Home Office, 2002). Since this review, however, the English Drug Strategy has been updated twice, with both subsequent strategies having a much clearer focus on families and communities (Home Office, 2008; Home Office, 2010), problematic parental substance use is included in *Working Together to Safeguard Children* (Department for Children, Schools and Families (DfCSF), 2010), and more specific guidance relating to families at risk (for example, *Think Family*) includes parental problematic substance use (Cabinet Office, 2008; Department for Children, Schools and Families (DfCSF)/National Treatment Agency (NTA)/Department of Health (DoH), 2009).

Think Family: Improving the Life Chances of Families at Risk (Cabinet Office, 2008) sets out plans that are aimed at supporting families who have the most entrenched problems, including problematic substance use, and requires both childrens' and adults' services to work effectively with families. This push to get adult and childrens' services to work together and think about a whole family approach is a long-overdue development, which is also a focus of the Scottish document *Getting it Right for Every Child* (Scottish Government, 2008b).

> 'Think Family' practice depends on children's services developing arrangements with local adult services so that the impact of any problems that mothers, fathers and other key carers are experiencing are seen in the context of the welfare of the children for whom they are responsible. (Department for Children, Schools and Families (DfCSF), 2010: 289)

Since 2009, local authorities in England have been able to access extra funding to begin implementing the recommendations in *Think Family*; however, at this time it is too early to tell if the recommendations outlined in this guidance will make a substantial difference to families for whom substance use is a problem. Clear joint guidance for drawing up local protocols between drug and alcohol treatment services and local safeguarding and families' services certainly shows promise (DfCSF/NTA/DoH, 2009). Importantly, it appears that parental problematic substance use, and the importance of children, family and adults services working together has finally made it onto the political agenda.

Parental problematic substance use in child and family social work settings

It is estimated that between 780,000 and 1.3 million children in the UK are negatively affected by parental problematic alcohol use (Templeton et al., 2009), and that between 250,000 and 350,000 children are affected by parental drug use (ACMD, 2003). Parental problematic substance use does not necessarily mean that cared-for children will be neglected or abused; however, it does increase the likelihood of these things occurring. According to research, parental problematic substance use can adversely affect attachment, family dynamics, relationships and functioning, increase the risk of violence and exacerbate mental health problems (Kroll, 2004: 129–30). Parental problematic substance use has also been linked to child neglect, emotional, physical and sexual abuse (Taylor et al., 2008). So while these outcomes are not a given, the potential for these types of problems to make a significant impact on the lives of children and their families is considerable. That is not to say that all children whose parents have problematic substance use will develop behavioural, emotional or psychological difficulties, because we know that children can be incredibly resilient in the face of adversity. What it does mean, however, is that there is a potential for neglect and abuse which can certainly take its toll on even the most resilient of children.

Parental problematic substance use is one of the most common difficulties for child and family social workers, with studies estimating that between 20 and 60 per cent of childcare cases involve problematic substance use (Cleaver et al., 1999; Forrester and Harwin, 2006; Fraser et al., 2009). Comparatively little is known about families that have issues related to parental problematic substance use and who are involved with childcare services; however, one study provides us with some further insight. According to the study by Forrester and Harwin (2006), the first of its kind on the subject in the UK, children involved in care services whose caregivers have problematic substance use tend to be younger than other children involved with services, with parental problematic 'drug misuse' being more common among parents with babies aged less than a year (p. 328). Also of note from this study is that there were twice as many problems related to alcohol use as opposed to problematic drug use among the sample.

Clearly social disadvantage is often a problem for children and families referred to childcare services. It appears, however, that social disadvantage is even more striking for families where problematic substance use is a problem in this sample.

Substance misuse families were half as likely to have a working parent (18 per cent compared with 35 per cent); they were twice as likely to be living in temporary accommodation (23 per cent compared with 12 per cent) and three times as likely to have identified housing concerns (26 per cent compared with 8 per cent). (Forrester and Harwin, 2006: 329)

This study also highlighted the complete lack of referrals to child protection services from 'substance misuse' services in the sample that was studied. While this is of primary concern to specialist 'substance misuse' services themselves, what it does indicate generally is that better liaison and communication between these services is urgently needed. While this study showed that when 'substance misuse' services were involved there were few if any difficulties with this working relationship, the majority of cases did not involve 'substance misuse' specialists at all. When they were involved they tended to be for severe end cases and when families were motivated towards behaviour change. This study therefore highlights the need for child and family social workers to have some skills and knowledge in dealing with issues of parental problematic substance use in their own practice. It may not always be essential or possible to make a referral to a specialist team, and/or some initial motivational work with parents and caregivers may be required prior to making a referral. Where 'substance misuse' services are not directly involved at all it is recommended that child and family social workers work closely with them and liaise for advice and support.

Effective social work with parental problematic substance use

If you are a child and family social worker, or intend to become one, it should be of no surprise to you that you will at some stage work with families where parental problematic substance use is an issue. While there are no set patterns of behaviour that indicate parental problematic substance use, if children are having behavioural difficulties it is worth considering this as a potential issue (Kroll, 2004). While it is not always the easiest of topics to engage families in, there are some key recommendations for your work with children and families that will be important for you to consider in your role (also see Standing Conference on Drug Abuse (SCODA), 1997).

- Routinely ask the question about whether there is a problem with substance use in the family, and whether they would like a referral to a specialist service. Record these discussions in the families file.
- Assess and manage risk in relation to any problematic substance use. There are specific strategies that may be implemented to reduce potential harm to children from parental substance use (for example, parents should keep substances and paraphernalia locked away from children, not use substances in their presence, and find alternative childcare arrangements if parents are going to become intoxicated) (please see Chapter 10 on harm reduction).
- Think about establishing and developing strong links and relationships with local 'substance misuse' services, so that you are aware of referral paths and can call them for advice and support if necessary (don't forget that this relationship will work both ways and you could become a vital 'link' person for their team too).
- If family members are involved with specialist 'substance misuse' services, it is vital that they are invited to relevant statutory and non-statutory meetings that you may be holding for the family. Consideration needs to be given to agreed mechanisms of open communication and issues of confidentiality.
- Work with specialist services to inform them of any significant changes happening in the life of the family that may impact on substance use, for example if a child is going to be removed from the home.
- Consider whether the parent's problematic substance use is potentially having an impact on the caring responsibilities of the children in the family.
- Consider some further training in working with problematic substance use. (DfCSF/ NTA/DH, 2009: 13–14)

You will already have a number of skills in engaging with and working with families, so it is important that the issue of parental problematic substance use does not cause you anxiety. If you seek adequate supervision when concerned, working with this issue will not be so very different from working with a number of other complex needs that you will no doubt be good at, or get used to dealing with. It will be useful to read Part 3 of this book that discusses a range of useful models for working with problematic substance use (which are appropriate for using with family members), which you can use alongside your core skills and in the family context. Remember that the number of affected children is only likely to decrease when the number of problem substance users decreases. Engaging families, including the children, in discussions about problematic substance use, and reducing their fear about disclosing the issues has to be the first step. 'If trust could be established sufficiently for workers to be allowed to actually see what is really going on, then more purposeful assessment and intervention might be possible' (Kroll, 2004: 138).

Case Study – a local Family Intervention Project (DfCSF/NTA/DH, 2009)

Family Intervention Projects (FIPs) appear to be making some headway with difficult-to-engage families who are experiencing poor outcomes, poverty, long-standing worklessness, legal action and the threat of eviction (DfCSF, 2010). There are three types of FIP across England, the first of which were established in 2006. These are Anti-Social FIPs (AS FIP), Child Poverty FIPs (CP FIP) and Youth Crime FIPs (YC FIP), which have all been set up to focus on identified areas of need. Parental problematic substance use may be dealt with alongside other complex needs (mental health, violence, poverty) under any of these FIP's (DfCSF, 2010). One such initiative helped transform the life of 'Jenny' (not her real name), a problematic substance-using mother of two (DfCSF/NTA/DH, 2009).

This Family Intervention Project was started in 2007 as part of this network of teams across England funded by the Department for Children, Schools and Families. Jenny used crack and heroin on a daily basis, and was sex working to support her habit. Her two children had come to the notice of child services and the family were referred to the FIP team. Through FIP, Jenny and her family were assigned an individual key worker who co-ordinated and provided practical support and more specialist interventions. FIP key workers use 'assertive and persistent' working methods to maximise engagement, and expectations of the families themselves are clearly defined in their family support plan. The types of support offered to Jenny included parenting support, help with diet and nutrition, budgeting, life skills, help to make sure that the children accessed education and specialist health and behavioural interventions, including accessing appropriate 'substance misuse' services. Jenny's children also received counselling. Over a period of time, as trust was built up between Jenny, her children and the key worker, Jenny was able to sort out her finances and avoid eviction. Eventually, when she was ready, Jenny was able to access 'substance misuse' services that prescribed her methadone and helped address her liver damage. Her key worker made the initial referral and attended, with Jenny, all of her appointments at the 'substance misuse' clinic. The trust-building and motivational work done prior to making this referral was critical. By the time that Jenny attended the clinic she was motivated to change her behaviour and this has led to the increased likelihood of success. Jenny's children went into foster care while she worked on her problematic substance use, but Jenny continues to work towards her own wellness so that her children will be able to live with her again soon. Jenny sees that FIP, through her keyworker, has provided help in a patient, consistent, supportive and nurturing way that has meant that she has been able to make huge changes in her life.

FIP recognises the whole family approach and understands that it is no longer feasible for child and family services to see parental problematic substance use as 'someone else's problem', or just as an issue that only specialists should deal with. Jenny's keyworker used a motivational approach (see Chapter 11) to get Jenny ready for behaviour change and a referral to a specialist 'substance misuse' service; in effect providing a form of problematic substance-use intervention until Jenny was ready for more in-depth specialist work (DfCSF/NTA/DH, 2009). The background knowledge and skill base to work in this way with parental problematic substance use is useful and important in FIP, but also across other child and family services. Knowledge of, and effective communication, liaison and referral to and with specialist substance misuse services is also critical if children and their families are to be supported to negotiate this difficult issue. Please see DfCSF (2010) for a variety of other FIP case studies.

Summary

Substance use, and even parental problematic substance use, is not necessarily inconsistent with being a good parent. When it occurs, however, there is an increased risk of neglect, emotional, physical and sexual abuse and problems with attachment, relationships, family dynamics and functioning. There is also an increased risk of violence and the potential for an exacerbation of any mental health problems. Parental problematic substance use is a common issue within child and family social work. It is estimated that between 20 and 60 per cent of childcare cases involve problematic substance use, that these families have significantly more social problems, and that the children in these families are considerably younger than in other cases allocated to social workers (Cleaver et al., 1999; Forrester and Harwin, 2006; Fraser et al., 2009). There are a number of pieces of key guidance and policy in relation to working with children and families where parental problematic substance use is an issue, and most of these have been influenced by *Hidden Harm* (ACMD, 2003). This document made a number of recommendations which included the need for a coherent 'joined-up' approach across children, family and adult services as well as the recommendation that all social workers should learn about problematic substance use in their pre-qualification and in-service training.

Think Family and Family Intervention Projects (FIPs) are initiatives aimed at 'at-risk' families. *Think Family* takes a whole family approach and encourages children, family and adult services to work together in the best interests of everyone in the family, especially the children. FIPs offer at-risk families intensive, ongoing and persistent interventions aimed at a number of complex social issues that families may be dealing with, including problematic substance use.

Child and family social workers will encounter families with issues related to problematic substance use, and when they do so it will be important to be aware of a number of key strategies that can be used, coupled with their existing skills in the family context (see Part 3 of this book). Especially important will be the use of the motivational approach to encourage family members to work towards behaviour change, and harm reduction strategies that keep substance users and their children safe. Parental problematic substance misuse can no longer be seen by child and family services as someone else's problem. The challenge is for all social workers who work in these practice settings to develop skills and knowledge in the area of parental problematic substance use, so as to offer these families the services that they need and deserve:

> Social workers need to be better prepared for working with substance misuse. Improved interagency working, while important, is not enough. Families referred to social services are not bundles of discrete problems that can be dealt with by separate specialists. Rather, complex social and individual problems coexist and interact, and social workers need to be able to understand and intervene in relation to these. (Forrester and Harwin, 2006: 333)

Reflections

How do you feel about parents who use drugs? Do you really believe it is possible for a drug-using parent to be a 'good parent'?

Do you feel differently about parents who use alcohol problematically? If so, why do you think that this is?

If you work or have a placement in a child and family social service how well do you think the service works with parental problematic substance use?

Further readings

Advisory Council on the Misuse of Drugs (ACMD) (2003) *Hidden Harm: Responding to the needs of Children of Problem Drug Users*. London: ACMD.

Cleaver, H., Nicholson, D., Tarr, S. and Cleaver, D. (2007) *Child Protection, Domestic Violence and Parental Substance Misuse: Family Experiences and Effective Practice*. London: Jessica Kingsley Publishers.

Kroll, B. and Taylor, A. (2003) *Parental Substance Misuse and Child Welfare*. London: Jessica Kingsley Publishers.

Problematic Substance Use in Health Care Settings – Pain, HIV and HCV

Social workers can and do work in a variety of health care settings, including hospitals, primary health care, hospice, disability and specialist services (for example, HIV, infectious disease services). Given the nature of problematic substance use and its potential negative effects on the users' health, it is essential that social workers working in these settings are aware of the potential for their service users to have problematic substance use, and how some health concerns might be specifically related to problematic substance use. This chapter will overview the complex relationship between problematic substance use and pain, as well as the link between problematic substance use and human immunodeficiency virus (HIV), and the hepatitis C virus (HCV). For more of an overview of the variety of negative health effects related to substance use please see Chapter 3.

Problematic substance use and pain

Persistent pain affects approximately 13 per cent of the general population but may be higher in people with problematic drug use, although there is a lack of knowledge about the true prevalence of this problem (Colvin and Orgel, 2008). It appears that drug users are often given inadequate pain relief, including for painful physical disabilities and palliative care. There seem to be two main reasons for this. First, it appears that prescribers are often unaware of the problematic drug use of their patient and therefore their potential tolerance to some pain medication; and second, if the patient is a known drug user, the prescriber may be overly concerned about prescribing for them and therefore underprescribe the necessary dose. Adequate pain relief is a basic human right for all service users and problematic drug use should not preclude the therapeutic use of opioids to relieve pain (British Pain Society, 2007). While recommending amounts or types of medication is outside the scope of the social work role, the complex nature of these types of issues are important and relevant for social workers to be aware of.

These complex problems are well covered in *Pain and Substance Misuse: Improving the Patient Experience* (British Pain Society, 2007) which provides a good overview of best practice with this service user group in this practice setting. This resource is listed in the Further reading section at the end of this chapter.

Because of the nature of most pain medication, users of them will likely become physically dependent on them. That is, they will develop a tolerance to them and may require more medication to get the same pain relief over time and will experience withdrawal symptoms if they do not have them. These physiological symptoms of dependence that occur for people on prescribed pain medications are similar for people who are experiencing problematic substance use. This does not mean, however, that people using medication as prescribed are developing problematic substance use. Problematic substance use is indicated when there is aberrant use of the medication coupled with psychological features (pleasure seeking and distress avoidance) and social concerns (British Pain Society, 2007).

> Social concerns are a vital component when defining substance misuse or addiction. In the social context where a drug which induces dependence is available in a secure supply, is affordable, and is not sanctioned socially, much of the problematic behaviour associated with substance misuse is not observed. (British Pain Society, 2007: 31)

Although potentially concerning for service users, becoming dependent on pain medication alone is not indicative of problematic substance use. It is useful for social workers, in support of other health professionals involved, to be aware of this difference and be alert to the behaviour changes that may be associated with problematic substance use. Offering information, education and early interventions (if required) to service users regarding this will also be important. It is not uncommon for people who are prescribed pain medication to begin to use it problematically and develop serious problems with it, but it is certainly not inevitable.

Working with service users who may have had histories of problematic substance use but who are now abstinent, is also a challenge. People who have worked hard to remain abstinent and who have histories of problematic substance use (especially opioid use) may become very anxious about 'relapsing' into old substance-using behaviours if they have to be prescribed opioids for pain management. The management of any anxiety around this will be key, coupled with a clear plan for cessation of the pain medication and follow-up support in the community. While both pain and anxiety can be potential triggers for relapse, it is essential that service users understand the difference between becoming physically dependent on their prescribed medication and the other aspects of behaviour that need to be present to indicate the return of problematic substance use. Knowing this may help allay service users' fears, so it is essential information for social workers working in this practice setting.

While there is little research in the area, anecdotal evidence suggests that a variety of substances may be used by people to alleviate lower-grade and/or persistent pain that does not require any prescribed medication. Examples of this type of pain might include problems like persistent headaches and back pain, which are reasonably common in the general population, or people with more distressing physical disabilities using cannabis to alleviate pain. A study by Brennan et al. (2005), for example, found that older people were especially vulnerable to using alcohol to manage pain. According to this research, people experience more pain as they get older and more pain is associated with more use of alcohol to manage the pain.

HIV and hepatitis C (HCV)

Injecting drug users constitute a major risk group for the contraction of HIV and hepatitis C (HCV) in the UK. HIV and HCV are bloodborne viruses, so injecting drug users are at risk of catching these viruses if they share injecting equipment where the virus may be passed from user to user. Social workers who may specialise in working with those living with HIV and/or AIDS and/or HCV should have an awareness of the potential of ongoing problematic substance use, as well as an understanding of the key risk factors and health effects that this ongoing use may have for this service user population (for example, exacerbation of health problems, risk of spreading infection).

HIV/AIDS became a key health concern in the 1980s. This concern saw a fundamental change in the direction of UK drug policy and the implementation of harm reduction strategies that sought to reduce the spread of HIV infection (see Chapter 10). HIV is a condition in which the failure of the immune system can lead to life-threatening opportunistic infections. Once a person with HIV develops an opportunistic infection they have Acquired Immune Deficiency Syndrome (AIDS). Opportunistic infections include Pneumocystis pneumonia and Kaposi's sarcoma and because of the reduced and failed immune system people with AIDS usually die from these sorts of infections. HIV is treated primarily with anti-retroviral drugs, which can help suppress HIV in the body. It is estimated that approximately 1 in 73 injecting drug users in the UK is infected with HIV, and while this figure is still relatively low compared to many other countries, the incidence of HIV among injecting drug users has been rising since 2002 (Health Protection Agency (HPA) et al., 2009).

Harm-reduction initiatives established back in the 1980s to reduce the spread of the HIV infection in injecting drug users included engagement of and education for problematic drug users about safer drug-using practices and the introduction of new services such as needle exchanges. These services remain to this day. It is likely that these types of harm-reduction initiatives have kept the incidence of HIV among injectors in the UK relatively low (Paylor and Orgel, 2004). Unfortunately, harm-reduction measures that appear to have been effective in reducing the incidence of HIV in the drug-injecting population, have not worked as well for HCV.

HCV is a bloodborne virus that affects the liver causing chronic infection, cirrhosis and cancer (HPA et al., 2009). The risk of catching it appears to be much greater than with HIV, and because of this it is the most important disease affecting injecting drug users. While education aimed at reducing the incidence of HIV included making sure that people knew that they should have clean needles, it also included a 'cleaning regime' for injecting equipment (see Exchange Supplies, n.d.).

It appears that these types of regimes are not stringent enough to get rid of HCV, primarily because people are not aware that as well as cleaning the needles and syringes (as suggested for HIV), all other paraphernalia should also be cleaned (spoons, filters and water) (Paylor and Orgel, 2004). HCV is also more easily spread through paraphernalia associated with snorting drugs (paper, paper currency/notes or straws), and sharing of pipes used to smoke drugs where there is the potential for cuts, burns and bleeding (Paylor and Mack, 2009). It is thought that the majority of people who are infected with HCV are unaware that they have it because they have little if any symptoms and it is slow to flourish in the body. It can take between 10 and 40 years for serious liver disease to develop. The estimates of those infected in the UK therefore vary from between 250,000 and 600,000 because so many people are undiagnosed (Paylor and Mack, 2009: 2). According to the Advisory Council on the Misuse of Drugs (2009), 80 per cent of those infected with HCV are likely to have been infected through injecting drug use, and up to 50 per cent of current injecting drug users are likely to have HCV; most of whom will not know they have it. Social workers practising in the physical health care setting may work with service users who have HIV or HCV and it is essential that they know the links between these viruses and problematic substance use.

Key guidance and policy

The most useful guidance written to cover working with people who experience pain and problematic substance use is *Pain and Substance Misuse: Improving the Patient Experience* (British Pain Society, 2007). This document (which was due for review in 2010) provides non-specialists with the appropriate information they need to manage the pain of people who may currently or previously have experienced problematic substance use. While primarily aimed at medical professionals, this document is also extremely useful for social workers working in this practice setting. It provides specific information about this service user group, the law relating to prescribed medication, and relevant clinical issues for this complex work. For reference to this guidance, please see the Further reading section of this chapter.

Guidance and policy relating to HIV and HCV in the UK varies across England and the devolved governments of Scotland, Wales and Northern Ireland; however, it is not within the scope of this chapter to elaborate on each of these. The provision of services for bloodborne viruses is addressed in a number of national action plans and various guidance documents. These documents include (but are not limited to): *The National Strategy for Sexual Health and HIV* (DoH, 2001); the *Department of Health Action Plan: HIV-Related Stigma and Discrimination* (DoH, 2006b); *HIV in Healthcare* (National AIDS Trust, 2005); *HIV Action Plan* in Scotland, (2009); the *Hepatitis C Action Plan for England* (DoH, 2004); in Scotland a *Hepatitis C Action Plan* (initiated in 2006, and its second phase launched in May 2008); an *Action Plan for the Prevention, Management and Control of Hepatitis C in Northern Ireland* (2007); and, in Wales, a consultation on a proposed bloodborne viral hepatitis action plan held in the summer of 2009 (Health Protection Agency et al., 2009: 6).

A further key document *The Primary Prevention of Hepatitis C among Injecting Drug Users* (Advisory Council on the Misuse of Drugs, 2009) provides key recommendations for services in the bid to reduce the number of new HCV infections. Some of these recommendations include the need for an increase in the availability of sterile injecting equipment (especially to those receiving substitution therapy), more testing of at-risk groups, and training for staff so that they can do these tests as well as an evaluation of the effectiveness of education and harm-reduction strategies.

Concern abounds about the ineffectiveness of much of this policy and guidance, especially in relation to HCV. According to the All-Party Parliamentary Hepatology Group (APPHG) (2008), while the Scottish government's response to HCV should be commended, the English HCV action plan has thus far been ineffective. The English action plan has not yet yielded the necessary results as most Primary Care Trusts (PCTs) had only partially implemented the action plan at the time of the APPHG review, and some had not implemented it at all (p. 5). The group also expressed real concern about the delay in the launch of the Welsh HCV action plan (APPHG, 2008: 5). The APPHG in finding fault with current action plans made some of their own recommendations about HCV policy and guidance development. These recommendations included the need for detailed planning, accountability (targets and benchmarks), a robust governance structure, managed care networks, improved infrastructure and a co-ordinated approach to tackling HCV and Hepatitis B together.

Effective social work with problematic substance use, pain, HCV and HIV

The dual challenge of effectively and safely managing long-term persistent or palliative pain for the person who has problematic opioid use and may or may not also be on prescribed substitute medication (for example, methadone) is a complex one. While not the direct role of the social worker, it is one that the social worker working in these practice settings needs to be aware of as they support the service user with the psychosocial consequences of this pain and problematic substance use. Pain can have significant affective (emotional) and cognitive influences as well as social and environmental consequences. It is likely that the social work role in these instances will be around these issues alongside any concerns about problematic substance use that can significantly influence the service user's well-being.

Because of the nature of problematic substance use it is essential that social workers and other health professionals are aware of the possibility of service users diverting their medication (selling it, giving it away), or the prescribers' practices being a target for drug diversion (theft and/or prescription fraud). Social workers must be equally aware, however, of any discrimination faced by people with histories of problematic substance use when seeking health services that may result in them not getting adequate care and/or pain relief.

Social workers working with service users who experience pain should also be aware of the possibility that any service user who is prescribed pain mediation can become dependent on this, regardless of whether they have a history of problematic substance use. When prescribing medication prescribers are usually very careful to explain this likelihood, but if service users have ongoing questions or concerns about this, it is important that social workers can answer them.

Social workers may want to put in place relapse prevention plans (see Chapter 12) to lessen the likelihood of a return to old behaviours for people who have had previous problematic substance use and are being prescribed pain medication. If problematic substance use does occur again, social workers can be there in support of service users to act fast to help stop problem behaviours becoming entrenched. Using some of the models and strategies outlined in Part 3 of this book may also be useful. Referral to specialist 'substance misuse' services may be required for these services users, so an ongoing and close relationship with local specialist and/or peer-led support services will be important when referrals are necessary.

According to Paylor and Mack (2009: 1), 'Social care workers, particularly those working with physically disabled adults or older adults, will find themselves with vastly increased caseloads as HCV diagnoses increase.' When working with people who have been diagnosed with HCV or HIV, or who are at risk of having these viruses and are going to be tested, there are a number of key roles for the social worker in the health care setting. While each individual and their family will have different presenting needs, the key tasks of the social worker will include:

- Taking a non-judgemental and non-stigmatising approach.
- Using a motivational approach to encourage testing or reduce substance use.
- Accessing financial support for additional costs such as transport, dietary requirements, and homecare (through accessing direct payments and/or benefits such as Disability Living Allowance or Carer's Allowance).
- Giving service users information about safe injecting practices, transmission risks and how to access needle exchange services.
- Referral to specialist services that can test.
- Supporting service users undergoing testing.
- Providing educational material about testing and what the results mean.
- Providing educational material about both fatigue and depression (major symptoms of HCV).
- Providing general educational material about the viruses (for example, that drinking alcohol for those with HCV and/or while receiving treatment is contraindicated).
- Supporting carers.
- Supporting service users to adhere to treatment (medication and otherwise).
- Helping service users access peer support or a buddy system. (Paylor and Mack, 2009)

Coupled with these key tasks (and the above is not an exhaustive list), the social worker may also want to use some of the relevant practice models outlined in Part 3 of this book.

Case study – the specialist hepatitis C social worker (Department of Health, 2002)

This example of improving services and practice for people experiencing HCV is outlined in *Hepatitis C Strategy in England* (Department of Health, 2002); however, this case study could relate to any relevant health care setting where HCV is treated. An Infectious Disease Unit at a hospital and the local City Council collaborated to employ a HCV specialist social worker to support clients referred to the hepatitis C clinic. The Infectious Diseases Unit offers a comprehensive clinical service for outpatient and inpatient care of individuals infected with HIV, hepatitis, tuberculosis and tropical infections. It is supported by medical staff, a clinical nurse specialist, a dietician, a psychologist and social workers. It also provides specialist counselling, a family clinic and HIV and hepatitis testing as required. The specialist HCV social worker provides a wide range of psychosocial supports, including pre- and post-test discussions; information about HCV, including risk reduction; advice on housing, financial and employment issues; liaison with other agencies such as drugs and mental health services; adherence to treatment (medication and otherwise); home visits; and facilitation a self-help group (p. 37). There is certainly a role for social work in working with people who have bloodborne viruses such as HCV as there are a number of psychosocial issues that arise when people are diagnosed. The specialist social worker must have an informed understanding of the link between problematic substance use, injecting drug use and HCV. Reducing the harms associated with injecting drug use and working closely with local 'substance misuse' teams is paramount as it is estimated that up to 80 per cent of those infected with HCV have been infected due to the sharing of injecting drug using equipment.

Summary

Due to the nature of problematic substance use, it is likely that at some stage problematic users will develop some negative health effects due to their use. Social workers working in health related practice need to be aware of a variety of physical health problems that may result as well as the complex issues associated with pain and problematic substance use. There are a number of key concerns for service users who experience pain and require pain medication. First, it is paramount that problematic substance users receive enough pain relief and that they are not left in pain due to inadequate assessment of their substance use, or because prescribers are overly concerned with diversion of the medication or untrusting of service users. While social workers do need to be aware of the potential for service users to divert their pain medication, as it can be worth a lot of money on the black market, this potential should be mitigated wherever possible by the prescriber and is not of primary concern in the social work role. Second, social workers need to be aware of, and able to explain to their service user, the difference between using medication as prescribed and becoming physically dependent on it, and developing problematic substance use. Problematic substance use only occurs when a number of other psychological and social factors are present alongside aberrant use of the medication. Third, social workers need to closely monitor and support service users who may have had previous problematic substance use and who are concerned that being prescribed pain medication may result in their 'relapsing' into old substance-using behaviours.

Two of the main bloodborne viruses that are associated with drug use and specifically injecting drug use are HIV and HCV. These viruses can be passed from user to user by the sharing of drug-using equipment (needles, syringes, spoons, water, filters). HCV is the biggest concern because it is estimated that approximately half of all injecting drug users in the UK have HCV, and many of them will not be aware that they have it. When working with service users who have HIV/AIDS and/or HCV, it is imperative that social workers are alerted to the possibility of continued substance use and are aware of the negative health effects this may have on the service user, over and above any symptoms they may have developed. Working with service users to reduce their own substance use as well as educating them in harm-reduction measures (not sharing needles, using condoms) to decrease the likelihood of passing the infection on is paramount.

Reflections

How would you feel discussing a service user's medication with them?

Do you think that you would feel confident enough discussing potential dependence and/or problematic use of the medication?

What is your attitude towards people with bloodborne viruses like HIV?

Further readings

Advisory Council on the Misuse of Drugs (2009) *The Primary Prevention of Hepatitis C among Injecting Drug Users*. London: Crown Copyright.

British Pain Society (2007) *Pain and Substance Misuse: Improving the Patient Experience*. London: British Pain Society.

Paylor, I. and Mack, H. (2009) 'Gazing into the scarlet crystal ball: Social work and Hepatitis C', *British Journal of Social Work*, 40(7): 2291–307.

Conclusion

The majority of people who use substances, whether legal or illegal, do not develop problems as a result of this use. When problematic substance use does develop, however, it touches the lives of people in every corner of the UK and beyond. The use of mind-altering substances is not a new phenomenon. There is evidence that people from all around the world have used a variety of substances, and sometimes developed problems with this use, for centuries. Understanding the history of problematic substance use, prohibition and the criminalisation of drug users, as well as theories that seek to understand the phenomenon should help you understand the importance of anti-discriminatory social work practice with this service user group, and see past the demanding behaviours that may present. The reasons why people continue to use substances even though this use has become problematic will be many and varied, and no one has a complete understanding of problematic substance use that explains the phenomenon in all people, at all times. The issue is complex and often individualised, so working in partnership with service users and their families in order to understand the problem as they see it for themselves is integral.

It is often difficult to understand why people may continue to use substances problematically in the face of some particularly dire consequences and it may seem as though substance use may exacerbate some unscrupulous behaviour, but using substances in and of itself does not make people wicked, evil or corrupt. While there is no doubt that the use of substances can have negative effects on the individual, their families and the community, as Chapter 3 outlines, the stigma attached to people who use substances problematically is a social construction that is entirely unnecessary. People with problematic substance use deserve to be treated with dignity and respect, not with moral judgement or suspicion. As social workers we need to challenge the stigma associated with problematic substance use in our professional roles, as well as any personal prejudice we may hold.

It is vital that we recognise that we can seek to understand and work with people who have problematic substance use regardless of the type of social work that we do, and that while referral to specialist services may be required, social workers do not need to be specialist 'substance misuse' workers to deal with this issue. Using the key skills outlined in this book like screening and assessment, brief intervention, motivational approaches and relapse prevention, coupled with an understanding of the key concepts of 'recovery', harm reduction and abstinence will provide a foundation for your work with people who have problematic substance use, whoever they are and wherever you met with them.

Appendix A1   The Alcohol Use Disorders Identification Test: Self-Report Version

Source: Babor et al., 2001. Reproduced with permission from WHO

The Alcohol Use Disorders Identification Test: Self-Report Version PATIENT: Because alcohol use can affect your health and can interfere with certain medications and treatments, it is important that we ask some questions about your use of alcohol. Your answers will remain confidential so please be honest. Place an X in one box that best describes your answer to each question.						
Questions	**0**	**1**	**2**	**3**	**4**	
1. How often do you have a drink containing alcohol?	Never	Monthly or less	2–4 times a month	2–3 times a week	4 or more times a week	
2. How many drinks containing alcohol do you have on a typical day when you are drinking?	1 or 2	3 or 4	5 or 6	7 to 9	10 or more	
3. How often do you have six or more drinks on one occasion?	Never	Less than monthly	Monthly	Weekly	Daily or almost daily	
4. How often during the last year have you found that you were not able to stop drinking once you had started?	Never	Less than monthly	Monthly	Weekly	Daily or almost daily	
5. How often during the last year have you failed to do what was normally expected of you because of drinking?	Never	Less than monthly	Monthly	Weekly	Daily or almost daily	
6. How often during the last year hare you needed a first drink in the morning to get yourself going after a heavy drinking session?	Never	Less than monthly	Monthly	Weekly	Daily or almost daily	

Questions	0	1	2	3	4	
7. How often during the last year have you had a feeling of guilt or remorse after drinking?	Never	Less than monthly	Monthly	Weekly	Daily or almost daily	
8. How often during the last year have you been unable to remember what happened the night before because of your drinking?	Never	Less than monthly	Monthly	Weekly	Daily or almost daily	
9. Have you or someone else been injured because of your drinking?	No		Yes, but not in the last year		Yes, during the last year	
10. Has a relative, friend, doctor, or other health care worker been concerned about your drinking or suggested you cut down?	No		Yes, but not in the last year		Yes, during the last year	
					Total	

Appendix A2 The Alcohol Use Disorders Identification Test: Interview Version

Source: Babor et al., 2001. Reproduced with permission from WHO

The Alcohol Use Disorders Identification Test: Interview Version

Read questions as written. Record answers carefully. Begin the AUDIT by saying "Now I am going to ask you some questions about your use of alcoholic beverages during this past year". Explain what is meant by "alcoholic beverages" by using local examples of beer, wine, vodka, etc. Code answers in terms of "standard drinks". Place the correct answer number in the box at the right.

1. How often do you have a drink containing alcohol?

   (0) Never [Skip to Qs 9–10]
   (1) Monthly or less
   (2) 2 to 4 times a month
   (3) 2 to 3 times a week
   (4) 4 or more times a week

2. How many drinks containing alcohol do you have on a typical day when you are drinking?

   (0) 1 or 2
   (1) 3 or 4
   (2) 5 or 6
   (3) 7, 8, or 9
   (4) 10 or more

3. How often do you have six or more drinks on one occasion?

   (0) Never
   (1) Less than monthly
   (2) Monthly
   (3) Weekly
   (4) Daily or almost daily

   Skip to Questions 9 and 10 if Total Score for Questions 2 and 3 = 0

4. How often during the last year have you found that you were not able to stop drinking once you had started?

   (0) Never
   (1) Less than monthly
   (2) Monthly
   (3) Weekly
   (4) Daily or almost daily

5. How often during the last year have you failed to do what was normally expected from you because of drinking?

   (0) Never
   (1) Less than monthly
   (2) Monthly
   (3) Weekly
   (4) Daily or almost daily

6. How often during the last year have you needed a first drink in the morning to get yourself going after a heavy drinking session?

   (0) Never
   (1) Less than monthly
   (2) Monthly
   (3) Weekly
   (4) Daily or almost daily

7. How often during the last year have you had a feeling of guilt or remorse after drinking? (0) Never (1) Less than monthly (2) Monthly (3) Weekly (4) Daily or almost daily	9. Have you or someone else been injured as a result of your drinking? (0) No (2) Yes, but not in the last year (4) Yes, during the last year
8. How often during the last year have you been unable to remember what happened the night before because you had been drinking? (0) Never (1) Less than monthly (2) Monthly (3 Weekly (4) Dally or almost daily	10. Has a relative or friend or a doctor or another health worker been concerned about your drinking or suggested you cut down? (0) No (2) Yes, but not in the last year (4) Yes, during the last year

Record total of specific items here

If total is greater than recommended cut-off, consult User's Manual.

Appendix B

Source: Adapted from Skinner, H. (1982) 'The drug abuse screening test', *Addictive Behaviors*, 7: 363–71.
Available from www.drugslibrary.stir.ac.uk/documents/dast.pdf

DRUG USE QUESTIONNAIRE (DAST-10)

NAME: _____ Date:_____

The following questions concern information about your potential involvement with drugs excluding alcohol and tobacco during the past 12 months. Carefully read each countyment and decide if your answer is "YES" or "NO". Then, check the appropriate box beside the question.

When the words "drug abuse" are used, they mean the use of prescribed or over-the-counter medications used in excess of the directions and any non-medical use of any drugs. The various classes of drugs may include but are not limited to: cannabis (e.g., marijuana, hash), solvents (e.g., gas, paints etc....), tranquilizers (e.g., Valium), barbiturates, cocaine, and stimulants (e.g., speed), hallucinogens (e.g., LSD) or narcotics (e.g., Heroin). Remember that the questions do not include alcohol or tobacco.

Please answer every question. If you have difficulty with a countyment, then choose the response that is mostly right.

These questions refer to the past 12 months only.
YES NO

1. Have you used drugs other than those required for medical reasons?........
2. Do you abuse more than one drug at a time?..
3. Are you always able to stop using drugs when you want to?....................
4. Have you had "blackouts" or "flashbacks" as a result of drug use?...........
5. Do you ever feel bad or guilty about your drug use?................................
6. Does your spouse (or parent) ever complain about your involvement with drugs?..
7. Have you neglected your family because of your use of drugs?..................
8. Have you engaged in illegal activities in order to obtain drugs?..................

9. Have you ever experienced withdrawal symptoms (felt sick) when you stopped taking drugs?..

10. Have you had medical problems as a result of your drug use (e.g., memory loss, hepatitis, convulsions, bleeding etc....)?......................................

* DAST Score.....................................
* See scoring instructions for correct scoring procedure

DRUG USE QUESTIONNAIRE (DAST-10)

Administration & Interpretation

Instructions

The DAST-10 is a 10-item, yes/no, self-report instrument that has been shortened from the 28-item DAST and should take less than 8 minutes to complete. The DAST-10 was designed to provide a brief instrument for clinical screening and treatment evaluation and can be used with adults and older youth. It is strongly recommended that the SMAST be used along with the DAST-10 unless there is a clear indication that the client uses NO ALCOHOL at all. The answer options for each item are "YES" or "NO". The DAST-10 is a self-administered screening instrument.

Scoring and Interpretation – For the DAST-10, score 1 point for each question answered, "YES", except for question (3) for which a "NO" answer receives 1 point and (0) for a "YES". Add up the points and interpretations are as followed:

DAST-10
Score
Degree of Problem
Related to Drug Abuse
SuggestedAction
0 No problems reported None at this time.
1 – 2 Low Level Monitor, reassess at a later date.
3 – 5 Moderate Level Further investigation is required.
6 – 8 Substantial Level Assessment required.
9 – 10 Severe Level Assessment required.

Appendix C   The Twelve Steps of Alcoholics Anonymous

1. We admitted we were powerless over alcohol – that our lives had become unmanageable.
2. Came to believe that a Power greater than ourselves could restore us to sanity.
3. Made a decision to turn our will and our lives over to the care of God *as we understood Him*.
4. Made a searching and fearless moral inventory of ourselves.
5. Admitted to God, to ourselves, and to another human being the exact nature of our wrongs.
6. Were entirely ready to have God remove all these defects of character.
7. Humbly asked Him to remove our shortcomings.
8. Made a list of all persons we had harmed, and became willing to make amends to them all.
9. Made direct amends to such people wherever possible, except when to do so would injure them or others.
10. Continued to take personal inventory and when we were wrong promptly admitted it.
11. Sought through prayer and meditation to improve our conscious contact with God, *as we understood Him*, praying only for knowledge of His will for us and the power to carry that out.
12. Having had a spiritual awakening as the result of these Steps, we tried to carry this message to alcoholics, and to practice these principles in all our affairs.

Source: The Twelve Steps are reprinted with permission of Alcoholics Anonymous World Services, Inc. ('AAWS') Permission to reprint the Twelve Steps does not mean that AAWS has reviewed or approved the contents of this publication, or that AAWS necessarily agrees with the views expressed herein. AA is a programme of recovery from alcoholism *only* – use of the Twelve Steps in connection with programmes and activities which are patterned after AA, but which address other problems, or in any other non-AA context, does not imply otherwise.

References

Abel, E. (2001) 'The gin epidemic: much ado about what?', *Alcohol and Alcoholism*, 36(5): 401–5.

Addaction (2007) 'Social workers left out of drugs training equation', *Community Care*, 9 August.

Adfam (2010) *What Can I Do to Help?* [Online]. Available at: http://www.adfam.org.uk/what_can_i_do_to_help.html [accessed 30 July 2010].

Advisory Council on the Misuse of Drugs (ACMD) (2003) *Hidden Harm: Responding to the Needs of Children of Problem Drug Users*. London: ACMD.

Advisory Council on the Misuse of Drugs (ACMD) (2007) *Hidden Harm Three Years on: Realties, Challenges and Opportunities*. London: ACMD.

Advisory Council on the Misuse of Drugs (ACMD) (2009) *The Primary Prevention of Hepatitis C among Injecting Drug Users*. London: Home Office.

Ahmed, M. (2007) 'Social workers left out of drugs training equation', *Community Care*, 9 August.

Alcoholics Anonymous (2001) 'How it works', *Alcoholics Anonymous* (4th edn): 58–71. Alcoholics Anonymous World Services [Online]. Available at: http://www.aa.org/bigbookonline/en_bigbook_chapt5.pdf [accessed 20 October 2009].

All-Party Parliamentary Hepatology Group (APPHG) (2008) *Divided Nations: Tackling the Hepatitis C Challenge across the UK*. London: APPHG. [Online]. Available at: http://www.hepctrust.org.uk/Resources/HepC/HCV%20Reports/APPHG%20Report%20-%20Divided%20Nations.pdf [accessed 7 July 2010].

American National Institute on Drug Abuse (NIDA) (2008) *Preventing Drug Abuse among Children and Adolescents: Risk and Protective Factors*. NIDA [Online]. Available at: http://drugabuse.gov/scienceofaddiction/addiction.html [accessed 8 November 2010].

American Psychiatric Association (APA) (2000) *Diagnostic and Statistical Manual of Mental Disorders* (revised 4th edn). Washington, DC: APA.

Ashton, M. (2007) 'The new abstentionists', *DrugLink*, insert Dec./Jan. 2008.

Awiah, J., Butt, S. and Dorn, N. (1990) 'The last place I would go: Black people and drug services in Britain', *DrugLink*, Sept./Oct.: 14–15.

Babor, T. and Higgins-Biddle, J. (2001) *Brief Intervention for Hazardous and Harmful Drinking: A Manual for Use in Primary Care*. World Health Organization [Online]. Available at: http://whqlibdoc.who.int/hq/2001/WHO_MSD_MSB_01.6b.pdf [accessed 1 February 2010].

Babor, T.F., Higgins-Biddle, J.C., Saunders, J.B. and Monteiro, M.G (2001) *The Alcohol Use Disorders Identification Test (AUDIT): Guidelines for Use in Primary Care* (2nd edn). World Health Organization [Online]. Available at: http://whqlibdoc.who.int/hq/2001/who_msd_msb_01.6a.pdf [accessed 25 July 2010].

Baker, A., Boggs, T. and Lewin, T. (2001) 'Randomised controlled trial of brief cognitive-behavioural interventions among regular users of amphetamine', *Addiction*, 96: 1279–87.

Barber, J. (2002) *Social Work with Addictions.* Basingstoke: Palgrave Macmillan.

Beail, N. (1995) 'Outcome of psychoanalysis, psychoanalytic and psychodynamic psychotherapy with people with intellectual disabilities: A review',*Changes*, 13: 186–91.

Becker, J. and Duffy, C. (2002) *Women Drug Users and Drug Service Provision: Service Level Responses to Engagement and Retention.* London: Home Office.

Bennett, L. and O'Brien, P. (2007) 'Effects of co-ordinated services for drug abusing women who are victims of intimate partner violence', *Violence Against Women*, 13(4): 395–411.

Bennett, T. and Holloway, K. (2004) *Drug Use and Offending: Summary Results of the First Two Years of the NEW-ADAM Programme.* Research, Development and Statistics Directorate. London: Home Office.

Bennett, T. and Holloway, K. (2005) *Understanding Drugs, Alcohol and Crime.* Maidenhead: Open University Press.

Bhui, K., Warfa, N., Edonya, P., McKenzie K. and Bhugra D. (2007) 'Cultural competence in mental health care: a review of model evaluations', *BMC Health Services Research*, 7(1).

Bliss, D. and Pecukonis, E. (2009) 'Screening and Brief Intervention Practice Model for social workers in non-substance-abuse practice settings', *Journal of Social Work Practice in Addictions*, 9(1): 21–40.

Blum, K., Noble, E. and Sheridan, P. (1990) 'Allelic association of human domain D2 receptor gene in alcoholism', *Journal of the American Medical Association*, 263: 2055–60.

Bootle, K. (2007) Personal communication with Training Officer at Southwark Social Services.

Borkman, T. (2008) 'The Twelve-Step Recovery Model of AA: A voluntary mutual help association', in M. Galanter and L. Kaskutas (eds), *Recent Developments in Alcoholism. Volume 18: Research on Alcoholics Anonymous and Spirituality in Addiction Recovery.* New York: Springer Science and Business Media.

Brako, M. and Saleh, A. (2001) *Community Engagement Project: Report of the Drugs Misuse Needs Assessment Carried out by AHEAD (African Health for Empowerment and Development) amongst the Sierra Leonean and Ugandan Community in Greenwich and Bexley Borough.* London, Department of Health/Preston, Centre for Ethnicity and Health/ University of Central Lancashire.

Brems, C., Johnson, M.., Neal, D. and Freemon, M. (2004) 'Childhood abuse history and substance use among men and women receiving detoxification services', *American Journal of Drug and Alcohol Abuse*, 4: 799–821.

Brennan, P., Schutte, K. and Moos, R. (2005) 'Pain and use of alcohol to manage pain: Prevalence and 3-year outcomes among older problem and non-problem drinkers', *Addiction*, 100: 777–86.

British Pain Society (2007) *Pain and Substance Misuse: Improving the Patient Experience.* London: The British Pain Society.

Brown, G. and Coldwell, B. (2006) 'Developing a controlled drinking programme for people with learning disabilities living in conditions of medium security', *Addiction Research and Theory*, 14(1): 87–95.

Brown, R. and Rounds, L. (1995) 'Conjoint screening questionnaires for alcohol and drug abuse', *Wisconsin Medical Journal*, 94: 135–40.

Brownlee, K., Spakes, A., Saini, M., O'Hare, R., Kortes-Miller, K. and Graham, J. (2005) 'Heterosexism among social work students', *Social Work Education*, 24(5): 485–94.

Bywater, J. and Jones, R. (2007) *Sexuality and Social Work.* Exeter: Learning Matters.

Cabinet Office (2008) *Think Family: Improving the Life Chances of Families at Risk*. London: Cabinet Office.

Carson DeWitt, R. (ed) (2009) *Encyclopedia of Drugs, Alcohol and Addictive Behavior* (2nd edn). Durham, NC: Macmillan Reference USA.

Chong, M., Wolff, K., Wise, K., Tanton, C., Winstock, C. and Silber, E. (2006) 'Cannabis use in patients with multiple sclerosis', *Multiple Sclerosis*, 12: 646–51.

Christie, G., Marsh, R., Sheridan, J., Wheeler, A., Suaalii-Sauni, T., Black, S. and Butler, R. (2007) 'The Substances and Choices Scale (SACS) – the development and testing of a new alcohol and other drug screening and outcome measurement instrument for young people', *Addiction*, 102: 1390–8.

Clawson, R. (2008) 'Working with disabled children and adults', in K. Wilson, G. Ruch, A. Brammer, R. Clawson, B. Littlechild, I. Paylor and R. Smith (eds), *Social Work: An Introduction to Contemporary Practice*. London: Pearson Education Limited, pp. 537–63.

Cleaver, H., Unell, I. and Aldgate, J. (1999) *Children's Needs–Parenting Capacity: The Impact of Parental Mental Illness, Problem Alcohol and Drug Use and Domestic Violence on Children's Development*. London: The Stationery Office.

Collins, S. (1999) 'Treatment and therapeutic interventions: psychological approaches', *Tizard Learning Disability Review*, 4(2): 20–7.

Colvin, L. and Orgel, M. (2008) 'The forgotten co-morbidity: chronic pain and substance misuse – an update of the issues and exploration of collaborative clinical solutions', 2008 Drug Treatment Conference. Glasgow, Scotland.

Commission for Social Care Inspection (CSCI) (2008) *Putting People First: Equality and Diversity Matters: Providing Appropriate Services for Lesbian, Gay, Bisexual and Transgender People*. London: CSCI.

Cormier, R., Dell, C. and Poole, N. (2003) *Women's Health Surveillance Report. A Multi-Dimensional Look at the Health of Canadian Women*. Ontario: Institute for Health Information.

Cox, G. and Lawless, M. (2000) *Making Contact: An Evaluation of a Syringe Exchange Programme*. Dublin: Merchants' Quay Project.

Cox, G. and Rampes, H. (2003) *Adverse Effects of Khat: A Review* [Online]. Available at: http://apt.rcpsych.org/cgi/reprint/9/6/456.pdf [accessed 6 November 2010].

Crawford, K. and Walker, J. (2003) *Social Work and Human Development*. Exeter: Learning Matters.

Dalrympole, J. and Burke, B. (2006) *Anti-Oppressive Practice, Social Care and the Law*. (2nd edn). Buckingham: Open University Press.

Davenport-Hines, R. (2004) *The Pursuit of Oblivion: A Social History of Drugs*. London: Phoenix Press.

Davies, M. and Petersen, T. (2002) 'Motivationally based interventions for behavior change', in T. Petersen and A. McBride (eds), *Working with Substance Misusers: A Guide to Theory and Practice*. London: Routledge.

Department for Children, Schools and Families (DfCSF) (n.d.) *Drug Use Screening Tool* [Online]. Available at: http://www.dcsf.gov.uk/datastats1/guidelines/children/pdf/DUST-DFES.pdf.

Department for Children, Schools and Families (DfCSF) (2010) *Working Together to Safeguard Children: A Guide to Interagency Working to Safeguard and Promote the Welfare of Children*. London: HM Government.

Department for Children, Schools and Families (DfCSF)/National Treatment Agency (NTA)/Department of Health (DoH) (2009) *Joint Guidance on Development of*

Local Protocols between Drug and Alcohol Treatment Services and Local Safeguarding and Family Service. London: DfCSF/NTA/DoH.

Department for Education and Skills (DfES) (2003) *Every Child Matters.* London: DfES.

Department for Education and Skills (DfES) (2004) *Every Child Matters: Change for Children.* London: DfES.

Department of Health (DoH) (1998) *Modernising Social Services.* London: Department of Health.

Department of Health (DoH) (2001) *The National Strategy for Sexual Health and HIV.* London: Department of Health.

Department of Health (DoH) (2002) *Mental Health Policy Implementation Guide: Dual Diagnosis Good Practice Guide.* London: Department of Health [Online]. Available at: http://www.dh.gov.uk/prod_consum_dh/groups/dh_digitalassets/@ dh/@en/documents/digitalasset/dh_4060435.pdf [accessed 25 July 2010].

Department of Health (DoH) (2004) *Hepatitis C Action Plan for England.* London: Department of Health [Online]. Available at: www.dh.gov.uk/assetRoot/04/08/47/ 13/04084713.pdf [accessed 7 July 2010].

Department of Health (DoH) (2006a) *Dual Diagnosis in Mental Health Inpatient and Day Hospital Settings: Guidance on the Assessment and Management of Patients in Mental Health Inpatient and Day Hospital Settings who have Mental Ill-Health and Substance Use Problems.* London: Department of Health [Online]. Available at: http:// www.dh.gov.uk/prod_consum_dh/groups/dh_digitalassets/@dh/@en/documents/ digitalasset/dh_062652.pdf [accessed 25 July 2010].

Department of Health (DoH) (2006b) *Department of Health Action Plan: HIV-Related Stigma and Discrimination.* London: Department of Health.

Department of Health (DoH) (2008) *Refocusing the Care Programme Approach: Policy and Positive Practice Guidance.* London: Department of Health.

Department of Health (DoH) (2009) *New Horizons: A Shared Vision for Mental Health.* London: Department of Health [Online]. Available at: http://www.dh.gov. uk/prod_consum_dh/groups/dh_digitalassets/@dh/@en/documents/digitalasset/ dh_109708.pdf [accessed 25 July 2010].

Department of Health (DoH), Home Office, Department for Education and Skills (DfES), Department of Culture, Media and Sport (DCMS) (2007) *Safe. Sensible. Sociable. The Next Steps in the National Alcohol Strategy.* London: Home Office [Online]. Available at: http://www.dh.gov.uk/en/Publicationsandstatistics/ Publications/PublicationsPolicy AndGuidance/DH_075218 [accessed 25 July 2010].

Department of Health (DoH), Social Services and Public Policy (2006) *New Strategic Direction for Alcohol and Drugs.* Belfast: Department of Health, Social Services and Public Policy.

Dodds, C., Keogh, P. and Hickson, F. (2005) *It Makes Me Sick: Hetereosexism, Homophobia and the Health of Gay Men and Bisexual Men.* Sigma Research [Online]. Available at: http://www.sigmaresearch.org.uk/files/report2005a.pdf [accessed 25 July 2010].

Dominelli, L. (1998) 'Anti-oppressive practice in context', in R. Adams, L. Dominelli and M. Payne (eds), *Social Work: Themes, Issues and Critical Debates.* Houndmills: Macmillan Press, pp. 3–22.

Dominellli, L. (2002) *Anti-Oppressive Social Work Theory and Practice.* Basingstoke: Palgrave Macmillan.

Donovan, D. and Floyd, A. (2008) 'Facilitating involvement in twelve-step programs', in M. Galanter and L. Kaskutas (eds), *Recent Developments in Alcoholism. Volume 18: Research on Alcoholics Anonymous and Spirituality in Addiction Recovery.* New York: Springer Science and Business Media, pp. 303–20.

Drake, R. (2007) 'Dual diagnosis', *Psychiatry*, 6(90):381–4.

Drug Policy Alliance (2001) *The Racial History of US Drug Prohibition* [Online]. Available at: http://www.drugpolicy.org/about/position/race_paper_history.cfm [accessed 7 August 2008].

DrugScope (2009) *Drug Treatment at the Crossroads: What it's for, Where it's at and How to Make it Even Better.* London: DrugScope.

DrugScope (2010) *Khat: What is Khat?* [Online]. Available at: http://www.drugscope.org.uk/resources/drugsearch/drugsearchpages/khat [accessed 6 November 2010].

Emmett, D. and Nice, G. (2006) *Understanding Street Drugs: A Handbook of Substance Misuse for Parents, Teachers and Other Professionals.* London: Jessica Kingsley Publishers.

European Monitoring Centre for Drugs and Drug Addiction (EMCDDA) (2006) *Annual Report 2006. Selected Issue 2: A Gender Perspective on Drug Use and Responding to Drug Problems.* Luxembourg: EMCDDA.

Ewing, J. (1984) 'Detecting alcoholism: The CAGE questionnaire', *Journal of the American Medical Association*, 252: 1905–7.

Exchange Supplies (n.d.) *Cleaning Works* [Online]. Available at: http://www.exchange-supplies.org/shopdisp_P106.php [accessed 25 July 2010].

Fagan, J., Naughton, L. and Smyth, B. (2008) 'Opiate-dependent adolescents in Ireland: A descriptive study at treatment entry', *Irish Journal of Psychiatric Medicine*, 25: 46–51.

Farrall, S. (2002) *Rethinking what Works with Offenders: Probation, Social Context and Desistance from Crime.* Cullompton: Willan Publishing.

Farrell, M., Gowing, L., Marsden, J., Ling, W. and Ali, R. (2005) 'Effectiveness of drug dependence treatment in HIV prevention', *International Journal of Drug Policy*, 16: 67–75.

Fischer, J., Jenkins, N., Bloor, M., Neale, J. and Berney, L. (2007) *Drug User Involvement in Treatment Decisions.* London: Joseph Rowntree Foundation.

Forrester, D. and Harwin, J. (2006) 'Parental substance misuse and child care social work: Findings from the first stage of a study of 100 families', *Child and Family Social Work*, 11: 325–35.

Fountain, J. (2009a) *Issues Surrounding Drug Use and Drug Services among the Black African Communities in England.* London: NTA and University of Central Lancashire. [Online]. Available at: http://www.nta.nhs.uk/uploads/2_black_african_final.pdf [accessed 8 May 2010].

Fountain, J. (2009b) *Issues Surrounding Drug Use and Drug Services among the Black Caribbean Communities in England.* London: NTA and University of Central Lancashire. [Online]. Available at: http://www.nta.nhs.uk/uploads/3_black_carib-bean_final.pdf [accessed 8 May 2010].

Fountain, J. (2009c) *Issues Surrounding Drug Use and Drug Services among the Chinese and Vietnamese Communities in England.* London: NTA and University of Central Lancashire. [Online]. Available at: http://www.nta.nhs.uk/uploads/5_chinese_vietnamese_final.pdf [accessed 8 May 2010].

Fountain, J. (2009d) *Issues Surrounding Drug Use and Drug Services among the Kurdish, Turkish Cypriot and Turkish Communities in England.* London: NTA and

University of Central Lancashire. [Online]. Available at: http://www.nta.nhs.uk/uploads/4_kurdish_turkish_cypriot_turkish_final.pdf [accessed 8 May 2010].

Fountain, J. (2009e) *Issues Surrounding Drug Use and Drug Services among the South Asian Communities in England*. London: NTA and University of Central Lancashire. [Online]. Available at: http://www.nta.nhs.uk/uploads/1_south_asian_final.pdf [accessed 8 May 2010].

FRANK (2005) 'Talking diversity', *FRANK Action Update*, 11 April: 1–48.

Fraser, C., McIntyre, A. and Manby, M. (2009) 'Exploring the impact of parental drug/alcohol problems on children and parents in a Midlands County in 2005/06', *British Journal of Social Work*, 39: 846–66.

Furnham, A. and Thompson, L. (1996) 'Lay theories of heroin addiction', *Social Science and Medicine*, 43: 29–40.

Galvani, S. (2007) 'Refusing to listen: Are we failing the needs of people with alcohol and drug problems?', *Social Work Education*, 26(7): 697–707.

Galvani, S. and Forrester, D. (2008) *What Works in Training Social Workers about Drug and Alcohol Use? A Survey of Student Learning and Readiness to Practice*. London: University of Warwick and University of Bedfordshire. [Online]. Available at: http://www.beds.ac.uk/departments/appliedsocialstudies/staff/sarah-galvani/galvani-forrester-horeport2008pdf [accessed 25 July 2010].

Galvani, S. and Forrester, D. (2009) *Social Work and Substance Use: Teaching the Basics*. London: SWAP.

George, W. (1989) 'Marlatt and Gordon's relapse prevention model: A cognitice behavioural approach to understanding and preventing relapse', *Journal of Chemical dependence Treatment*, 2: 125–52.

Ghaffer, O. and Feinstein, A. (2008) 'Multiple sclerosis and cannabis: A cognitive and psychiatric study', *Neurology*, 71: 164–9.

Gossop, M. (2000) *Living with Drugs* (5th edn). Aldershot: Ashgate.

Gossop, M. (2002) 'Relapse prevention', in T. Petersen and A. McBride (eds), *Working with Substance Misusers: A Guide to Theory and Practice*. London: Routledge, pp. 189–95.

Greater London Authority (GLA) (2004) *Young Refugees and Asylum Seekers in Greater London: Vulnerability to Problematic Drug Use*. London: Greater London Authority. [Online]. Available at: http://www.drugsandalcohol.ie/6035/2/youngrefugeessummary.pdf [accessed 31 March 2010].

Greater London Authority (GLA) (2005) *Domestic Violence and Substance Use: Overlapping Issues in Separate Services?* London: GLA.

Greaves, A., Best, D., Day, E. and Foster, A. (2009) 'Young people in coerced drug treatment: Does the UK Drug Intervention Programme provide as useful and effective service to young offenders?', *Addiction Research and Theory*, 17(1): 17–29.

Greenfield, S., Brooks, A., Gordon, S., Green, C., Kropp, F., McHugh, R., Lincoln, M., Hien, D. and Miele, G. (2007) 'Substance abuse treatment entry, retention, and outcome in women: A review of the literature', *Drug and Alcohol Dependence*, 86: 1–21.

Greenfield, S., Manwani, S. and Nargiso, J. (2003) 'Epidemiology of substance use disorders in women', *Obstetrics and Gynaecology Clinic of North America*, 30(3): 414–46.

Gregory, M. (2006) 'The offender as citizen: Socially inclusive strategies for working with offenders within the community', in K. Gorman, M. Gregory, M. Hayles and N. Parton (eds), *Constructive Work with Offenders*. London: Jessica Kingsley, pp. 49–67.

Haden, M. (2006) 'The evolution of the four pillars: Acknowledging the harms of drug prohibition', *International Journal of Drug Policy*, 17(2): 124–6.

Hafford-Letchfield, T. and Nelson, A. (2008) 'Closeness equals pathology: Working with issues of sexual desire and intimacy within the substance misuse field', *Diversity in Health and Social Care*, 5: 215–24.

Harris, S. (2003) 'Inter-agency practice and professional collaboration: The case of drug education and prevention', *Journal of Education Policy*, 18(3): 303–14.

Hatton, K. (2008) *New Directions in Social Work Practice*. Exeter: Learning Matters.

Havell, C. (2004) *Khat Use in Somali, Ethiopian, and Yemeni Communities in England: Issues and Solutions*. London: Turning Point.

Hawkings, C. and Gilburt, H. (2004) *Dual Diagnosis Toolkit: Mental Health and Substance Misuse*. London: Rethink and Turning Point. [Online]. Available at: http://www.rethink.org/dualdiagnosis/toolkit.html [accessed 25 July 2010].

Health Protection Agency (HPA), Health Protection Scotland, National Public Health Service for Wales, CDSC Northern Ireland, CRDHB (2009) *Shooting Up: Infections among Injecting Drug Users in the United Kingdom 2008*. London: Health Protection Agency.

Health and Social Care Information Centre (2010) *Statistics on Alcohol: England 2010*. London: Health and Social Care Information Centre.

Heather, N. (1998) 'Using brief opportunities to change', in W. Miller and N. Heather (eds), *Treating Addictive Behaviours* (2nd edn). New York: Plenum.

Hettema J., Steele, J. and Miller, W. (2005) 'Motivational interviewing', *Annual Review of Clinical Psychology*, 1: 91–111.

Hill, R., Harris, J., Cloherty, M., Cooper, W., Graham, J and Wanigaratne, S. (n.d.) *A Compendium of Psychological Therapies for Preventing Relapse*. London: South London and Maudsley Trust.

Hoare, J. (2009) *Drug Misuse Declared: Findings from the 2008/09 British Crime Survey, England and Wales*. London: Home Office.

Hohman, M., Clapp, J. and Carrillo, T. (2006) 'Development and validation of the Alcohol and Other Drug Identification (AODI) scale', *Journal of Social Work Practice in the Addictions*, 6(3): 3–12.

Hollins, S. and Sinason, V. (2000) 'Psychotherapy, learning disabilities and trauma: New perspectives', *British Journal of Psychiatry*, 176: 32–6.

Holloway, K., Bennett, T. and Farrington, D. (2005) *The Effectiveness of Criminal Justice and Treatment Programmes in Reducing Drug-Related Crime: A Systemic Review*. London: Home Office.

Homayoun, S., Best, D., Witton, J., Manning, V. and Day, E. (n.d.) *Is the Harm Still Hidden? Inconsistent Responses to Hidden Harm in Specialist Addiction Services* [Online]. Available at: http://learnx.iriss.ac.uk/IntraLibrary?command=open-previewandlearning_object_key=i4631n182755t [accessed 21 June 2010].

Home Office (1998) *Tackling Drugs to Build a Better Britain* [Online]. Available at: http://www.archive.official-documents.co.uk/document/cm39/3945/problem.htm [accessed 5 April 2009].

Home Office (2002) *The Updated Drug Strategy for England*. London: Home Office.

Home Office (2005) *Developing Peer-Led Support for Individuals Leaving Substance Misuse Treatment: Emerging Themes and Findings from Five Peer-Led Support Projects*. London: Home Office.

Home Office (2006) *Home Office Diversity Manual*. London: Home Office.

Home Office (2008) *Drugs: Protecting Families and Communities: The 2008 Drug Strategy*. London: HM Government.

Home Office (2009a) *Drugs and the Law* [Online]. Available at: http://www.homeoffice.gov.uk/drugs/drug-law/ [accessed 25 July 2010].

Home Office (2009b) *Crime in England and Wales 2008/09. Volume 1: Findings from the British Crime Survey and Police Recorded Crime.* London: Home Office.

Home Office (2010) *Drug Strategy 2010. Reducing Demand, Restricting Supply, Building Recovery: Supporting People to Live a Drug Free Life.* London: Home Office.

House of Commons Science and Technology Committee (2006) *Drug Classification: Making a Hash of it? Fifth Report of Session 2005–06.* London: The Stationery Office. [Online]. Available at: http://www.publications.parliament.uk/pa/cm200506/cmselect/cmsctech/1031/1031.pdf [accessed 25 July 2010].

Hser, Y., Huang, D., Teruya, C. and Anglin, D. (2003) 'Gender comparisons of drug abuse treatment outcomes and predictors', *Drug and Alcohol Dependence,* 72: 255–64.

Hughes, L. (2006) *Closing the Gap: A Capability Framework for Working Effectively with People with Combined Mental Health and Substance Use Problems (Dual Diagnosis).* London: Department of Health.

Hunt, N., Trace, M. and Bewley-Taylor, D. (2006) *Reducing Drug Related Harm to Health: An Overview of Global Evidence.* Oxford: Beckley Foundation Drug Policy Programme.

Institute of Alcohol Studies (IAS) (2009) *Alcohol and the Elderly.* Cambridge: IAS [online] http://www.ias.org.uk/resources/factsheets/elderly.pdf [accessed 14 January].

Isse, H. (2004) *Khat Training Workshop* [Online]. Available at: www.fdap.org.uk/fdapevents/documents/Khat.ppt [accessed 6 November 2010].

Jarvis, T., Tebutt, J., Mattick, R. and Shand, F. (eds) (2005) *Treatment Approaches for Alcohol and Drug Dependence: An Introductory Guide* (2nd edn). Chichester: John Wiley and Sons.

Jellinek, E. (1960) *The Disease Concept of Alcoholism.* New Haven, CT: Hillhouse Press.

Kalunta-Crumpton, A. (2003) 'Black people, drugs and criminal justice', *DrugLink,* May/June: 13–14.

Kellogg, S. (2003) 'On "gradualism" and the building of the harm reduction-abstinence continuum', *Journal of Substance Abuse Treatment,* 25(4): 241–7.

Keogh, P., Reid, D., Bourne, A., Weatherburn, P., Hickson, F., Jessup, K. and Hammond, G. (2009) *Wasted Opportunities: Problematic Alcohol and Drug Use among Gay and Bisexual Men.* Sigma Research [Online]. Available at: http://www.sigmaresearch.org.uk/files/report2009c.pdf [accessed 25 July 2010].

Khan, F. (1999) *Drus Prevention, Care and Treatment in Greater London Area, Focusing on Race.* London: Race and Drugs Project, T3E/University of Middlesex.

Klag, S., O'Callaghan, F. and Creed, P. (2005) 'The use of legal coercion in the treatment of substance abusers: An overview and critical analysis of thirty years of research', *Substance Use and Misuse,* 40: 1777–95.

Kroll, B. (2004) 'Living with an elephant: Growing up with parental substance misuse', *Child and Family Social Work,* 9: 129–40.

Kvaternik, I. and Grebenc, V. (2009) 'The role of social work in the field of mental health: Dual diagnoses as a challenge for social workers', *European Journal of Social Work,* 12(4): 509–21.

Laming, Lord (2003) *The Victoria Climbie Inquiry Report.* London: Crown Copyright. [Online]. Available at: http://www.dh.gov.uk/prod_consum_dh/groups/dh_digitalassets/documents/digitalasset/dh_110711.pdf [accessed 4 August 2008].

Larimer, M., Palmer, R. and Marlatt, G. (1999) 'Relapse prevention: An overview of Marlatt's Cognitive Behavioural Model', *Alcohol Research and Health,* 23(2): 151–60.

Lart, R. (2006) 'Drugs and health policy', in R. Hughes, R. Lart and P. Highgate (eds), *Drugs: Policy and Politics.* Maidenhead: Open University Press, pp. 92–112.

Levine, H. (1978) 'The discovery of addiction: Changing conception of habitual drunkenness in America', *Journal of Studies on Alcohol*, 39: 143–74.

Littlechild, B. and Smith, R. (2008) 'Social work with young offenders', in K. Wilson, G. Ruch, M. Lymbery and A. Cooper (eds), *Social Work: An Introduction to Contemporary Practice*. Harlow: Pearson Longman Education, pp. 512–36.

Lloyd, C. (2010) 'How we got to where we are now', in J. Barlow (ed.), *Substance Misuse: The Implications of Research, Policy and Practice*. London: Jessica Kingsley Publishers.

London Borough of Greenwich (1987) *A Child in Mind: Protection of Children in a Responsible Society: The Report of the Commission of Inquiry into the Circumstances Surrounding the Death of Kimberley Carlisle: Presented to the London Borough of Greenwich and the Greenwich Health Authority by Members of the Commission of Inquiry*. Greenwich: London Borough of Greenwich.

Luckock, B., Lefevre, M., Orr, D., Jones, M., Marchant, R. and Tanner, K. (2006) *Teaching, Learning and Assessing Communication Skills with Children and Young People in Social Work Education*. London: SCIE.

Luty, J. and Rao, H. (2008) 'Survey of professional attitudes to addiction treatment policy', *Journal of Substance Use*, 13(2): 115–20.

Lymbery, M. (2006) 'United we stand? Partnership working in health and social care and the role of social work in services for older people', *British Journal of Social Work*, 36: 1119–34.

Marlatt, G. (1996) 'Harm reduction: Come as you are', *Addictive Behaviours*, 21: 779–88.

Marlatt, G. and Gordon, J. (eds) (1985) *Relapse Prevention: Maintenance Strategies in the Treatment of Addictive Behaviors*. New York: Guilford.

Marlatt, G. and Witkiewitz, K. (2005) 'Relapse prevention for alcohol and drug problems', in G. Marlatt and D. Donovan (eds), *Relapse Prevention: Maintenance Strategies in the Treatment of Addictive Behaviors* (2nd edn). New York: Guilford Press, pp. 1–44.

Matrix Knowledge Group (2008) *Dedicated Drug Court Pilots: A Process Report*. London: Ministry of Justice [Online] http://www.justice.gov.uk/publications/docs/dedicated-drug-courts.pdf [accessed 11 March 2010].

Matthew, S. and Richardson, A. (2005) *Findings from the 2003 Offending, Crime and Justice Survey: Alcohol-Related Crime and Disorder*. London: Home Office. [Online]. Available at: http://www.homeoffice.gov.uk/rds/pdfs05/r261.pdf [accessed 13 March 2010].

McCambridge, J. and Strang, J. (2005) 'Can it really be this black and white? An analysis of the relative importance of ethnic group and other sociodemographic factors to patterns of drug use and related risk among young Londoners', *Drugs, Education, Prevention and Policy*, 12(2): 149–59.

McCormack, M. and Walker, R. (2005) *Drug Prevention for Young Asylum Seekers and Refugees: A Review of Current Knowledge*. London: Mentor UK. [Online]. Available at: http://www.mentorfoundation.org/uploads/UK_Drug_Prevention_Lit_Review.pdf [accessed 31 March 2010].

McLaughlin, D., Taggart, L., Quinn, B. and Milligan, V. (2007) 'The experiences of professionals who care for people with intellectual disability who have substance-related problems', *Journal of Substance Use*, 12(2): 133–43.

McNeill, F. (2006) *A New Paradigm for Social Work with Offenders?* CjScotland. [Online]. Available at: http://www.cjscotland.org.uk/index.php/articles/desistance/ [accessed 11 March 2010].

Mendel, E. and Hipkins, J. (2002) 'Motivating learning disabled offenders with alcohol-related problems: A pilot study', *British Journal of Learning Disabilities*, 30: 153–8.

Miller, N. (1995) *Treatment of Addictions: Applications of Outcome Research*. New York: Hawthorn Press.

Miller, W. and Moyers, T. (2006) 'Eight stages in learning motivational interviewing', *Journal of Teaching in the Addictions*, 5(1): 3–17.

Miller, W. and Rollnick, S. (2002) *Motivational Interviewing: Preparing People for Change* (2nd edn). New York: Guilford Press.

Miller, W. and Sanchez, V. (1993) 'Motivating young adults for treatment and lifestyle change', in G. Howard (ed.), *Issues in Alcohol Use and Misuse by Young Adults*. Notre Dame, IN: University of Notre Dame Press.

Miller, W., Zweben, A., DiClemente, C. and Rychtarik, R. (1992) *Motivational Enhancement Therapy Manual: A Clinical Research Guide for Therapists Treating Individuals with Alcohol Abuse and Dependence*. Rockville, MD: National Institute on Alcohol Abuse and Alcoholism.

Ministry of Justice (2009) *Statistics on Race and the Criminal Justice System 2007/8: A Ministry of Justice Publication under Section 95 of the Criminal Justice Act 1991*. London: HM Stationery Office.

Mold, A. (2007) 'Consuming habits: Histories of drugs in modern societies', *Social and Cultural History*, 4(2): 261–70.

Moss, B. (2008) *Communication Skills for Health and Social Care*. London: Sage.

Moss, H. and Kirisic, L. (1995) 'Aggressivity in adolescent alcohol abusers: Relationship with conduct disorder', *Alcoholism: Clinical and Experimental Research*, 19(3): 642–6.

National AIDS Trust (2005) *HIV in Healthcare: Facts about HIV and AIDS* [Online]. Available at: http://www.nat.org.uk/Media%20Library/Files/PDF%20Documents/HIV-in-Healthcare.pdf [accessed 7 July 2010].

National Center on Addiction and Substance Abuse (CASA) (2010) *Behind Bars II: Substance Abuse and America's Prison Population*. New York: CASA, Columbia University. [Online]. Available at: http://www.casacolumbia.org/absolutenm/templates/print-article.aspx?articleid=592andzoneid=79 [accessed 11 March 2010].

National Health Service (NHS) (2010) *Smoking (Quitting) – Facts* [Online]. Available at: http://www.nhs.uk/Conditions/Smoking-(quitting)/Pages/Facts.aspx [accessed 6 November 2010].

National Treatment Agency for Substance Misuse (NTA) (2002) *Models of Care for the Treatment of Drug Misusers*. London: NTA.

National Treatment Agency for Substance Misuse and Centre for Ethnicity and Health (2003) *Black and Minority Ethnic Communities in England: A Review of the Literature on Drug Use and Related Service Provision*. London: National Treatment Agency for Substance Misuse and Centre for Ethnicity and Health.

National Treatment Agency for Substance Misuse (NTA) (2004) *Promoting Safer Drinking: A Briefing Paper for Drugs Workers*. London: NTA.

National Treatment Agency for Substance Misuse (NTA) (2005) *Women in Drug Treatment Services. Research Briefing: 6*. London: NTA.

National Treatment Agency for Substance Misuse (NTA) (2006) *Models of Care for the Treatment of Adult Drug Users: Update 2006*. London: NTA.

National Treatment Agency for Substance Misuse (NTA) (2008a) *Good Practice in Harm Reduction*. London: NTA.

National Treatment Agency for Substance Misuse (NTA) (2008b) *Statistics from the National Drug Treatment Monitoring System (NDTMS) 1 April 2001–31 March 2008*. London: NTA.

National Treatment Agency for Substance Misuse (NTA) (2009a) *Media Release: Rise in Number of Cocaine Dependent Women Entering Treatment* [Online]. Available at: http://www.nta.nhs.uk/uploads/2_12_09_rise_in_number_of_cocaine_dependent_women_entering_treatment.pdf [accessed 12 February 2010].

National Treatment Agency for Substance Misuse (NTA) (2009b) *Breaking the Link: The Role of Drug Treatment in Tackling Crime*. London: NTA. [Online]. Available at: http://www.nta.nhs.uk/uploads/nta_criminaljustice_0809.pdf [accessed 25 July 2010].

National Treatment Agency for Substance Misuse (NTA) (2009c) *Young People's Specialist Substance Misuse Treatment: Exploring the Evidence*. London: NTA. [Online]. Available at: http://www.nta.nhs.uk/uploads/yp_exploring_the_evidence_0109.pdf [accessed 15 February 2010].

National Treatment Agency for Substance Misuse (NTA) (2010) *Substance Misuse among Young People – The Data for 2008/09*. London: NTA.

Neaigus, A., Miller, M., Friedman, S., Hagn, D. et al. (2001) 'Potential risk factors for the transition to injecting among non-injecting heroin users: A comparison of former injectors and never injectors', *Addiction*, 96(6): 984–7.

Nutt, D., King, L., Saulsbury, W. and Blakemore, C. (2007) 'Development of a rational scale to assess the harms of drugs of potential misuse', *The Lancet*, 369: 1047–53.

Office for National Statistics (ONS) (2008) *Gender: Health* [Online]. Available at: http://www.statistics.gov.uk/cci/nugget.asp?id=1657 [accessed 14 November 2010].

Office for National Statistics (ONS) (2009) *New Guidance on Measuring Sexual Identity in Social Surveys*. ONS News Release: ONS. [Online]. Available at: http://www.statistics.gov.uk/pdfdir/siug0509.pdf [accessed 24 April 2010].

Office of Substance Abuse Services (2004) *Gender Differences and their Implications for Substance Use Disorder Treatment*. VA: Virginia Department of Mental Health, Mental Retardation and Substance Abuse Services.

Orford, J., Johnson, M. and Purser, B. (2004) 'Drinking in second-generation Black and Asian communities in the English Midlands', *Addiction, Research and Theory*, 12 (1): 11–30.

Owen, R., Hughes, P., Baker, C. and Chesterman, L. (2008) 'Addressing substance misuse in a medium secure unit', *Drugs and Alcohol Today*, 8(3): 17–21.

Patel, S. (2008) 'Attitudes to khat use within the Somali community in England', *Drugs: Education, Prevention and Policy*, 15(1): 37–53.

Paylor, I. and Mack, H. (2009) 'Gazing into the scarlet crystal ball: Social work and Hepatitis C', *British Journal of Social Work*, 40(7): 2291–307.

Paylor, I. and Orgel, M. (2004) 'Sleepwalking through an epidemic – Why social work should wake up to the treatment of Hepatitis C', *British Journal of Social Work*, 34: 897–906.

Pega, F. and MacEwan, I. (2010) *Making Visible: Improving Services for Sexual Minority People in Alcohol and Other Drug Prevention and Treatment* (2nd edn). Wellington, New Zealand: Matua Raki.

Perera, J., Power, R. And Gibsom, N. (1993) *Assessing the Needs of Black Drug Users in North Westminster, London*. London: Hungerford Drug project and the Centre for Research on Drugs and Health Behaviour.

Petersen, T. and McBride, A. (2002) *Working with Substance Misusers: A Guide to Theory and Practice*. London: Routledge.

Prime Minister's Strategy Unit, Cabinet Office (2004) *Alcohol Harm Reduction Strategy for England*. London: Cabinet Office.

Prochaska, J. and DiClemente, C. (1982) 'Transtheoretical therapy: Towards a more integrative model of change', *Psychotherapy: Theory, Research, and Practice*, 19: 276–88.

Project MATCH Research Group (1997) 'Matching alcoholism treatments to client heterogeneity: Project MATCH post treatment drinking outcomes', *Journal of Studies on Alcohol*, 58(1): 7–29.

Provine, D. (2007) *Unequal Under Law: Race in the War on Drugs*. Chicago, IL: University of Chicago Press.

Rao, R. (2006) 'Alcohol misuse and ethnicity', *British Medical Journal*, 332: 682.

Reinout, W. and Stacy, A. (eds) (2005) *Handbook of Implicit Cognition and Addiction*. London: Sage.

Reuter, P. and Stevens, A. (2007) *An Analysis of UK Drug Policy: A Monograph Prepared for the UK Drug Policy Commission*. London: UK Drug Policy Commission.

Richmond, R., Heather, N., Wodak, A., Kehoe, L. and Webster, I. (1995) 'Controlled evaluation of a general practice-based brief intervention for excessive drinking', *Addiction*, 90: 119–32.

Rimke, H. and Hunt, A. (2002) 'From sinners to degenerates: The medicalization of morality in the 19th century', *History of the Human Sciences*, 15(1): 59–88.

Rollnick, S. and Miller, W.R. (1995) 'What is motivational interviewing?', *Behavioural and Cognitive Psychotherapy*, 23: 325–34.

Rostami, R., Zarei, J., Zamiri Nejad, S. and Larijani, R. (2010) 'Childhood abuse history among male addicts in comparison with non-addict population', *Procedia Social and Behavioural Sciences*, 5: 738–40.

Royal College of Obstetricians and Gynaecologists (RCOG) (2006) *Alcohol and Pregnancy: Information for You* [Online]. Available at: http://www.rcog.org.uk/womens-health/clinical-guidance/alcohol-and-pregnancy-information-you [accessed 23 February 2010].

Royal Society of Arts (RSA) (2007) *The Report of the RSA Commission on Illegal Drugs, Communities and Public Policy*. London: RSA.

Rush, B. (1790) *An Inquiry into the Effects of Spirituous Liquors on the Human Body and the Mind*. Boston, MA: Thomas and Andrews.

Save the Children and Glasgow Greater Council (2002) *Starting Again*. London: Save the Children/Glasgow City Council.

Schulte, S., Moring, J., Meier, P. and Barrowclough, C. (2007) 'User involvement and desired service developments in drug treatment: Service user and provider views', *Drugs Education, Prevention and Policy*, 14(3): 277–87.

Scotland, P., Kelly, H. and Devaux, M. (1998) *The Report of the Luke Warm Luke Mental Health Inquiry Presented to the Chairman of Lambeth, Southwark and Lewisham Health Authority 13 November 1998*.

Scottish Executive (2003) *Mind the Gaps – Meeting the Needs of People with Co-occurring Substance Misuse and Mental Health Problems*. Edinburgh: Scottish Government.

Scottish Government (2008a) *The Road to Recovery: A New Approach to Tackling Scotland's Drug Problem*. Edinburgh: Scottish Government.

Scottish Government (2008b) *Getting it Right for Every Child*. Edinburgh: Scottish Government.

Selzer, M. (1971) 'The Michigan Alcoholism Screening Test (MAST): The quest for a new diagnostic instrument', *American Journal of Psychiatry*, 127: 1653–8.

Skinner, H. (1971) 'The drug abuse screening test', *Addictive Behaviours*, 7: 363–71.

Skinner H. (2001) 'Assessment of drug abuse: Drug abuse screening test', in R. Carson-Dewitt (ed.) *Encyclopedia of Drugs, Alcohol and Addiction Behaviour*. 2nd edn. Durham, NC: Macmillan Reference USA, pp. 147–8.

Slayter, E. (2010) 'Disparities in access to substance abuse treatment among people with intellectual disabilities and serious mental illness', *Health and Social Work*, 35(1): 49–59.

Smith, R. (2008) *Social Work and Power*. Basingstoke: Palgrave Macmillan.

Social Care Institute for Excellence (SCIE) (2006) *The Social Care Needs of Refugees and Asylum Seekers*. London: SCIE. [Online]. Available at: http://www.scie.org.uk/publications/raceequalitydiscussionpapers/rcdp02.pdf [accessed 25 July 2010].

Standing Conference on Drug Abuse (SCODA) (1997) *Drug Using Parents: Policy Guidelines for Inter-Agency Working*. London: Local Government Association Publications.

Stella Project, The (2007) *Domestic Violence, Drugs and Alcohol: Good Practice Guidelines*. London: The Stella Project.

Stephens, R.S., Roffman, R.A. and Curtin, L. (2000) 'Comparison of extended versus brief treatments for marijuana use', *Journal of Consulting and Clinical Psychology*, 68(5): 898–908.

Strang, J. and Gossop, M. (eds) (2005) *Heroin Addiction and the British System, Volume 1: Origins and Evolution*. London: Routledge.

Straussner, S. (2004) 'The role of social workers in the treatment of addictions: A brief history', *Journal of Social Work Practice in the Addictions*, 1(1): 3–9.

Substance Abuse and Mental Health Services Administration (SAMHSA)/Center for Substance Abuse Treatment (CSAT) (2001) *A Providers Guide to Substance Abuse Treatment for Lesbian, Gay, Bisexual and Transgendered Individuals*. Rockville, MD: SAMHSA/CSAT. [Online]. Available at: http://download.ncadi.samhsa.gov/prevline/pdfs/BKD392/index.pdf [accessed 24 April 2010].

Taggart, L., McLaughlin, D.F., Quinn, B. and Milligan, V. (2006). 'An exploration of substance misuse in people with intellectual disabilities', *Journal of Intellectual Disability Research*, 50: 227–36.

Taggart, L., McLaughlin, D., Quinn, B. and McFarlane, C. (2007) 'Listening to people with intellectual disabilities who misuse alcohol and drugs', *Health and Social Care in the Community*, 15(4): 360–8.

Tatarsky, A. (2003) 'Harm reduction psychotherapy: Extending the reach of traditional substance use treatment', *Journal of Substance Abuse Treatment*, 25(4): 249–56.

Taylor, A., Toner, P., Templeton, L. and Velleman, R. (2008) 'Parental alcohol misuse in complex families: The implications for engagement', *British Journal of Social Work*, 38: 843–64.

Templeton, L., Velleman, R., Hardy, E. and Boon, S. (2009) 'Young people living with parental alcohol misuse and parental violence: "No-one has ever asked me how I feel in any of this"', *Journal of Substance Use*, 14(3–4): 139–50.

Thompson, N. (2001) *Anti-Discriminatory Practice*. Basingstoke: Palgrave Macmillan.

Thompson, N. (2006) *Anti-Discriminatory Practice* (4th edn). Basingstoke: Palgrave Macmillan.

Timpson, S., Ross, M., Williams, M. and Atkinson, J. (2007) 'Characteristics, drug use and sex partners of a sample of male sex workers', *American Journal of Drug and Alcohol Abuse*, 33: 63–9.

Todd, F. (2010) *Te Ariari o te Oranga: The Assessment and Management of People with Co-existing Mental Health and Substance Use Problems 2010*. Wellington,

New Zealand: Ministry of Health. [Online]. Available at: http://www.moh.govt.nz/moh.nsf/pagesmh/10055/$File/te-ariari-o-te-orang-teariari-13-04-10.pdf [accessed 14 January 2011].

Transform Drugs Policy Foundation (2009) *A History of Drug Prohibition and a Prediction for its Abolition and Replacement* [Online]. Available at: http://www.tdpf.org.uk/Policy_Timeline.htm [accessed 5 April 2009].

Turning Point Alcohol and Drug Centre (2000) *Relapse Prevention*. Melbourne, Australia: Turning Point Alcohol and Drug Centre.

UK Alcohol Alert (2010) *Which Direction for Alcohol Policy under the Coalition* [Online]. Available at: http://www.ias.org.uk/resources/publications/alcoholalert/alert201002/al201002.pdf [accessed 14 November 2010].

UK Drugs Policy Commission (UKDPC) (2007) *A Response to Drugs: Our Community, Your Say Consultation Paper*. London: UKDPC.

UK Drugs Policy Commission (UKDPC) (2008) *The UK Drugs Policy Commission Recovery Concensus Group: A Vision of Recovery*. London: UKDPC.

UN Refugee Agency (2007) *Convention and Protocol Relating to the Status of Refugees* [Online]. Available at: http://www.unhcr.org/3b66c2aa10.html [accessed 25 July 2010].

VanderWaal, C.J., McBride, D.C., McElrath, T. and Van Buren, H. (2001) *Breaking the Juvenile Drug–Crime Cycle: A Guide for Practitioners and Policymakers*. Washington, DC: Department of Justice, National Institute of Justice.

Wahab, S. (2005) 'Motivational interviewing and social work practice', *Journal of Social Work*, 5(1): 51–60.

Waine, B., Tunstill, J., Meadows, P. and Peel, M. (2005) *Developing Social Care Values and Principles*. London: Social Care Institute for Excellence (SCIE). [Online]. Available at: http://www.scie.org.uk/publications/positionpapers/pp04/values.pdf [accessed 11 March 2010].

Watson, H. (1999) 'Minimal intervention for problem drinkers: A review of the literature', *Journal of Advanced Nursing*, 30: 513–19.

Watson, S. and Hawkings, C. (2007) *Dual Diagnosis Good Practice Handbook*. London: Turning Point. [Online]. Available at: http://www.turning-point.co.uk/inthenews/Documents/DualDiagnosisGoodPracticeHandbook.pdf [accessed 6 June 2010].

Welsh Assembly Government (2007) *A Service Framework to Meet the Needs of People with a Co-occurring Substance Misuse and Mental Health Problem*. Wales: Welsh Assembly Government. [Online]. Available at: http://wales.gov.uk/topics/housingandcommunity/safety/substancemisuse/publications/cooccuring/?lang=en [accessed 6 June 2010].

Wilk, A., Jensen, N. and Havighurst, T. (1997) 'Meta analysis of randomised control trials addressing brief interventions in heavy alcohol drinkers', *Journal General Intern Medicine*, 12: 274–83.

Williams, C. (2004) 'Twelve-step approaches', in T. Petersen and A. McBride (eds), *Working with Substance Misusers: A Guide to Theory and Practice*. London: Routledge, pp. 134–44.

Williamson, K. (2002) 'Substance misuse and older people', in T. Petersen and A. McBride (eds), *Working with Substance Misusers: A Guide to Theory and Practice*. London: Routledge, pp. 317–26.

Wilson, K., Ruch, G., Lymbery, M. and Cooper, A. (2008) *Social Work: An Introduction to Contemporary Practice*. Harlow: Pearson Education Limited.

Witkiewitz, K. and Marlatt, G. (2004) 'Relapse prevention for alcohol and drug problems: That was Xen, this is Tao', *American Psychologist*, 59: 224–35.

Witkiewitz, K. and Marlatt, G. (eds) (2007) *Therapist's Guide to Evidence-Based Relapse Prevention*. CA: Elsevier.

Wolfensberger, W. (1998) *A Brief Introduction to Social Role Valorization: A High-Order Concept for Addressing the Plight of Societally Devalued People, and for Structuring Human Services*. 3rd edn. New York: Training Institute for Human Service Planning, Leadership and Change Agentry, Syracuse University.

Women's Health Council (2009) *Women and Substance Misuse in Ireland: Overview*. Dublin: Women's Health Council.

Woodiwiss, M. (1998) 'Reform, racism and rackets: Alcohol and drug prohibition in the United States', in R. Coomber (ed.), *The Control of Drugs and Drug Users: Reason or Reaction?* London: Harwood Academic Publishers, pp. 13–30.

World Health Organization (WHO) (1992) *The ICD: 10 International Classification of Mental and Behavioural Disorders*. Geneva: WHO.

World Health Organization (WHO) (2006) *Harm Reduction: Good Practice in Asia. Integration of Harm Reduction into Abstinence-Based Therapeutic Communities. A Case Study of We Help Ourselves, Australia*. Western Pacific Region: WHO.

Yates, R. (2002) 'A brief history of British drug policy, 1950–2001', *Drugs: Education, Prevention and Policy*, 9(2): 113–24.

Zweben, A. and Fleming, M. (1999) 'Brief interventions for alcohol and drug problems', in J. Tucker, D. Donovan and G. Marlatt (eds), *Changing Addictive Behavior: Bridging Clinical and Public Health Strategies*. New York: Guilford Press, pp. 251–82.

Index